Strengthening Your Grip

By the same author:

IMPROVING YOUR SERVE

Strengthening Your Grip

Essentials in an Aimless World

Charles R. Swindoll

HODDER AND STOUGHTON
LONDON SYDNEY AUCKLAND

British Library Cataloguing in Publication Data

Swindoll, Charles R.
  Strengthening your grip.
  1. Christian life
  I. Title
  248.4   BV4501.2

ISBN 0 340 33904 7

*Hodder and Stoughton Editorial Office: 47 Bedford Square, London,
WC1B 3DP.*

Contents

With much gratitude this volume
is dedicated to four men, each of whom
helped strengthen my grip
more than he ever realized

In the 1950s.............. Bob Newkirk
Who gave the encouragement I needed

In the 1960s...........Howie Hendricks
Who modeled the skills I admired

In the 1970s.............. Ray Stedman
Who had the wisdom I appreciated

In the 1980s................. Al Sanders
Who provided the vision I lacked

I count it a privilege today
to call each man my friend

Acknowledgments

UNLESS OTHERWISE INDICATED, Scripture quotations are from *The New American Standard Bible,* (NASB) copyright © The Lockman Foundation 1960, 1962, 1963, 1968, 1971, 1972, 1973, 1975.

Other Scripture quotations in this publication are from the following sources:

The Living Bible, Paraphrased (TLB), copyright © 1971 by Tyndale House Publishers, Wheaton, Illinois.

The Amplified New Testament (AMPLIFIED), copyright © 1958 by The Lockman Foundation.

The New International Version of the Bible (NIV), published by The Zondervan Corporation, copyright © 1978 by the New York International Bible Society.

The New Berkeley Version in Modern English, Revised Edition: copyright 1945, 1959, © 1969 by Zondervan Publishing House. Old Testament © 1959 by Zondervan Publishing House. New Testament © 1945 by Gerrit Verkuyl; assigned 1958 to Zondervan Publishing House.

The Revised Standard Version of the Bible (RSV), copyright © 1946, 1952, © 1971 and 1973 by the Division of Christian Education of the National Council of the Churches of Christ in the U.S.A.

The King James Version of the Bible (KJV).

Introduction

EVERY DECADE POSSESSES a particular characteristic. It comes into focus without announcement or awareness as the years unfold. Not suddenly, but quietly. Almost imperceptibly. Like random pieces of a puzzle—each a different shape and size—the events and people and ideas of a decade begin to come together in a meaningful form. First a corner, then a side, finally the entire border falls into place. But the scene is not immediately clear.

Years must pass. As they do, more sections fit together, and meaningfulness starts to emerge. By the end of the decade, the seasoned picture is obvious, including the shading, harmony of colors, and even our feelings about the finished product. Every decade puts a frame around its own particular scene.

I was born in 1934. As I reflect on the decade of the 1930s through the lens of history (and discussion with those who were adults during that era), I get the distinct impression that it was a decade of *idealism*. Renewed hope clawed its way from beneath the devastation of the Great Depression. Optimism and diligence joined hands with determination, giving our country a needed boost out of the ominous shadows of the late 1920s.

I was a growing youngster in the 1940s—a decade of *patriotism*. Nationalistic zeal reached its zenith as "our boys" slugged it out in Europe and the Far East. Simultaneous gasoline and food rationing, plus an unconditional commitment to win, gave us a feeling of pride and partnership as we rallied around the flag. Nobody, it seemed, questioned authority or tolerated the slightest action that smacked of insubordination. Babies born in the forties learned the pledge of allegiance as early in life as they learned the alphabet. Patriotism characterized the 1940s.

By the 1950s, I was a young man. My high school years in East Houston could have been the perfect place to film "Happy Days." My education continued, and a hitch in the Marine Corps, a new bride, and a change in careers marked those days in my life. Looking back, I have little trouble identifying that era. It was a decade of *materialism*, a time of dreaming, learning, earning, and succeeding. "The good life" became attainable to all who would work longer hours and push for the top. War was behind us, new frontiers were open to us, if only we would pay the price—advanced education and additional hours on the job. What we overlooked was the growing number of children and adolescents who got caught in the backwash of our materialistic greed. They would sit down and be quiet only so long. The fuse burned shorter each year that decade. It was only a matter of time before the powder keg would blow.

Then came the 1960s. Who could ever forget the anger, the riots, the frenzy of the sixties? A decade of *rebellion*. A new music with a heavy beat made parents frown in disapproval and kids scream with excitement. The foundations of our new frontiers came unglued. Campus riots, civil rights marches, political assassinations, the growing addiction to television, domestic runaways, sit-ins, drug abuse, unemployment, the threat of nuclear attack, and burning cities and draft cards made the President's job a hell-on-earth nightmare. Snarling defiance replaced submissive allegiance. On top of it all was that weird war in

Southeast Asia—the black eye on Uncle Sam's face—the no-win wound that refused to heal. Nothing was quiet on the Western Front in the 1960s.

The overt rebellion of that stormy era led us, limping and licking our wounds, into the 1970s. Depressing folk songs and the strumming of a guitar had now become our national emblem. Increased passivity characterized much of the leadership in the 1970s as more of our youth began to rethink the work-hard-so-you-can-get-rich materialism mentality. Confusion began to replace confidence, ushering us into a decade of *disillusionment*. You name it, a question mark could be attached to it. The integrity of our Oval Office? The "proper" role of women? The need for national defense? Capital punishment? The media? The home? The school? The church? The prisons? The establishment? Nuclear energy? Ecology? Marriage? Education? Rights? And I may as well add: Purpose? Direction? Hope? We lost our grip on absolutes in the 1970s.

All of which brought us into the "aimless 1980s" with a table full of pieces that initially defied reason. The grim-faced, tight-lipped, double-fisted fight of the sixties had turned into a lazy yawn twenty years later. The slogan of the 1940s, "Remember Pearl Harbor!" and the 1960s' "We shall overcome!" were now slowly eroding into the new slogan of the 1980s, "Who really cares?" The muscular patriot who once rolled up his sleeves and dared any enemy to step foot on our shores was now listening to the clicks of a computer, preoccupied in his silent, isolated world of code language all day and the glare of color television half the night. The tide of apathy has risen, and we are seeing the sand castles that once housed our hopes washed out to sea.

Face it, ours is simply not the same world as it was a few short decades ago. The full picture hidden in the puzzle is still unclear, but the border is in place. The scene has changed drastically.

For some reason the truth of all this began to impact me shortly after we entered the decade of the 1980s. I felt jolted as the changes seized my attention. I guess such thoughts occur when one approaches a half century in age. But, more important, as a communicator of God's timeless truth, I found myself having to face the frightening facts of reality. We cannot drift on the ship of aimless indifference very long without encountering disaster. God's eternal and essential principles must be firmly grasped and communicated afresh if we hope to survive. None of them are new. But for too long, too many of them have been buried under the debris of tired clichés and predictable talk of yesteryear. Most people I know who are coping with the complexities and stress of this decade are not at all interested in religious bromides that come across in a dated and dull fashion. We can no longer speak to the issues of the 1980s in the terms of the 1940s or the 1960s or even the 1970s, for that matter. Much of that is now awash.

We need biblical fixed points to hang onto—firm, solid handles that will help us steer our lives in a meaningful manner. What we really want is something to grab—believable, reliable truth that makes sense for today's generation, essential principles for our aimless world.

I have only that to offer in this volume. Within these pages are ancient truths presented in today's terms for today's person, facing today's demands. Each chapter deals with a different essential that will, if applied in a personal manner, increase your confidence and your ability to cope with current crises, because it rests on the bedrock of inspired revelation, the Holy Bible. When these insights are lived out in your life, you will soon discover that they will strengthen your grip on the Life Preserver that won't submerge when the tide rises. And best of all, these principles won't change on you at the dawning of a new decade in the next few years. We have our Lord to thank for that! He is "the same yesterday and today, yes, and forever" (Heb. 13:8).

The puzzle of every new decade rests firmly in His hands. He is still in charge. In spite of how things may appear, our times are still in His hands.

If the aimlessness of the eighties is starting to loosen your confidence in God's sovereign control, this book will help strengthen your grip.

CHARLES R. SWINDOLL
Fullerton, California

Strengthening Your Grip on Priorities

THE TYRANNY OF THE URGENT is a small booklet with a big fist. Its message is uncomplicated and direct. Actually, it's a warning to all of us. There are times when its penetrating blow punches my lights out! Like a guided missile, it assaults and destroys all excuses I may use.

Here, in one sentence, is the warning: Don't let the urgent take the place of the important in your life.[1] Oh, the urgent will really fight, claw, and scream for attention. It will plead for our time and even make us think we've done the right thing by calming its nerves. But the tragedy of it all is this: While you and I were putting out the fires of the urgent (an everyday affair), the important was again left in a holding pattern. And interestingly, the important is neither noisy nor demanding. Unlike the urgent, it patiently and quietly waits for us to realize its significance.

WHAT IS IMPORTANT TO YOU?

Forgetting the urgent for a few minutes, ask yourself what is really important to you. What do you consider "top

priority" in your life? That is a big question, maybe one you need
some time to think about. I began to think about it over a year
and a half ago. Because I am a minister in a sizable church where
I face a busy schedule week after week, I decided to think seriously about my priorities *and* the priorities of our growing ministry. It helped. What I discovered is worth passing on to others.
Who knows? It may be just what you need to hear today.

Let me give you a little background. In some ways,
people and organizations are alike. Both tend to lose vitality
rather than gain it as time passes. Both also tend to give greater
attention to what they *were* rather than what they are *becoming*.
It's easier to look back into the past and smile on yesterday's
accomplishments than it is to look ahead into the future and
think about tomorrow's possibilities.

I realized my own tendency to do that when our
congregation moved into brand new facilities in March 1980.
Almost twelve acres of choice land in a suburb of Los Angeles.
Five new, lovely, spacious, efficient structures to house our
church family. The answer to years of praying and sacrificial
giving. A dream come true. God had again done wonders among
us.

It soon became apparent, however, that if we
weren't alert and careful, we would slump into a continuous
focus on where we had been rather than on where we were
going . . . what we were in the process of becoming. God's people
are not museum pieces, placed and anchored on a shelf to collect
dust. We are alive, moving, and active people called by Him to
make an impact on a world that isn't quite sure which end is up.
But to do that, we need to determine our priorities.

As I opened my Bible and began to search for direction, I came across the second chapter of 1 Thessalonians, a
letter Paul wrote centuries ago to a growing group of Christians.
He began this chapter by saying: "For you yourselves know,
brethren, that our coming to you was not in vain . . . " (v. 1).

Although he certainly had not stayed there among
them very long, his coming was no wasted effort. It may have

been brief and, on occasion, discouraging, but it wasn't in vain.

FOUR PRIORITIES FOR LIVING

After declaring this fact, Paul then pinpoints the characteristics of his life and ministry in Thessalonica. In doing so he sets forth four essential priorities for every church in any era—or, for that matter, any life.

Be Biblical

Looking back over the weeks they were together, he recalls his initial impressions.

> But after we had already suffered and been mistreated in Philippi, as you know, we had the boldness in our God to speak to you the gospel of God amid much opposition. For our exhortation does not come from error or impurity or by way of deceit; but just as we have been approved by God to be entrusted with the gospel, so we speak, not as pleasing men but God, who examines our hearts (vv. 2–4).

I'm confident that there was a constant barrage of urgent needs pounding away on Paul's mind, but he made sure that his life and ministry were firmly fixed on the important—the Scriptures.

Did you catch these thoughts as you read those verses?

• When he spoke amidst the strong current of public opposition, it was "the gospel of God" he shared (v. 2).

• The very foundation of his being was not "error" or "impurity" or "deceit," but rather the truth of the Scriptures (v. 3).

• Furthermore, he considered the Word of God as something "entrusted" to him. And it gave him such security and confidence that he didn't feel the need to compromise and become a "people pleaser" (v. 4).

Even though it may sound old-fashioned, the first and most significant priority we can cultivate is to make the Scriptures a part of our lives. A biblical mentality is the secret to surviving the aimlessness of our day.

> ... We must daily soak ourselves in the Scriptures. We must not just study, as through a microscope, the linguistic minutiae of a few verses, but take our telescope and scan the wide expanses of God's Word, assimilating its grand theme of divine sovereignty in the redemption of mankind. 'It is blessed,' wrote C. H. Spurgeon, 'to eat into the very soul of the Bible until, at last, you come to talk in scriptural language, and your spirit is flavoured with the words of the Lord, so that your blood is Bibline and the very essence of the Bible flows from you.'[2]

I find it interesting that being committed to a biblical mentality and lifestyle is so old it's new! For sure, it's rare. It also leads to a good deal of self-examination. Did you observe this at the end of verse 4? As we begin to soak up the truths of God's Book, He goes to work on us!

> The word of God is living and active. Sharper than any double-edged sword, it penetrates even to dividing soul and spirit, joints and marrow; it judges the thoughts and attitudes of the heart. Nothing in all creation is hidden from God's sight. Everything is uncovered and laid bare before the eyes of him to whom we must give account (Heb. 4:12–13, NIV).

Descriptive, isn't it? The principles and precepts of Scripture touch what no surgeon's scalpel can touch—the soul, the spirit, thoughts, attitudes, the very essence of our being. And God uses His truths to help shape us and clean us up and mature us in our walk with Him.

Let's take this to heart. Let's determine that we are not going to allow the tyranny of the urgent to steal from us those all-important moments with our God in His Word. First and foremost, let's become people who are thoroughly committed to biblical thinking and action.

I find a second priority in this same part of 1 Thessalonians.

Be Authentic

Listen to the way Paul talks about himself. For a moment he shifts the emphasis from the message to the messenger.

> For we never came with flattering speech, as you know, nor with a pretext for greed—God is witness—nor did we seek glory from men, either from you or from others, even though as apostles of Christ we might have asserted our authority (1 Thess. 2:5–6).

The man was real. He was so secure he peeled off all masks, all cover-ups, and stood vulnerably before God and others. It's beautiful! Even though he was an apostle—a genuine first-century bigwig—he did not push for the limelight. He consciously resisted being a power abuser.

Ronald Enroth, author and professor of sociology at Westmont College, is correct in his analysis of a leader's use of power.

> . . . Bible scholars point out that the New Testament concept of authority as expressed in the Greek word *exousia* does not have the connotation of jurisdiction over the lives of others. Rather, it is the authority of truth, the authority of wisdom and experience which can be evidenced in a leader who is held up as a special example, who can commend himself "to every man's conscience in the sight of God" (2 Cor. 4:2).[3]

Paul was that kind of leader. He did not take unfair advantage of his role as an apostle. Of top priority to him, right alongside being a strong believer in the Scriptures, was being authentic.

Webster's dictionary defines the term *authentic* by suggesting three things "authentic" is *not*: It is *not* imaginary, it is *not* false, it is *not* an imitation. Today we would say that being authentic means not being phony... free of the standard hype that often accompanies public gatherings.

Let's make this a priority in the 1980s! Surrounded by numerous religious types to whom everything is "fantastic," "super," and "incredible," let's work hard at being real. This means we are free to question, to admit failure or weakness, to confess wrong, to declare the truth. When a person is authentic, he or she does not have to win or always be in the top ten or make a big impression or look super-duper pious.

A man I deeply appreciate—a fine student and teacher of the Bible—admitted in a public meeting that the more he studied prophecy the *less* he knew about it! I smiled with understanding and admiration.

Robert Wise, pastor of Our Lord's Community Church in Oklahoma City, helped take some of the tension out of my own tendency to compete and continually achieve, always fearing failure. In his intriguing book *Your Churning Place*, he mentions an experience that encouraged him to be real.

> I had a friend who used to call me on the phone on Monday mornings. I'd pick up the phone and this minister would say, "Hello, this is God. I have a gift for you today. I want to give you the gift of failing. Today you do not have to succeed. I grant that to you." Then he would hang up. I would sit there for 10 minutes, staring at the wall.
>
> The first time I couldn't believe it. It was really the gospel. God's love means it's even OK to fail. You don't have to be the greatest thing in the world. You can just be you.[4]

Authentic people usually enjoy life more than most. They don't take themselves so seriously. They actually laugh and cry and think more freely because they have nothing to prove—no big image to protect, no role to play. They have no fear of being found out, because they're not hiding anything. Let's make the Bible our foundation in the '80s. And as we apply its insights and guidelines, let's also cultivate a style that is authentic.

In doing so we'll need to watch our attitude—our next priority.

Be Gracious

Paul deals with this third priority in 1 Thessalonians 2:7–11 where he writes of the value of being gracious.

But we proved to be gentle among you, as a nursing mother tenderly cares for her own children.

Having thus a fond affection for you, we were well pleased to impart to you not only the gospel but also our own lives, because you had become very dear to us.

For you recall, brethren, our labor and hardship, how working night and day so as not to be a burden to any of you, we proclaimed to you the gospel of God.

You are witnesses, and so is God, how devoutly and uprightly and blamelessly we behaved toward you believers; just as you know how we were exhorting and encouraging and imploring each one of you as a father would his own children (vv. 7–11).

What a gracious, tolerant spirit! The man was both approachable and tender. Did you notice the word pictures? He cared for others "as a nursing mother" (v. 7) and dealt with them in their needs "as a father" (v. 11). He had compassion. Of high priority to this capable, brilliant man of God was a gracious, compassionate attitude.

He admits that he was interested in doing more than dumping a truckload of theological and doctrinal data on them . . . he wanted to share not only the gospel, but his life.

If there is one specific criticism we hear against our evangelical "camp" more than any other, it is this: We lack compassion. We are more abrasive and judgmental than thoughtful, tactful, compassionate, and tolerant. If we're not careful, we tend to use people rather than love them, don't we? We try to change them and later help them, rather than accept them as they are.

A greatly needed priority for this decade is an attitude or disposition that is characterized by *grace.* Do you recall Peter's final bit of counsel?

> But grow in the grace and knowledge of our Lord and Savior Jesus Christ. To Him be the glory, both now and to the day of eternity. Amen (2 Pet. 3:18).

Am I saying there is no place for conviction or a firm commitment to truth? Of course not. All I plead for are threads of grace woven through the garment of truth. If I live to be one hundred fifty, I will never buy the idea that it is an either-or matter. Our world of hungry, hurting humanity longs for and deserves the message of truth presented in attractive, gentle, gracious wrappings. Don't forget: "As a mother... as a father." There is positive affirmation implied rather than negative nitpicking.

Charlie Shedd illustrates this so perfectly as he tells of an experience he had with Philip, one of his sons. The story revolved around a bale of binder twine.

> ... When we moved from Nebraska to Oklahoma, we brought [the binder twine] along. I had used it there to tie sacks of feed and miscellaneous items. It cost something like $1.15. So I said, "Now, Philip, you see this binder twine? I want you to leave it alone." But it held a strange fascination for him and he began to use it any time he wanted. I would say, "Don't," "No," and "You can't!" But all to no avail.
>
> That went on for six or eight months. Then one day I came home tired. There was the garage, looking like a no-man's land with binder twine across, back and forth, up and down. I had to cut my way through to get the car in. And was I provoked! I ground

my teeth as I slashed at that binder twine. Suddenly, when I was halfway through the maze, a light dawned. I asked myself, "Why do you want this binder twine? What if Philip does use it?"

So when I went in to supper that night, Philip was there and I began, "Say, about that binder twine!" He hung his head and mumbled, "Yes, Daddy." Then I said, "Philip, I've changed my mind. You can use that old binder twine any time you want. What's more, all those tools out in the garage I've labeled 'No'—you go ahead and use them. I can buy new tools, but I can't buy new boys." There never was a sunrise like that smile. "Thanks, Daddy," he beamed. And guess what, Peter. He hasn't touched that binder twine since![5]

That's the way it works in a gracious, accepting climate. People become far more important than rigid rules and demanding expectations.

Thus far we've deposited into our memory banks three vital priorities: those of being biblical, authentic, and gracious. In 1 Thessalonians 2:12–13 Paul deals with yet another priority.

So that you may walk in a manner worthy of the God who calls you into His own kingdom and glory.

And for this reason we also constantly thank God that when you received from us the word of God's message, you accepted it not as the word of men, but for what it really is, the word of God, which also performs its work in you who believe.

Be Relevant

There is a direct link here between talk and walk. Paul's message always has a relevant ring to it. Even though the truth of the Scriptures is ancient, when it is received, it goes to work today; . . . it is up to date and continually at "work in you who believe" (v. 13).

If we are hoping to reach our generation in the '80s, we must make relevance a high priority. That is exactly what Jesus Christ did. He met people as they *were*, not as they "ought to have been." Angry young men, blind beggars, proud politicians, loose-living streetwalkers, dirty and naked victims of demonism, and grieving parents got equal time. They all hung on His every word. Even though He could have blown them away with his knowledge and authority, He purposely stayed on their level. Jesus was the epitome of relevance. And still is.

It is *we* who have hauled His cross out of sight. It is *we* who have left the impression that it belongs only in the sophisticated, cloistered halls of a seminary or beautified beneath the soft shadows of stained glass and cold marble statues. I applaud the one who put it this way:

> I simply argue that the cross be raised again
>   at the center of the market place
>   as well as on the steeple of the church,
>
> I am recovering the claim that
>   Jesus was not crucified in a cathedral
>   between two candles:
>
> But on a cross between two thieves;
>   on a town garbage heap;
>   At a crossroad of politics so cosmopolitan
>   that they had to write His title
>   in Hebrew and in Latin and in Greek...
>
> And at the kind of place where cynics talk smut,
>   and thieves curse and soldiers gamble.
>
> Because that is where He died,
>   and that is what He died about.
>   And that is where Christ's men ought to be,
>   and what church people ought to be about.[6]

GEORGE MacLEOD

REVIEW AND WRAP-UP

The tyranny of the urgent will always outshout the essential nature of the important . . . if we let it. We have determined not to let that happen. The secret is establishing personal priorities. I have suggested four:

- Set a firm foundation—be *biblical.*
- Apply the truth of the Scriptures—be *authentic.*
- Develop a compassionate attitude—be *gracious.*
- Stay current, always up to date—be *relevant.*

As we begin to do this, Christianity becomes something that is absorbed, not just worn. It is more than believed; it is incarnated.

And if there is anything that will catch the attention of preoccupied people fighting the fires of the urgent, it is God's truth incarnated. It happened in the first century and it can happen in the twentieth. Even in an aimless world like ours.

DISCUSSION QUESTIONS AND IDEAS TO HELP YOU STRENGTHEN YOUR GRIP ON PRIORITIES

Before going on to the next chapter, pause and reflect. Take time to review and apply.

- All of us face the tyranny of the urgent. It has a way of casting an eclipse over the important. Think about the urgent demands on your life. Name a few to yourself. Now consider this: What important things are being ignored because of the urgent?

- In this chapter we thought about four top priority items, according to 1 Thessalonians 2:1–13. Can you name each one as you read this section of Scripture?

- Why are these so important? What happens if they are missing from a person's life? Or from one's church?

    • Now consider seriously what you could change in your schedule or your way of living to make room for these priorities. Be specific.

    • Spend a minute or two in prayer. Thank God for speaking to you about these essentials. Ask Him to help you give less attention to the urgent and more to the important.

CHAPTER TWO

Strengthening Your Grip on Involvement

"I KNOW OF NO MORE potent killer than isolation. There is no more destructive influence on physical and mental health than the isolation of you from me and us from them. It has been shown to be a central agent in the etiology of depression, paranoia, schizophrenia, rape, suicide, mass murder, and a wide variety of disease states."[1]

Those are the words of Professor Philip Zimbardo, a respected authority on psychology from Stanford University, a man who faces the blunt blows of reality in daily doses. His words are not only true, they are downright frightening. No longer are we a share-and-share-alike people. We are independent cogs in complex corporate structures. We wear headsets as we jog or do our lawns or walk to class or eat in cafeterias. Our watchword is "privacy;" our commitments are short-term. Our world is fast adopting the unwritten regulation so often observed in elevators, "Absolutely no eye contact, talking, smiling, or relating without written permission from the management." The Lone Ranger, once a fantasy hero, is now our model, mask and all.

How times have changed! John Donne, a seventeenth-century sage from the Old Country, would never have thought it possible. He wrote these once-familiar, but soon-to-be-forgotten thoughts:

> No man is an island, entire of itself; every man is a piece of the continent, a part of the main; if a clod be washed away by the sea, Europe is the less... any man's death diminishes me, because I am involved in mankind; and therefore never send to know for whom the bell tolls; it tolls for thee.[2]

Our aimless, lonely generation has great difficulty understanding such concepts as the interrelatedness of mankind. Thanks to the now-accepted policy of many businesses to transfer a man and his family across the nation with each promotion, even the extended family bonds are now being loosened. Involvement with our roots is reduced to snapshots and phone calls at Christmas. Family reunions and seasonal rituals are nearly extinct as relatives become curious aliens to our children. All this and much, much more, plus the inevitable, irritating hassles connected with cultivating close relationships, causes us to move away from each other into our own separate houses where we isolate ourselves still further in our own separate bedrooms. We pursue self-sufficient lifestyles that make sharing unnecessary.

As one man observes, "The well-tended front lawn is the modern moat that keeps the barbarians at bay."[3] Anonymity, cynicism, and indifference are fast replacing mutual support and genuine interest. It may seem on the surface to be more efficient, but remember the counsel of Dr. Zimbardo: isolation is actually a "potent killer."

WHAT IS "INVOLVEMENT"?

In the Webster's dictionary, we find that *being involved* means "to draw in as a participant, to relate closely, to connect, to include." When you and I involve ourselves with someone, we "connect" with them. We think of them as we make our plans. We actually operate our lives with others in clear focus. We draw them in as participants in our activities. We include them.

To break this down into manageable terms, Christians have at least four areas of involvement to maintain:

• **Our involvement with God.**

In the past, this involvement resulted in our salvation—our new birth through faith in Jesus Christ. Currently it is our everyday walk with Christ through life. To maintain a close connection with our Lord, we think of Him as we make our plans, we pray, we explore the rich treasures of His Word. This is the single most significant involvement in all of life, but it is not automatic.

• **Our involvement with members of our family.**

Parents, children, relatives, mates... Christian or not—all of these people comprise our circle of close contact. We include them in our thinking, some, of course, more closely than others.

• **Our involvement with other Christians.**

Usually, these people are selected from the church we attend. The number grows as we "connect" with others through areas of mutual interest. Some of us could list literally *hundreds* of Christian friends with whom we have a relationship. This becomes a major factor in our ability to cope with life on this planet, an otherwise lonely and discouraging pilgrimage.

• **Our involvement with non-Christians.**

We work alongside them, do business with them, live near them, go to school next to them, and are usually entertained by them. Unfortunately, most Christians cut off *all* close ties with non-Christians within a few months after salvation. Small wonder we find it difficult to share our faith with others. I'll talk more about that in chapter 14.

BEING INVOLVED WITH OTHER CHRISTIANS

For the balance of this chapter, let's center our attention on the third area of involvement—our relationship with others in God's family. If you are not a Christian *or* if you are a new believer, you might think that the Christian-with-Christian relationship is one step short of heavenly bliss. On the contrary. Although there are some beautiful exceptions, it has been my observation that we Christians are often at odds with each other.

Someone once suggested that we are like a pack of porcupines on a frigid wintry night. The cold drives us closer together into a tight huddle to keep warm. As we begin to snuggle really close, our sharp quills cause us to jab and prick each other—a condition which forces us apart. But before long we start getting cold, so we move back to get warm again, only to stab and puncture each other once more. And so we participate in this strange, rhythmic "tribal dance." We cannot deny it, we need each other, yet we needle each other!

> To dwell above with saints we love,
>   That will be grace and glory.
> To live below with saints we know;
>   That's another story![4]

How can we break ye olde porcupine syndrome? The answer in one word is involvement. Or, to use the biblical term, it is *fellowship*.

> And they were continually devoting themselves to the apostles' teaching and to fellowship, to the breaking of bread and to prayer (Acts 2:42).

This verse of Scripture is a statement of immense significance. Historically, the church has just come into existence. About three thousand new Christians are huddled together in the streets of Jerusalem. They have nothing tangible to lean on—no building, no organization, no church constitution and bylaws, no "pastor," not even a completed copy of the Scriptures. What did they do? This verse says they devoted themselves to the instruction of the apostles, to the ordinances, to prayer, *and* to fellowship.

The Greek term for fellowship is *koinonia*. The root meaning is "common." The next three verses from Acts 2 reveal just how closely they were bound together.

And everyone kept feeling a sense of awe; and many wonders and signs were taking place through the apostles.

And all those who had believed were together, and had all things in common; and they began selling their property and possessions, and were sharing them with all, as anyone might have need (vv. 43–45).

To borrow from the familiar words of John Fawcett's hymn, "Blest Be the Tie," these first-century Christians shared their mutual woes, their mutual burdens they bore, and often for each other flowed a sympathizing tear.

OBSERVATIONS OF FIRST-CENTURY INVOLVEMENT

I observe that their mutual involvement had four characteristics:

1. It was entered into by everyone (three times we read "all").
2. It helped hold them together in times of great need.
3. It was genuine, spontaneous, never forced. Sincerity was there.
4. It added to their sense of unity and harmony.

In Acts 4 we read more about the early days of the church:

And the congregation of those who believed were of one heart and soul; and not one of them claimed that anything belonging to him was his own; but all things were common property to them.

For there was not a needy person among them, for all who were owners of lands or houses would sell them and bring the proceeds of the sales, and lay them at the apostles' feet; and they would be distributed to each, as any had need (Acts 4:32, 34–35).

Amazing!

Ancient *koinonia* must have been something to behold. As I try to form a mental picture of it, I come up with this description: *Koinonia is expressions of authentic Christianity freely shared among members of God's family.* It is mentioned about twenty times in the New Testament. Without exception it is invariably expressed in one of two directions.

First, it is used in the sense of sharing something *with* someone such as food, money, supplies, encouragement, time, and concern. And second, it is used in the sense of sharing *in* something with someone, like a project, a success, a failure, a need, a hurt.

The significance of all this is that biblical *koinonia* is *never something done alone*. In other words, God's desire for His children is that we be personally and deeply involved in each other's lives. It is not His will that we start looking like touch-me-not automatons covered over with a thin layer of shiny chrome. Our superficial "How ya' doin'" and "Have a nice day" won't cut it. There was none of this lack of involvement in that group of first-century Christians. There wasn't a porcupine among them!

Why Get Involved?

As I search God's Word for reasons to break with the isolationism of this age, I find two inescapable facts: God commands it and the Church needs it.

God Commands It

We read in Romans 12:9–16 a series of commands:

Let love be without hypocrisy. Abhor what is evil; cleave to what is good.

Be devoted to one another in brotherly love; give preference to one another in honor; not lagging behind in diligence, fervent in spirit, serving the Lord; rejoicing in hope, persevering in tribulation, devoted to prayer, contributing to the needs of the saints, practicing hospitality.

Bless those who persecute you; bless and curse not.

Rejoice with those who rejoice, and weep with those who weep.

Be of the same mind toward one another; do not be haughty in mind, but associate with the lowly. Do not be wise in your own estimation.

All those verses are actually an outgrowth of the first command, "Let love be without hypocrisy." Look at the way *The Living Bible* presents verses 9 and 10:

Don't just pretend that you love others: really love them. Hate what is wrong. Stand on the side of the good. Love each other with brotherly affection and take delight in honoring each other.

Away with hypocrisy! Farewell to indifference! God commands that we reach out, accept, and affirm one another. This means that we consciously resist the strong current of the stream we are in . . . the one that dictates all those excuses:

"I'm just too busy."

"It's not worth the risk."

"I don't really need anyone."

"I'll get burned if I get too close."

"If I reach out, I'll look foolish."

The devil's strategy for our times is working. He has deluded us into believing that we really shouldn't concern ourselves with being our brother's keeper. After all, we have time pressures and work demands (that relentless, fierce determination to be number one), not to mention, anxieties prompted by economic uncertainty. And who really needs our help anyway? I'll tell you who—just about every person we meet, that's who. Don't be fooled by the secure-looking, self-reliant veneer most of us wear. Deep down inside there's usually a scared little kid who is waiting for someone to care, to hold his or her hand, to affirm and love with authentic affection.

God commands us to be involved because He has made us dependent beings. Remember what He said to Adam just before He gave him Eve? "It is not good for the man to be alone" (Gen. 2:18).

This brings up the second reason we are to be involved.

The Body Needs It

Read again these familiar words:

As it is, there are many parts, but one body.
The eye cannot say to the hand, "I don't need you!" And the head cannot say to the feet, "I don't need you!"
On the contrary, those parts of the body that seem to be weaker are indispensable, and the parts that we think are less honorable we treat with special honor. And the parts that are unpresentable are treated with special modesty, while our presentable parts need no special treatment. But God has combined the members of the body and has given greater honor to the parts that lacked it, so that there should be no division in the body, but that its parts should have equal concern for each other.
If one part suffers, every part suffers with it; if one part is honored, every part rejoices with it.
Now you are the body of Christ, and each one of you is a part of it (1 Cor. 12:20–27, NIV).

In order for Christ's body, the Church, to do its thing, we must be working together as a team. To dispel division, we are to be involved with one another. To keep down disease, to mend fractures, to accelerate healing, we must be interdependent. Furthermore, we need to assist each other as servants and friends—just like a human body comes to the aid of its injured parts.

During an adolescent period in my own spiritual growth, I went through a stage where I felt I really didn't need anyone. I "used" a few people during that time, and I occasionally acted out a role that looked like I was willing to be involved, but deep down inside I kept my distance. Hidden pride played games within me, I am ashamed to admit, as I mouthed the right stuff, but I had no interest whatever in reaching out or allowing anyone else to reach in.

It was at that time God went to work on my attitude. He used every possible means, it seemed, to get my attention and reveal to me my need for others. Looking back, I can now see why He didn't let up. With relentless regularity He stayed on my case, punching, pushing, pulling, pressing, penetrating. The best part of all was the beautiful way others ministered to me—and I was forced to face the fact that *I needed them* just like Paul writes in 1 Corinthians 12. I learned by experience: "The eye cannot say to the hand, 'I have no need of you'" (v. 21, RSV).

In the family of God, there is no such thing as a completely independent member of the body. We may act like it for awhile, but ultimately He shows us how much we need one another.

WHAT DOES INVOLVEMENT INCLUDE?

As I read verses 25 through 27 of 1 Corinthians 12, I find at least three particular ingredients in meaningful involvement: Spontaneity, vulnerability, and accountability.

Spontaneity

Read again verse 25.

So that there should be no division in the body, but that its parts should have equal concern for each other (NIV).

I'm glad God expresses Himself here like He does. "Should." Not "must." Not "You better, or else!" Spontaneous willingness is implied in "should."

When God prompts involvement, it is not contrived. It's never forced. It flows. There is no legislation, no galling obligation. It's done because the person wants to, not because he *has* to.

Vulnerability

Look at verse 26:

If one part suffers, every part suffers with it; if one part is honored, every part rejoices with it (NIV).

There is a lot of personal feeling in these words. The one who gets involved doesn't play the role of prim-and-proper Mr. Clean. No, he is human, vulnerable—capable of being wounded, open to attack, misunderstanding, or damage. He is unguarded.

When wounds ooze, vulnerable people get soiled. There is genuine sharing in the hurt. Vulnerable people are fearless, however, when it comes to being broken. In her own, inimitable style, Anne Ortlund writes of this as she reflects on a sermon her husband Ray preached on Mark 14:3.

... "Here came Mary," he said, "with her alabaster vase of nard to the dinner where Jesus was. She broke the bottle and poured it on Him."

An alabaster vase—milky white, veined, smooth, precious.

And pure nard inside! Gone forever. According to John 12:3, the whole house became filled with the fragrance. Some story.

Christians file into church on a Sunday morning. One by one by one they march in—like separate alabaster vases.
Contained.
Self-sufficient.
Encased.
Individually complete.
Contents undisclosed.
No perfume emitting at all.

Their vases aren't bad looking. In fact, some of them are the Beautiful People, and they become Vase-Conscious: conscious of their own vase and of one another's. They're aware of clothes, personalities, of position in this world—of exteriors.

So before and after church (maybe during) they're apt to talk Vase Talk. *Your ring is darling; what stone is that? Did you hear if Harry got that job? What is Lisa's boy doing for the summer? Is that all your own hair? I may take tennis lessons if George wants to.*

Mary broke her vase.

Broke it! How shocking. How controversial. Was everybody doing it? Was it a vase-breaking party? No, she just did it all by herself. What happened then? The obvious: all the contents were forever released. She could never hug her precious nard to herself again.[5]

That's the way it is with vulnerability. It's risky, but it's so essential.

There is one final ingredient in meaningful involvement found in this 1 Corinthians passage.

Accountability

Now you are the body of Christ, and each one of you is a part of it (v. 27, NIV).

We are not only one massive body, we are *individuals*, single units who carry out vital functions. This means we are accountable to one another. As I quoted earlier, "No man is an island... every man is a piece of the continent."

In our indifferent, preoccupied world of isolation and anonymity, it's a comfort to know we are linked together. Someone cares about us. Someone is interested. Someone notices. That's another benefit of being involved.

I am the senior pastor of a rather large congregation in Southern California. It is easy for a person to get completely lost in the shuffle... to be a nameless face in a crowd. To feel no sense of identity. To accept no responsibility. To drift dangerously near perilous extremes without anyone even knowing it. That's why those of us in leadership are constantly thinking of ways to cultivate an identity, to bring people out of anonymity, to assure them that involvement includes accountability. It is easy to think that all who come for worship are involved—are being noticed and encouraged. But such is not the case.

The grim reality of all this struck home to my heart some time ago as I read the true account of an experience my friend, Dr. James Dobson, had at a seminary. Jim had spoken on the subject of the need for self-esteem among men in the ministry. Strangely, many people have the mistaken idea that those preparing for ministry seldom struggle with inferiority. One young man was brave enough to admit that he found himself paralyzed with fear, even though he sincerely desired to help others as he served God. Dr. Dobson spoke openly of this common predicament that gnaws on one's soul.

Sitting in the audience that same day was another student with the same kind of problems. However, he did not write me a letter. He never identified himself in any way. But three weeks after I left, he hanged himself in the basement of his apartment. One of the four men with whom he lived called long distance to inform me of the tragedy. He stated, deeply shaken, that the dead student's roommates were so unaware of his problems that he hanged there five days before he was missed![6]

Difficult though it may be to believe it, there are Christian people who are *that* out of touch and *that* uninvolved in the town or city where you live. And also in the church where you worship. They need you. What's more, *you need them.* And unless something is done to establish and maintain meaningful involvement, tragedies will continue to occur.

Never forget, isolation is a potent killer. Strengthening our grip on involvement is not simply an enjoyable luxury for those who have time on their hands. It's essential for survival.

DISCUSSION QUESTIONS AND IDEAS TO HELP YOU STRENGTHEN YOUR GRIP ON INVOLVEMENT

• In your own words, define *involvement.* Think and talk about how it provides the needed answer to isolation. On a scale of 1 (lowest) to 10 (highest), how high would you rate your level of involvement?

• Remember the "porcupine syndrome"? Be honest with yourself as you reflect on your own tendency to push back when people start getting too close. Is this true? Ever analyzed why?

• We looked into numerous helpful Scripture passages in this chapter. See if you can recall several that took on a deeper meaning. Turn to them and discuss this.

• As we thought about the reasons involvement is important, we considered two: (1) because God commands it, and (2) because the Body needs it. Think this over—especially the *second* reason. What specifically do you gain from someone else, which you yourself cannot provide?

• Spontaneity, vulnerability, and accountability are three vital ingredients in meaningful involvement. Choose one and think about its value. Can you recall an experience when you witnessed this in someone else?

CHAPTER THREE

Strengthening Your Grip on Encouragement

KEYSTONE, COLORADO, IS A SKI RESORT area about an hour and a half west of Denver. My family and I were invited to spend Thanksgiving week at that picturesque spot in 1980 with about five hundred single young adults, most of whom were staff personnel with Campus Crusade, an international Christian organization. I cannot recall a time when there was a greater spirit of teachability and enthusiasm among a group of people. The atmosphere was electric!

I spoke all week on the subject of servanthood, emphasizing the importance of today's leader being one who helps, encourages, affirms, and cares for others rather than one who pulls rank and takes advantage of them. Many of the things I presented have now found their way into a book.[1] God *really* changed some lives that week. I continue to hear from various men and women who were a part of that memorable experience.

By Friday of that week I decided to take a break and hit the slopes (emphasis on *hit*, since it was my first time in all my life to attempt to ski). It had snowed all day Thanksgiving. The ski areas were absolutely beautiful and in perfect condition. I struck out on my virgin voyage with a positive mental attitude, thinking, "I'm going to be the first person who learned to ski without falling down.*Guinness Book of World Records* will hear of this and write me up!"

Don't bother to check. I'm not in the book.

It was unbelievable! You have heard of the elephant man? On skis, I'm the rhinoceros man. It is doubtful that anyone else on planet earth has ever come down any ski slope more ways than I did. Or landed in more positions. Or did more creative things in the air *before* landing. I can still hear the words of a ski instructor as she stood before her class of children, staring at me as I zipped past them. I was by then on one leg, leaning dangerously to the starboard side, traveling about thirty-five miles an hour—completely out of control. "Now class, that is what I DON'T want you to do!" As I recall, I ended that slide a few miles from Denver in a field of buffalo. Even they looked surprised.

Working with me that humiliating day was the world's most encouraging ski instructor (yes, I had an instructor!) who set the new record in patience. She is the one whom Guinness needs to interview.

Never once did she lose her cool.

Never once did she laugh at me.

Never once did she yell, scream, threaten, or swear.

Never once did she call me "dummy."

Never once did she say, "You are absolutely impossible. I quit!"

That dear, gracious lady helped me up more times than I can number. She repeated the same basics time and again—like she had never said them before. Even though I was colder than an explorer in the Antarctic, irritable, impatient, and under the snow more than I was on it, she kept on offering words of reassurance. On top of all that, she didn't even charge me for those hours on the baby slope when she could have been enjoying the day with all her friends on the fabulous, long slope up above. That day God gave me a living, never-to-be-forgotten illustration of the value of encouragement. Had it not been for her spirit and her words, believe me, I would have hung 'em up and been back in the condo, warming my feet by the fire in less than an hour.

What is true for a novice on the snow once a year is all the more true for the people we meet every day. Harassed by demands and deadlines; bruised by worry, adversity, and failure; broken by disillusionment; and defeated by sin, they live somewhere between dull discouragement and sheer panic. Even Christians are not immune! We may give off this "I've got it all together" air of confidence, much like I did when I first snapped on the skis at Keystone. But realistically, we also struggle, lose our balance, slip and slide, tumble, and fall flat on our faces.

All of us need encouragement—somebody to believe in us. To reassure and reinforce us. To help us pick up the pieces and go on. To provide us with increased determination in spite of the odds.

THE MEANING OF ENCOURAGEMENT

When you stop to analyze the concept, "encourage" takes on new meaning. It's the act of inspiring others with renewed courage, spirit, or hope. When we encourage others we spur them on, we stimulate and affirm them. It is helpful to remember the distinction between appreciation and affirmation. We appreciate what a person does, but we affirm who a person is. Appreciation comes and goes because it is usually related to something someone accomplishes. Affirmation goes deeper. It is directed to the person himself or herself. While encouragement would encompass both, the rarer of the two is affirmation. To be appreciated, we get the distinct impression that we must earn it by some accomplishment. But affirmation requires no such prerequisite. This means that even when we don't earn the right to be appreciated (because we failed to succeed or because we lacked the accomplishment of some goal), we can still be affirmed—indeed, we need it then more than ever.

I do not care how influential or secure or mature a person may appear to be, genuine encouragement never fails to help. Most of us need massive doses of it as we slug it out in the trenches. But we are usually too proud to admit it. Unfortunately, this pride is as prevalent among members of God's family as it is on the streets of the world. Let's dig deeper into this issue of encouragement.

THERE'S MORE TO WORSHIP THAN PRAYING

Most people who go to church believe that a worship service consists only of a few hymns, a prayer or two, dropping some bucks in a plate, hearing a solo, and finally listening to a sermon. If you gave that answer to my one-question quiz "Why do Christians gather for worship?" I'd have to grade you "incomplete." Let me show you why.

Many centuries ago when Christians began meeting together, persecution was standard operating procedure. Martyrdom was as common to them as traffic jams are to us—an everyday occurrence. As a result, fear gripped congregations. Some believers defected, others sort of drifted to play it safe.

A letter, therefore, began to circulate among the converted Jews, addressed to those who were enduring the blast of persecution. We know the letter today as *Hebrews*. Nobody knows for sure who wrote the letter, but whoever it was understood the value of corporate worship. After warning them against compromising their walk of faith, he informed them of the importance of those special times they spent together.

Spend a few moments thinking through his words that were written, no doubt, with a great deal of emotion.

Since therefore, brethren, we have confidence to enter the holy place by the blood of Jesus, by a new and living way which He inaugurated for us through the veil, that is, His flesh, and since we have a great priest over the house of God, let us draw near with a sincere heart in full assurance of faith, having our hearts sprinkled clean from an evil conscience and our body washed with pure water.

Let us hold fast the confession of our hope without wavering, for He who promised is faithful; and let us consider how to stimulate one another to love and good deeds, not forsaking our own assembling together, as is the habit of some but encouraging one another; and all the more, as you see the day drawing near (Heb. 10:19–25).

He begins this section by describing what we *have:*
1. We have confidence to approach God (v. 19).
2. We have a priest who gives us access to God—referring to Christ (v. 21).

We Christians today tend to forget what magnificent benefits these are. The reason we forget is simple—we've never known it any other way! But back then, during the threatening era of the first century, worshipers *lacked* confidence. They approached God with a spirit of fear and trepidation. Their fathers and forefathers knew nothing of such familiarity with the Father. But now that Christ has opened the way to God (by His death on the cross), we come boldly, confidently. Why? Because Jesus Christ is our go-between. We have confidence because He has given us this immediate access to the throne room of God the Father.

Next, the writer of Hebrews describes what we are *to do.* Did you catch the cues? Three times he prefaces his remarks with "let us."

"*Let us draw near...*" (v. 22).

In other words, come up close. It's an invitation to become intimately acquainted with our God. There's no need for children of God to feel as if they are walking on eggs when they come before Him.

"Let us hold fast..." (v. 23).

This verse conveys the importance of standing firm in the reliable truth of God. Today we'd say, "Let's hang tough!"

"Let us consider how to stimulate one another..." (v. 24).

This verse seems to focus in on the point the writer has been trying to make. Ultimately, we are to think about ways to stir up each other so that the result is a deeper love for one another and a greater involvement in doing good things for one another. In a word, he is talking about encouragement. How can we know that for sure? Check out the very next verse:

> Not forsaking our own assembling together, as is the habit of some but encouraging one another; and all the more, as you see the day drawing near (v. 25).

You see, there's much more to worship than sitting and listening to a sermon or bowing in prayer. A major objective is that we give attention to what we might do to encourage each other.

One further thought on that passage of Scripture—did you notice that we are not told specifically what to do? We are simply exhorted, "Let us consider how to stimulate one another...." The details are left up to each new generation of people who face new and different challenges.

THE SIGNIFICANCE OF ENCOURAGEMENT

Certainly there is more to encouragement than a smile and a quick pat on the back. We need to realize just how valuable it really is.

A good place to start is with the word itself. *Encouragement,* as used in Hebrews 10:25, is from the same Greek root used for the Holy Spirit in John 14:26 and 16:7. In both those verses He is called "the Helper." The actual term, *para-*

kaleo, is from a combination of two smaller words, *kaleo,* "to call," and *para,* "alongside." Just as the Holy Spirit is called alongside to help us, so it is with us when you and I encourage someone else. In fact, when we encourage others, we come as close to the work of the Holy Spirit as anything we can do in God's family. Believe me, when Christians begin to realize the value of mutual encouragement, there is no limit to what we can be stimulated to accomplish. It is thrilling to realize that God has "called *us* alongside to help" others who are in need. How much better to be engaged in actions that lift others up rather than actions that tear them down!

Realizing this, one man writes:

> One of the highest of human duties is the duty of encouragement. . . . It is easy to pour cold water on their enthusiasm; it is easy to discourage others. The world is full of discouragers. We have a Christian duty to encourage one another. Many a time a word of praise or thanks or appreciation or cheer has kept a man on his feet.[2]

The beautiful part about encouragement is this: *Anybody* can do it. You don't need a lot of money to carry it out. You don't even need to be a certain age. In fact, some of the most encouraging actions or words I've received have come from my own children at a time when my heart was heavy. They saw the need and moved right in . . . they "came alongside and helped."

Local churches are beginning to catch on, too. I read of a congregation in Salem, Oregon, who decided to get serious about this. "Encouragement cards" are placed in the hymn racks on each pew. At the top of the card, the words "Encouraging One Another" appear in bold print. Those who use them place the name of the recipient on one side and their message of encouragement on the other. All cards must be signed—no unsigned cards are mailed. All cards are collected, and early that same week office personnel address, stamp, and mail the cards. Multiple cards to the same person are bunched together and mailed in a single envelope.

Since many are too busy to sit down during the week and write a word of encouragement, this congregation takes time as the worship service begins. Some bow in prayer while others grab a pencil and start encouraging. What a grand idea!

"Aw, it'll get old—lose its punch," you might think. "Not so," says the pastor. For nine years they have been involved in this process of putting encouragement into action, and it is more effective and meaningful today than ever before.[3]

I am absolutely convinced that there are many thousands of people who are drying up on the vine simply because of the lack of encouragement. Lonely, forgotten missionaries, military service men and women away from home, collegians and seminarians, the sick and the dying, the divorced and the grieving, those who serve faithfully behind the scenes with scarcely a glance or comment from anyone.

While I was studying at Dallas Theological Seminary, my wife and I became close friends with a graduate student working toward his doctor of theology degree. He was a winsome, brilliant young man whose future looked promising. He was single at the time, and Cynthia and I often spoke of how fortunate some young lady would be to claim him as her own! As time passed he not only earned the coveted degree, he met and married a young woman. Several years and two children later, our friend was well on his way toward an extremely successful career when suddenly his world collapsed. His wife left him, taking the children and the joys of a home with her.

I shall never forget his description of walking into the house and finding it cold and empty. A dozen emotions swept through him as the grim reality of loss bit deeply into his soul, spreading the paralyzing venom of despair. Time dragged on . . . no change, only memories. Reconciliation became a misty, distant dream, finally an absolute impossibility. The horror of endless hours of loneliness caused our friend to question many things. To say he was low is to understate the obvious—he was at rock bottom. While there, he wrote this piece which I repeat with his permission, but I shall leave it anonymous to protect his privacy.

The days are long, but the nights longer—and lonelier.
I wait for the daylight—
   but darkness holds me in her grip.
I struggle alone.

Sleep escapes me as memories of the good times—
   and the bad—
Crowd out the vestiges of euphoria and leave me restless—
   hurting—
Filling my mind with thoughts of love—
   and hostility,
Of thoughtlessness—
   and remorse,
Of guilt—
   and despair.

O God, I cry, is there no end to the hurt?
Must shame plague my steps forever?
Is there not another who will walk with me—
   accepting
     loving
       caring
         forgiving—
Willing to build with me a new life on foundations more sure—
To whom I will pledge, as will she, faithfulness forever?

Others have cried with me in the darkness—
   they have cared—
But in the confinements of our own humanness.
The demands of their lives must take precedence.
And in the end I stand alone—
   apart from Thee.

I have attempted to build again—
   on my own—
Too soon, unwise and unstable.
New hurts have come to tear open the wounds not yet healed.
The struggle is not ended.

And so I crawl—
   uneasy, yet unyielding to defeat and sure despair—
Toward better days,
   Toward light that is unending,
     Toward God who keeps me in His care.

Encouragement became this man's single oasis in the desert of defeat. A few people graciously and consistently reached out to him, giving him hope and the will to go on as many more turned away, rejecting him and questioning his character. The man has since remarried and is happily engaged in a fulfilling, challenging role as an executive in a Christian organization. Thanks to encouragement, he survived. His case is one in thousands—another example of the strategic significance encouragement plays in the lives of those who hurt.

IMPLEMENTING ENCOURAGEMENT

Going back to the statement found in Hebrews 10:25, we are to "consider how to stimulate one another to love and good deeds." In other words, we are to give thought to specific ways we can lift up, affirm, and help others. God's commands are not theoretical—especially those that relate to people in need. A couple of scriptures come to my mind:

If you have a friend who is in need of food and clothing, and you say to him, "Well, good-bye and God bless you; stay warm and eat hearty," and then don't give him clothes or food, what good does that do? (James 2:15–16, TLB).

But if someone who is supposed to be a Christian has money enough to live well, and sees a brother in need, and won't help him—how can God's love be within him? (1 John 3:17, TLB).

Maybe a few ideas will help spark an interest in putting our encouragement into action.

• Observe and mention admirable character qualities you see in others, such as:

Punctuality	Thoroughness
Tactfulness	Diligence
Faithfulness	Honesty
Good attitude	Compassion
Loyalty	Good Sense of Humor
Tolerance	Vision and Faith

• Correspondence, thank-you notes, small gifts with a note attached. Preferably not so much at birthdays or Christmas, but at unexpected times.

• Phone calls. Be brief and to the point. Express appreciation for something specific that you genuinely appreciate.

• Notice a job well done and say so. I know a few important people who are successful largely because they have splendid assistance from secretaries and support personnel within the ranks... but seldom are those people told what a fine job they are doing.

• Cultivate a positive, reassuring attitude. Think and respond along this line. Encouragement cannot thrive in a negative, squint-eyed atmosphere.

• Pick up the tab in a restaurant... provide free tickets to some event you know the person (or family) would enjoy... send flowers... give a gift of money when it seems appropriate.

• Be supportive to someone you know is hurting. Reach out without fear of what others may think or say.

A few final words of clarification are in order. Encouragement should take the sting out of life. But be careful not to create other burdens for those you want to encourage. Do what you do with no interest whatever in being paid back. Reciprocal expectations are guilt-giving trips, not encouraging actions! Also, try to be sensitive to the timing of your actions. A well-timed expression of encouragement is never forgotten. Never!

I often think of those who once did their job faithfully for an extended period of time and then were replaced—only to be forgotten. People like former teachers, former officers in a church, former board members, previous pastors, and those who discipled us become lost in the sea of distant memories. Spend some time recalling the important people who had part in building your life . . . and look for ways to encourage them. You and I may be surprised to know how much it means to them just to know they are not forgotten. If you need a tangible reminder of the encouragement this brings, call to mind our P.O.W.'s in Viet Nam and our hostages in Iran. Just the knowledge that they were not out of sight, out of mind, kept most of them going.

The ability to encourage is developed first in one's home. It is here that this vital virtue is cultivated. Children pick it up from their parents as they become the recipients of their mother's and dad's words of delight and approval. Numerous tests document the sad fact, however, that homes tend to be far more negative than positive, much less affirming than critical.

Allow me to challenge you to have a family that is different. Start taking whatever steps that need to be taken to develop in your home a spirit of positive, reinforcing, consistent encouragement. Your family will be forever grateful, believe me. And *you* will be a lot happier person.

I know a young man whose spinal cord was severed in an accident when he was four years old. He has absolutely no use of his legs today. They are like excess baggage stuck to his body. But thanks to a father who believed in him and a wife who absolutely adores him, Rick Leavenworth accomplishes feats today that you and I would call unbelievable. One of his more recent ones is backpacking and mountain climbing. In fact, a film[4] has been made (you *must* see it!) that shows him reaching the top of a mountain over 13,000 feet elevation ... all alone, just Rick, his wheelchair, and determination cultivated over years of encouragement.

I'm giving serious thought to giving up skiing and taking up backpacking. Maybe Rick will be willing to train me.

Discussion Questions and Ideas to Help You Strengthen Your Grip on Encouragement

• Encouragement plays a vital part in our relationship with one another. Talk about why. Be specific as you describe the things encouragement does for a person.

• Go back over the passage in Hebrews 10 that we referred to in this chapter. Read it aloud and slowly. Talk about the one part that seems most significant to you. Explain why.

• Now then, in your mind list three or four ways we *discourage* others. Be painfully honest with yourself as you answer the questions: Do you do this? If so, *why?* Next, mentally list some ways we *encourage* others. Talk about how you can start doing this more often.

• Can you think of a person who often lifts the spirits of others? Name the individual and describe how you have personally benefited from him or her. Have you ever told the person "Thanks"? Why not write a letter or make a phone call soon and communicate your gratitude?

• Strengthening your grip on encouragement is a slow process. Like the formation of any habit, it takes time. But in order for you to join the ranks of "encouragers," you need to start doing one or two things *daily* to encourage others. Think for a few moments, then share what you plan to start doing to form the habit of encouraging others.

CHAPTER FOUR

Strengthening Your Grip on Purity

"CHRISTIANITY IS SUPREMELY the champion of purity...."[1]

The words seemed to jump off the page. I grabbed the dictionary on my desk and looked up "champion." It means "a militant advocate or defender." A champion is one who fights for another's rights. As I went back to the original statement, I paraphrased it:

"Christianity is supremely the militant advocate, the defender of purity."

I then fantasized the sparkling image of a muscular man dressed in white with his brightly shining sword drawn. I named him Christianity and envisioned him as he stood in front of Purity, ready to slash to ribbons any enemy who attempted to attack her. She felt safe in his shadow, protected in his presence, like a little sister standing behind her big brother.

And then I thought, "Is that still true?" I checked the date on the book I was reading: 1959. With a sigh, I was forced to face reality, "We've come a long way since '59." Maybe a better word is *drifted*. Does Purity still have her champion?

Theoretically, she does. There has never been a more valiant defender of Purity than Christianity. Nothing can compare to the power of Christ when it comes to cleaning up a life. His liberating strength has broken the yoke of slavery to sin. His death and resurrection have come to our rescue, offering us dignity in place of moral misery and hope instead of degenerating despair. Unlike the helpless victims without the Savior who try and try to get their act together in their own strength—only to fail again and again—the person who knows Jesus Christ personally, having received Him by faith, has available to himself or herself all the power needed to walk in purity. But let's understand, that walk is not automatic. Ah, there's the rub.

It's not that Christianity has begun to lose its punch over the past twenty to twenty-five years; it's that more and more Christians (it seems to me) now opt for a lower standard when confronted with the choice of living in moral purity as set forth in the Scriptures or compromising (then rationalizing away the guilt). Well, just look around. You decide.

The battle of choices is certainly not new. Two sections of the New Testament, written in the first century (!), describe the internal warfare quite vividly:

> Your old evil desires were nailed to the cross with him; that part of you that loves to sin was crushed and fatally wounded, so that your sin-loving body is no longer under sin's control, no longer needs to be a slave to sin. . . .

> Do not let sin control your puny body any longer; do not give in to its sinful desires. Do not let any part of your bodies become tools of wickedness, to be used for sinning; but give yourselves completely to God—every part of you—for you are back from death and you want to be tools in the hands of God, to be used for his good purposes (Rom. 6:6, 12–13, TLB).

> For we naturally love to do evil things that are just the opposite from the things that the Holy Spirit tells us to do; and the good things we want to do when the Spirit has his way with us are just the opposite of our natural desires. These two forces within

us are constantly fighting each other to win control over us, and our wishes are never free from their pressures (Gal. 5:17, TLB).

How balanced the Bible is! Without denying the struggle or decreasing the strong appeal of our flesh, it announces that we need not yield as though we Christians are pathetic lumps of putty in the hands of temptation. In Christ, through Christ, because of Christ, we have all the internal equipment necessary to maintain moral purity. Yes, Christianity is *still* the champion of purity . . . but the challenges and attacks against purity have never been greater, and this complicates the problem.

MORAL EROSION: AN INESCAPABLE FACT

In case you are not ready to accept the idea that morals are on a downward trend, think back to 1939. That was the year *Gone With the Wind* was released, including in its script a scandal-making, four-letter word that raised the eyebrows of movie goers around the world. Has there been much change since '39? Do four-letter words still create scandals? What a joke!

Russian-born Pitirim Sorokin, the first professor and chairman of the Sociology Department at Harvard, is an astute observer of our times. His book, *The American Sex Revolution*, pulls no punches as he develops the theme: "Our civilization has become so preoccupied with sex that it now oozes from all pores of American life."[2] Grieved over our ever-increasing appetite for the sensual, Dr. Sorokin does a masterful job of describing the moral erosion of a nation once pure and proud:

. . . in the last century, much literature has centered on the personalities and adventures of subnormal and abnormal people,—prostitutes and mistresses, street urchins and criminals, the mentally and emotionally deranged, and other social derelicts.

There has been a growing preoccupation with the subsocial sewers,—the broken home of disloyal parents and unloved children, the bedroom of a prostitute, a "Canary Row" brothel, a den of criminals, a ward of the insane, a club of dishonest politicians, a street-corner gang of teen-age delinquents, the office of a huckster, the ostentatious mansion of a cynical business Mogul, a hate-laden prison, a "street car named desire," a crime-ridden waterfront, the courtroom of a dishonest judge, the jungle of cattle-murdering and meat-packing yards. These and hundreds of similar scenes are exemplary of a large part of modern Western literature, which has become increasingly a veritable museum of human pathology.

There has been a parallel transmutation of the experience of love. From the pure and noble or the tragic, it has progressively devolved. The common and prosaic, but usually licit sexual love that is portrayed in the literature of the eighteenth and nineteenth centuries has in the last fifty years been increasingly displaced by various forms of abnormal, perverse, vulgar, picaresque, exotic, and even monstrous forms,—the sex adventures of urbanized cavemen and rapists, the loves of adulterers and fornicators, of masochists and sadists, of prostitutes, mistresses, playboys, and entertainment personalities. Juicy "loves," "its," "ids," "orgasms," and "libidos" are seductively prepared and skillfully served with all the trimmings.

Designed to excite the fading lust of readers, and thereby increase the sales of these literary sex-tonics, much of contemporary Western literature has become Freudian through and through. It is preoccupied with "dirt-painting" of genital, anal, oral, cutaneous, homosexual, and incestuous "loves." It is absorbed in literary psychoanalysis of various complexes,—the castration, the Oedipus, the Tetanus, the Narcissus, and other pathological forms. It has degraded and denied the great, noble, and joyfully beautiful values of normal married love.[3]

Since Sorokin's book was written, we have degenerated beyond what even *he* would have imagined. Porno shops are now in every major American city. Hard-core X-rated films are now available on pay cable television as well as in some of the larger hotels. We have reached an all-time low with "kiddie porn" and "love" murders (yes, the actual crime) now captured on film. Even prime-time TV isn't exempt from intimate bedroom scenes, verbal explosions of profanity, and a rather frequent diet of so-called humor regarding sexual intercourse, homosexuality, nudity, and various parts of the human anatomy. One wonders when we shall reach the saturation level.

For sure, we've drifted a long way since '39! But this is not to suggest that up until then our land was as pure as the driven snow. No, it's just that there is a boldness, an un-blushing, uninhibited brashness in today's immorality that none can deny. And all of this assaults the senses with such relentless regularity that we need the power of God to walk in purity. The good news is this: *We have it!* But I remind you, putting His power into action is not automatic ... which brings us to one of the more potent biblical passages in the New Testament.

MORAL PURITY: AN ATTAINABLE GOAL

During Paul's second missionary journey, he trav-eled into Europe, a region of the world that had not heard of Christianity. In metropolitan cities like Philippi, Thessalonica, Athens, and Corinth he proclaimed the message of salvation, holding out hope and forgiveness to all who would listen. Later, after having had time to think about his ministry among them, he wrote letters to most of those places, desiring to clarify as well as intensify what he had taught them.

An example of this is found in 1 Thessalonians 4. Listen to the first five verses.

> Let me add this, dear brothers: You already know how to please God in your daily living, for you know the commands we gave you from the Lord Jesus himself. Now we beg you—yes, we demand of you in the name of the Lord Jesus—that you live more and more closely to that ideal.
>
> For God wants you to be holy and pure, and to keep clear of all sexual sin so that each of you will marry in holiness and

honor—not in lustful passion as the heathen do, in their ignorance of God and his ways (1 Thess. 4:1–5, TLB).

Like a pastor concerned about the flock among whom he ministers, Paul encourages them to do more than give a casual nod to sexual purity. Rather, he exhorts them to "excel still more" (NASB). He comes right out and commands them to "abstain from sexual immorality..." (NASB).

The Roman world of that day was a climate much like ours today. Impurity was viewed either with passive indifference or open favor. Christians back then (and now) were like tiny islands of morality surrounded by vast oceans of illicit sex and promiscuity. Knowing the current of temptation that swirled around them, he counseled them to "abstain"—an open and shut case for total abstention from sexual immorality. For Christianity to retain its role as "the champion of purity," the Christian is expected to be above reproach. The same is as true today as it was in the first century.

Christian holiness, says Paul, requires total abstinence from *porneias* ("sexual immorality," "fornication"). The word requires broad definition here as including all types of sexual sins between male and female.[4]

In our gray, hang-loose, swampy world of theological accommodation that adjusts to the mood of the moment, this passage of Scripture stands out like a lonely lighthouse on a stark, rugged hill. Interestingly, the verses go on to talk about the process of maintaining a pure lifestyle... that is to say, how to strengthen our grip on purity.

For this is the will of God, your sanctification; that is, that you abstain from sexual immorality; that each of you know how to possess his own vessel in sanctification and honor, not in lustful passion, like the Gentiles who do not know God; and that no man transgress and defraud his brother in the matter because the Lord is the avenger in all these things, just as we also told you before and solemnly warned you.

     For God has not called us for the purpose of impurity, but in sanctification (vv. 3–7).

Taking Control of the Body

     It is impossible to come to terms with moral purity without dealing with some practical facts related to the body—our flesh-and-blood appetites that crave satisfaction. Volumes are written about the mind, our emotional makeup, our "inner man," the soul, the spirit, and the spiritual dimension. But by comparison, very little is being said by evangelicals today about the physical body.

     • We are to present our bodies as living sacrifices to God (Rom. 12:1).

     • We are instructed *not* to yield any part of our bodies as instruments of unrighteousness to sin (Rom. 6:12–13).

     • Our bodies are actually "members of Christ"; they belong to Him (1 Cor. 6:15).

     • Our bodies are "temples" literally inhabited by the Holy Spirit (1 Cor. 6:19).

     • We are therefore expected to "glorify God" in our bodies (1 Cor. 6:20).

     • We are to become students of our bodies, knowing how to control them in honor (1 Thess. 4:4).

     You see, these bodies of ours can easily lead us off course. It isn't that the body itself is evil; it's just that it possesses any number of appetites that are ready to respond to the surrounding stimuli . . . all of which are terribly appealing and temporarily satisfying.

     Let me ask you: Do you know your body? Are you aware of the things that weaken your control of it? Have you stopped to consider the danger zones and how to stay clear of them—or at least hurriedly pass through them?

When I was in the Marines, I spent nearly a year and a half in the Orient. Some of the time I was stationed in Japan, most of the time on the island of Okinawa. Eight thousand lonely miles away from my wife and family. Lots of free time... and plenty of opportunities to drift into sexual escapades. Most of the men in my outfit regularly shacked up in the village. For those who didn't want the hassle of a "commitment" to one woman, there was an island full of available one-nighters. Brightly lit bars, with absolutely gorgeous (externally, that is) females of any nationality you pleased, were open seven nights a week, 365 days a year. And there wasn't anything they wouldn't do to satisfy their customers who were mostly Marines. The sensual temptation was fierce, to say the least.

I was in my midtwenties. I was a Christian. I was also one hundred percent human. It didn't take me long to realize that unless I learned how to force my body to behave, I'd be no different from any other Marine on liberty. Without getting into all the details, I developed ways to stay busy. I occupied my time with creative involvements. When walking along the streets, I walked fast. I refused to linger and allow my body to respond to the glaring come-on signals. My eyes looked straight ahead... and sometimes I literally *ran* to my destination. I consciously forced myself to tune out the sensual music. I disciplined my mind through intensive reading, plus a scripture memory program. And I began most days praying for God's strength to get me through. The battle was terribly difficult, but the commitment to sexual purity paid rich dividends, believe me.

It worked, and it will work for you too. Now, before you think I'm the monk type, let me declare to you *nothing could be further from the truth.* I simply refused to let my body dictate my convictions. Just as 1 Thessalonians 4:3–7 implies, moral purity paid off. And by the way, when the Lord began to open doors for me to talk about Christ with others, it is remarkable how willing they were to listen. Down deep inside, behind all that macho mask, the men longed to be rid of that awful, nagging guilt... the other side of sexual impurity that the merchants of hedonism never bother to mention. Purity won a hearing.

My whole point in sharing this with you is to underscore the fact that personal purity is an attainable goal. In our day of moral decline, it is easy to begin thinking that purity is some unachievable, outdated standard from the misty past of yesteryear. *Not so.* Hear again the timeless counsel of God's Word:

> For God has not called us for the purpose of impurity, but in sanctification.
>
> Consequently, he who rejects this is not rejecting man but the God who gives His Holy Spirit to you (1 Thess. 4:7–8),

and

> But examine everything carefully; hold fast to that which is good; abstain from every form of evil (1 Thess. 5:21–22),

and

> For the grace of God has appeared, bringing salvation to all men, instructing us to deny ungodliness and worldly desires and to live sensibly, righteously and godly in the present age, looking for the blessed hope and the appearing of the glory of our great God and Savior, Christ Jesus; who gave Himself for us, that HE MIGHT REDEEM US FROM EVERY LAWLESS DEED AND PURIFY FOR HIMSELF A PEOPLE FOR HIS OWN POSSESSION, zealous for good deeds (Titus 2:11–14),

and finally,

> Beloved, I urge you as aliens and strangers to abstain from fleshly lusts, which wage war against the soul.
>
> Keep your behavior excellent among the Gentiles, so that in the thing in which they slander you as evildoers, they may on account of your good deeds, as they observe them, glorify God ... (1 Pet. 2:11–12).

There is no question about it, God wants us, His people, to strengthen our grip on purity. His Spirit stands ready to assist us.

Being Accountable to the Body

Before leaving this vital subject, it's necessary that we think about *another* body that is affected by moral impurity—the larger Body of believers called in the Scriptures "the church." When a Christian willfully and deliberately chooses to walk in impurity, he or she is not the only one who suffers the consequences. That decision brings reproach to the whole Body to which he or she belongs. Since we are members of one another, we are accountable to one another. Even when one of us may not *want* that accountability, it is still an undeniable fact.

New Testament passages like 1 Corinthians 12:14–27 (please stop and read for yourself) paint a vivid picture of mutual concern, mutual interest, and mutual accountability. We are not isolated islands separate and without identity. Nor are we to respond with casual indifference when one of our brothers or sisters slides into immorality. Just listen:

> Dear brothers, if a Christian is overcome by some sin, you who are godly should gently and humbly help him back onto the right path, remembering that next time it might be one of you who is in the wrong. Share each other's troubles and problems, and so obey our Lord's command (Gal. 6:1–2, TLB).

> Dear brothers, if anyone has slipped away from God and no longer trusts the Lord, and someone helps him understand the Truth again, that person who brings him back to God will have saved a wandering soul from death, bringing about the forgiveness of his many sins (James 5:19–20, TLB).

The Savior Himself saw the need for this when He instructed His followers to pursue those who stray.

"And if your brother sins, go and reprove him in private; if he listens to you, you have won your brother.

"But if he does not listen to you, take one or two more with you, so that BY THE MOUTH OF TWO OR THREE WITNESSES EVERY FACT MAY BE CONFIRMED.

"And if he refuses to listen to them, tell it to the church; and if he refuses to listen even to the church, let him be to you as a Gentile and a tax-gatherer" (Matt. 18:15–17).

Very clear. Nothing that complicated. But how many congregations can you name who follow that plan to rescue those who have strayed? Or, for that matter, how many fellow Christians do you know who conscientiously follow Jesus' directions and confront the wayward? Now, I'm not suggesting a harsh, uncompassionate assault on all who temporarily lapse into sin and soon thereafter acknowledge and repent of the wrong. No, this involves much more than that. This is an open-and-shut case of sinful activity that is taking its toll on the person as well as others in the Body.

Who really cares anymore? Where is the Christian friend who is willing to risk being misunderstood to help another believer come to repentance and full restoration?

I'm not the only one concerned about this problem of indifference. On numerous occasions in my ministry I have received phone calls and letters from others who are deeply troubled over the lack of accountability within the Body. Here are a few excerpts from one such letter:

Dear Chuck:

During the past several years the Lord has been putting me into a number of situations involving accountability between Christians. I have and continue to struggle. And I want to share what I am learning.

Two couples in my Sunday school class began living with other partners before their eventual divorces. We didn't know how to respond, especially to the one woman who brought her boyfriend to class. So we ignored them. Just great, huh?

Some time later two... classmates started living with fellows. And that stirred up lots of things for me. There were a lot of Corinthian attitudes among my peers which I decided to assess methodically. About the same time a friend. . . dropped by on a business trip and discussed a current case with a rather well-known pastor in his locale who was sleeping around. At (a certain Christian school) coeds came for help with sexual involvements with married employees.

Talk about a thickening plot! In response I have been grappling with biblical and psychological concepts of relationship, confrontation, accountability, etc. Here are some of my observations to date:

. . . in a total of nineteen years... I have neither experienced nor heard of any community-level confrontation. It is as though the progressive confrontation of Matthew 18:15 and Paul's injunctions to Timothy on church leaders in 1 Timothy 5:19ff were not in Scripture. . . . I cannot help but conclude that the trend among Christians to divorce, to sin sexually, etc., will increase unless Scripture is taken seriously in the church in this area of confrontation. . . .

I believe that if our relationships in the church are not sufficiently developed such that others can see and respond to trouble brewing in our marriages, then we are in big trouble. Who will help us?...

Although the letter was addressed to me, think of it as addressed to you. Will *you* help? You see, purity is not only a personal matter; it is a group project. And when we strive for it, it isn't for the purpose of man's glory, but God's. It is *His* name that is at stake, in the final analysis.

Before anyone jumps to the conclusion that accountability is nothing more than a legalistic and systematic way to make an individual squirm, let me repeat that the ultimate objective is to *restore* fellow believers. It is to help them get back on their feet, free of the anchors of guilt and shame that once crippled their walk.

Quite frankly, I can think of few more powerful proofs that Christianity is the champion of purity than the compassionate efforts of one family member helping another brother or sister get out of the ditch. Even if it takes an initial jolt of upfront confrontation... or the full process of church discipline. Handled correctly, in a spirit of gentle, loving humility, it can result in the most beautiful, authentic display of repentance and grace one can imagine.

I greatly admire a particular congregation of believers who decided not to ignore the impure lifestyle of one of its members. The man, a Christian, was engaged in a series of illicit sexual relationships that began to bring shame to the name of Christ, not to mention the negative impact it was having on the local church to which he belonged. The leaders followed Christ's guidelines in Matthew 18 as they attempted to rescue the man out of his sensual syndrome... all to no avail. He refused their counsel. Finally, the inevitable. With grieving hearts and in obvious humility, they bit the bullet as they brought the case before the church and placed the man under discipline, refusing to fellowship with him until he repented. It was incredibly heartwrenching, an agonizing episode in the lives of those in leadership. They loved the man too much to let him continue in immorality. The fact that they were acting in obedience to God and the hope that it would someday result in the man's repentance and restoration were the *only* reasons they could carry out such a difficult assignment. They were determined to preserve the purity of the church, no matter the sacrifice or cost.

Years passed before the awful silence was broken. God ultimately honored their obedience. He used their words and actions to bring that man to his knees, broken and repentant before the Lord of absolute holiness. As a result, he wrote an open letter of confession to the church, affirming their efforts, acknowledging his wrong, and declaring his need for forgiveness. With a few deletions, this is what he wrote:

My fellow Christians,

Several years ago the congregation... took public action against me in accordance with Matthew 18:15–20. The charges against me were true.

I cannot reverse history and relive the events that led up to my downfall. I have harmed many people and brought ruin to myself. Because I was an outspoken, prominent member of the Christian community, my sins have been all the more deplorable and horrendous.

After I became a Christian some eighteen years ago I failed to deal thoroughly with lust, covetousness and immorality. In time I became self-deceived, proud and arrogant. Moreover, eventually God shouted upon the housetops that which I had tried desperately to keep hidden.... Twice I went through the horror and hell of manic-depressive psychoses (as Nebuchadnezzar did) that I might learn that God resists the proud, but gives grace to the humble.

I am very fortunate to be alive. I came very close to suicide and should have died in ignominy and disgrace....

I am in need of your forgiveness, for I have wronged you all. I earnestly desire your prayers for wholeness and complete deliverance....

It is impossible for me to retrace my footsteps and right every wrong. However, I welcome the opportunity to meet and pray with any individuals who have something against me that needs resolution. I am looking and waiting for the further grace and mercy of God in this matter. What you have bound on earth has been bound in heaven, and I now know your actions were done in love for my own good and that of the Body of Christ.

Sincerely,

What a classic example of the truth: "Christianity is supremely the champion of purity"... its militant advocate, its defender. Sin was crushed beneath the blows of the sword of the Spirit.

I cannot end this chapter without asking you a few direct questions:

• Are you a Christian who has started to slip morally?

• Will you be man or woman enough to deal with it? I mean *completely.*

• Realizing that you are truly accountable to others in the Body, would you be willing to get close to another Christian and openly admit your weakness . . . asking for his or her help in overcoming the problem?

• Perhaps you are currently holding a position of leadership in the Christian community and at the same time living an impure life. Will you be honest enough either to turn from your sin or resign your post?

• If you are close to a brother or sister in God's family who is compromising his or her testimony, would you pray about being God's instrument of reproof in confronting the person in a spirit of humility?

Since Christianity and purity belong together, some of us need to champion the cause. Let's get on the same team, I plead with you. Strengthening our grip on purity is a whole lot easier if we do it together.

DISCUSSION QUESTIONS AND IDEAS TO HELP YOU STRENGTHEN YOUR GRIP ON PURITY

• Go back through chapter 4 and read again each scriptural reference, preferably *aloud.* Following each reading, close your eyes and sit quietly for sixty to ninety seconds and let the truth speak for itself.

• In your own words, define *purity.* Try hard not to rely on clichés or traditional terms that aren't specific.

• What happens to a life when it becomes scarred by a lengthy period of sin? Can purity be recovered once a Christian has backslidden? Can you think of any scripture that supports your answer?

• Look deeply into two passages from the New Testament: Galatians 6:1–2 and James 5:19–20. Think and talk about their implications on a church fellowship. In light of 1 Corinthians 6:9–13 (please stop and read), discuss when and how this counsel should be applied.

• It is easy for our sincere interest in each other's walk in purity to degenerate into a judgmental legalism. How can there be cultivated a healthy and necessary sense of accountability without this happening?

• Openly admit your struggle with moral impurity. Ask for prayer in one or two particular areas of weakness. Pray for one another.

CHAPTER FIVE

Strengthening Your Grip on Money

NOW *THERE'S A FITTING TITLE!* Especially in a day when our checking accounts need month-to-month resuscitation to survive spiraling inflation and off-the-graph interest rates. Unlike those who receive incredible salaries for playing games, making movies, singing songs, and pumping oil, most of us are forced to face the fact that the only way we'll ever see daylight is to moonlight. Even then we feel like nothing more than members of the debt set. So when somebody mentions that there is a way to strengthen our grip on money, we're listening.

Don't misunderstand. I'm in no way interested in promoting greed. We get enough of that in the mercenary jungle-fighting on the job every day. And the flame of materialism is fanned anew each evening, thanks to the commercials that relentlessly pound their way into our heads. But even though we may get weary of that drumbeat, none can deny that money plays an enormous role in all our lives... even when we keep our perspective and steer clear of greed. As is often said, money cannot bring happiness—but it certainly puts our creditors in a better frame of mind.

I agree with the late heavyweight champ, Joe Louis: "I don't like money actually, but it quiets my nerves."

THE BIBLE TALKS ABOUT MONEY

To the surprise of many people, the Bible says a great deal about money. It talks about earning and spending, saving and giving, investing and even wasting our money. But in none of this does it ever come near to suggesting that money brings ultimate security. I love the proverb that paints this so vividly:

> Do not wear yourself out to get rich;
>   have the wisdom to show restraint.
> Cast but a glance at riches, and they are gone,
>   for they will surely sprout wings
>   and fly off to the sky like an eagle.
>   (Prov. 23:4–5, NIV)

Can't you just picture the scene? WHOOSH ... and the whole thing is gone for good.

This is not to say that money is evil. Or that those who have it are wicked. Let's once for all put to bed the old cliche: "God loves the poor and hates the rich." Nowhere does God condemn the rich for being rich. For sure, He hates false gain, wrong motives for getting rich, and lack of compassionate generosity among the wealthy. But some of the godliest biblical characters, even in today's terms, were exceedingly prosperous: Job, Abraham, Joseph, David, Solomon, Josiah, Barnabas, Philemon, and Lydia, to name a few.

It has been my observation that both the prosperous and those without an abundance must fight similar battles: envy of others and greed for more. The Scriptures clearly and frequently condemn both attitudes. This brings to mind a particular section of the Bible that addresses several of the attitudes that frequently accompany money.

ANCIENT COUNSEL THAT IS STILL RELIABLE

In 1 Timothy, a letter written to a young man who was a pastor, the writer (Paul) deals with the subject of money as he draws his thoughts to a close. While encouraging Timothy to carry on in spite of the odds against him, Paul exposes some of the characteristics of religious frauds in chapter 6, verses 4 and 5:

> He is conceited and understands nothing; but he has a morbid interest in controversial questions and disputes about words, out of which arise envy, strife, abusive language, evil suspicions, and constant friction between men of depraved mind and deprived of the truth, who suppose that godliness is a means of gain.

The *Good News Bible* renders the latter part of verse 5: ". . . they think that religion is a way to become rich."

Red flag! Keen-thinking Paul uses this as a launching pad into one of the most helpful discussions of money in all the Bible. Read carefully these words that follow:

> But godliness actually is a means of great gain, when accompanied by contentment.
>
> For we have brought nothing into the world, so we cannot take anything out of it either.
>
> And if we have food and covering, with these we shall be content.
>
> But those who want to get rich fall into temptation and a snare and many foolish and harmful desires which plunge men into ruin and destruction.
>
> For the love of money is a root of all sorts of evil, and some by longing for it have wandered away from the faith, and pierced themselves with many a pang. . . .
>
> Instruct those who are rich in this present world not to be conceited or to fix their hope on the uncertainty of riches, but on God, who richly supplies us with all things to enjoy.
>
> Instruct them to do good, to be rich in good works, to be generous and ready to share,

storing up for themselves the treasure of a good foundation for the future, so that they may take hold of that which is life indeed (vv. 6–10, 17–19).

Go back and check that out. The first series of thoughts is a *reminder* to those without much money. The second section is a *warning*. The third is simply *instruction*. Let's dig deeper.

Reminder to Those Who Are Not Rich (1 Tim. 6:6–8)

Picking up the term "godliness" from verse 5, Paul mentions it again in the next verse, linking it with contentment and offering a primary formula . . . a basic premise for happiness:

Godliness + Contentment = Great Gain

Meaning:

A consistent, authentic walk with God	+	An attitude of satisfaction and peace within (regardless of finances)	=	That which constitutes great wealth

If there were one great message I could deliver to those who struggle with not having an abundance of this world's goods, it would be this simple yet profound premise for happiness. For a moment, let's go at it backwards, from right to left.

That which constitutes great wealth is not related to money. It is an attitude of satisfaction ("enough is enough") coupled with inner peace (an absence of churning) plus a day-by-day, moment-by-moment walk with God. Sounds so simple, so right, so good, doesn't it? In our world of more, more, more . . . push, push, push . . . grab, grab, grab, this counsel is long overdue. In a word, the secret is *contentment*.

Consider Philippians 4:11–12:

> Not that I speak from want; for I have learned to be content in whatever circumstances I am.
>
> I know how to get along with humble means, and I also know how to live in prosperity; in any and every circumstance I have learned the secret of being filled and going hungry, both of having abundance and suffering need.

Contentment is something we must learn. It isn't a trait we're born with. But the question is *how?* Back in the 1 Timothy 6 passage, we find a couple of very practical answers to that question:

1. A current perspective on eternity: "For we have brought nothing into the world, so we cannot take anything out of it either" (v. 7).

2. A simple acceptance of essentials: "And if we have food and covering, with these we shall be content" (v. 8).

Both attitudes work beautifully.

First, it really helps us to quit striving for more if we read the eternal dimension into today's situation. We entered life empty-handed; we leave it the same way. I never saw a hearse pulling a U-Haul trailer!

The truth of all this was brought home forcefully to me when a minister friend of mine told of an experience he had several years ago. He was in need of a dark suit to wear at a funeral he had been asked to conduct. He had very little money, so he went to a local pawn shop in search of a good buy. To his surprise, they had just the right size, solid black, and very inexpensive. It was too good to be true. As he forked over the money, he inquired as to how they could afford to sell the suit so cheap. With a wry grin the pawnbroker admitted that all their suits had once been owned by a local mortuary, which they used on the deceased... then removed before burial.

He felt a little unusual wearing a suit that had once been on a dead man, but since no one else would know, why not? Everything was fine until he was in the middle of his sermon and casually started to stick his hand into the pocket of the pants... only to find *there were no pockets!* Talk about an unforgettable object lesson! There he stood preaching to all those people about the importance of living in light of eternity today, as he himself wore a pair of trousers without pockets that had been on a corpse.

Second, it also helps us model contentment if we'll boil life down to its essentials and try to simplify our lifestyle. Verse 8 spells out those essentials: something to eat, something to wear, and a roof over our heads. Everything beyond that we'd do well to consider as extra.

You see, society's plan of attack is to create dissatisfaction, to convince us that we must be in a constant pursuit for something "out there" that is sure to bring us happiness. When you reduce that lie to its lowest level, it is saying that contentment is impossible without striving for more. God's Word offers the exact opposite advice: Contentment is possible when we *stop* striving for more. Contentment never comes from externals. Never!

As a Greek sage once put it: "To whom little is not enough, nothing is enough."

In the *Third Part of King Henry the Sixth,* Shakespeare draws a picture of the king wandering alone in the country. He meets two men who recognize him as the king. One of them asks, "But, if thou be a king, where is thy crown?" The king gives a splendid answer:

> My crown is in my heart, not on my head;
> Not deck'd with diamonds and Indian stones,
> Nor to be seen; my crown is call'd content;
> A crown it is that seldom kings enjoy.[1]

Great story, but I'll be frank with you. My bottom-line interest is not the words of some Greek sage or the eloquent answer of a king borne in the mind of an English poet. It's *you.* It's helping you see the true values in life, the exceedingly significant importance of being contented with what you have rather than perpetually dissatisfied, always striving for more and more. I am certainly not alone in this desire to help people see through the mask of our world system:

PROMISES, PROMISES. Perhaps the most devastating and most demonic part of advertising is that it attempts to persuade us that material possessions will bring joy and fulfillment. "That happiness is to be attained through limitless material acquisition is denied by every religion and philosophy known to man, but is preached incessantly by every American television set." Advertisers promise that their products will satisfy our deepest needs and inner longings for love, acceptance, security and sexual fulfillment. The right deodorant, they promise, will bring acceptance and friendship. The newest toothpaste or shampoo will make one irresistible. A house or bank account will guarantee security and love.

Examples are everywhere. A bank in Washington, D.C., recently advertised for new savings accounts with the question: "Who's gonna love you when you're old and grey?" Our savings bank sponsors a particularly enticing ad: "Put a little love away. Everybody needs a penny for a rainy day. Put a little love away." Those words are unbiblical, heretical, demonic. They teach the big lie of our secular, materialistic society. But the words and music are so seductive that they dance through my head hundreds of times.

If no one paid any attention to these lies, they would be harmless. But that is impossible. Advertising has a powerful effect on all of us. It shapes the values of our children. Many people in our society truly believe that more possessions will bring acceptance and happiness. In its "Life-Style" section, *Newsweek* recently described the craze for $150 belt buckles, $695 rattlesnake belts and exceedingly expensive jewelry. A concluding comment by New York jewelry designer Barry Kieselstein shows how people search for meaning and friendship in things: "A nice piece of jewelry you can relate to is like having a friend who's always there."[2]

And speaking of the power of advertising, I recall hearing some pretty good counsel on how to overrule those television commercials that attempt to convince us we need this product or that new appliance to be happy. The guy suggested that every time we begin to feel that persuasive tug, we ought to shout back at the tube at the top of our voices: "Who are you kidding!"

It really works. My whole family and I tried it one afternoon during a televised football game. Not once did I feel dissatisfied with my present lot or sense the urge to jump up and go buy something. Our dog almost had a canine coronary; but other than that, the results were great.

Warning to Those Who Want to Get Rich (1 Tim. 6:9–10)

As we read on, the Scriptures turn our attention from those who are not rich to those who want to get rich. The warning is bold:

> But those who want to get rich fall into temptation and a snare and many foolish and harmful desires which plunge men into ruin and destruction.
> For the love of money is a root of all sorts of evil, and some by longing for it have wandered away from the faith, and pierced themselves with many a pang (1 Tim. 6:9–10).

This person is different from the first one we considered. This individual is one who cannot rest, cannot really relax until he or she has become affluent. The word *want* in verse 9, rather than meaning "like" or "desire" (like a passing fancy), suggests a firm resolve, a strong determination. It isn't an exaggeration to suggest that it would even include the idea of being possessed with the thought of getting rich... which helps us understand why such a severe warning follows: Those who *want* to get rich fall into temptation (unexpected traps) and many foolish or harmful desires leading ultimately to destruction.

Interestingly, contrary to popular opinion, the pursuit of wealth—even the acquiring of it—does not cause the bluebird of happiness to sing its way into our lives. Rather, the grim, diseased vulture of torment and misery circles over our carcass.

You need a 'fer instance?

Look at the faces of the super wealthy. Choose the group. The entertainers, *offstage*. How about the rock stars? Or even the comedians away from the camera? Let's name a few specifics: Elvis Presley, Howard Hughes, John Lennon. Those faces, captured in untold numbers of photographs, reflect strain and pain. And let's not forget the stress-ridden physician or executive pushing toward the top. Not much peace and calm, in my opinion.

Let's look at what Solomon said:

> A faithful man will be richly blessed,
> but one eager to get rich will not go unpunished. . . .
> A stingy man is eager to get rich
> and is unaware that poverty awaits him.
>
> (Prov. 28:20, 22, NIV)

Why? Why is the path of the greedy materialist so strewn with blind spots and traps that lead to ruin? Read again 1 Timothy 6:10, but don't *misread* it.

> For the love of money is a root of all sorts of evil, and some by longing for it have wandered away from the faith, and pierced themselves with many a pang (1 Tim. 6:10).

The verse does not say that money per se is the root of all evil, nor that the love of money is *the* root of all evil. This has reference to the LOVE of money (literally, "fondness of silver") being *a* (not "the") root—a basis of all kinds of evil. The verse also describes the kind of person who pursues money as being one who is "longing for it." The original Greek term means "to stretch oneself out in order to grasp something." And those on this pursuit experience two categories of perils:

- Spiritually, they wander away from the faith.
- Personally, they encounter many griefs.

It's worth remembering that most people with this kind of drive for more and more money really aren't generous; they are selfish. One writer put it all in perspective:

> Money in itself is neither good nor bad; it is simply dangerous in that the love of it may become bad. With money a man can do much good; and with money he can do much evil. With money a man can selfishly serve his own desires; and with money he can generously answer to the cry of his neighbor's need. With money a man can buy his way to the forbidden things and facilitate the path of wrongdoing; and with money he can make it easier for someone else to live as God meant him to live. Money brings power, and power is always a double-edged thing, for it is powerful to good and powerful to evil. [3]

The Bible offers two kinds of counsel: preventive and corrective . . . assistance before the fact and assistance after the fact. This verse is the former—a preventive warning. It stands like a yellow highway sign in a driving rainstorm.

DANGER, CURVE AHEAD
DRIVE SLOWLY

- Up-and-coming young executive, listen!
- Entertainer in the making, pay attention!
- Capable, youthful athlete, watch out!
- Recording artist, be careful!
- Visionary leader and entrepreneur, proceed with caution!
- Rapidly advancing salesperson, be on guard!
- Gifted minister with a lot of charisma, stop and think!

If you are not careful, you'll find yourself caught in the vortex of greed that will inevitably lead to your destruction. Materialism is a killer; at best, a crippler. Fight against it as you would a hungry pack of wolves.

Instruction to Those Who Are Rich (1 Tim. 6:17–19)

Before leaving this timely topic of money, consider one more classification deserving of our attention—those who have been blessed with prosperity. If you are in this category, you have your own unique battles. As I mentioned earlier in the chapter, you are neither suspect nor guilty in God's eyes simply because you are rich. You know if you acquired your wealth legally or illegally. If it has come from hard work, honest dealings, and wise planning, you have absolutely nothing of which to be ashamed. Only the Lord Himself knows how many ministries could not continue (humanly speaking) if it were not for people like you who are able to contribute large sums of money in support of these faith ventures. You are greatly blessed, and that carries with it great responsibility. As the object of innumerable attacks from the adversary (not to mention the envy of many people) you must be a wise servant of what God has entrusted into your care. I know of few paths filled with more dangerous traps and subtle temptations than the one you must walk every day. Hopefully, these things will help you as you attempt to live for Christ on that precarious tightrope.

To begin with, let's hear what the Scriptures say to you:

> Instruct those who are rich in this present world not to be conceited or to fix their hope on the uncertainty of riches, but on God, who richly supplies us with all things to enjoy.
> Instruct them to do good, to be rich in good works, to be generous and ready to share, storing up for themselves the treasure of a good foundation for the future, so that they may take hold of that which is life indeed (vv. 17–19).

If you look closely, you'll find three rather direct pieces of advice; the first two being negative and the third ending on a positive note.

First, Don't Be Conceited

This is a tough assignment, but it's essential. The term *conceited* means "high-minded." Proud, snobbish arrogance has no place in the life of the wealthy Christian. Because this is mentioned first, it is perhaps wise that we look upon it as the most frequent temptation the rich must guard against. One of the best ways to do that is to remember that everything you have has come from your heavenly Father. If it weren't for Him, think of where you'd be today. It's healthy for all of us to remember the hole of the pit from which He rescued us. That will do a lot to keep conceit conquered.

Marian Anderson, the black American contralto who deserved and won worldwide acclaim as a concert soloist, didn't simply grow great; she grew great simply. In spite of her fame, she has remained the same gracious, approachable lady... never one to "put on airs"—a beautiful model of humility.

A reporter, while interviewing Miss Anderson, asked her to name the greatest moment in her life. The choice seemed difficult to others who were in the room that day, because she had had many big moments. For example:

• There was the night Conductor Arturo Toscanini announced, "A voice like hers comes once in a century."

• In 1955 she became the first Negro to sing with the Metropolitan Opera Company of New York.

• The following year her autobiography, *My Lord, What a Morning*, was published... a bestseller.

• In 1958 she became a United States delegate to the United Nations.

• On several occasions during her illustrious career, she received medals from various countries around the world.

• There was that memorable time she gave a private concert at the White House for the Roosevelts and the King and Queen of England.

• Her hometown, Philadelphia, had, on one occasion, awarded her the $10,000 Bok Award as the person who had done the most for that city.

• In 1963 she was awarded the coveted Presidential Medal of Freedom.

• There was that Easter Sunday in Washington D.C. when she stood beneath the Lincoln statue and sang for a crowd of 75,000, which included Cabinet members, Supreme Court justices, and most members of Congress.

Which of those big moments did she choose? None of them. Miss Anderson quietly told the reporter that the greatest moment of her life was the day she went home and told her mother she wouldn't have to take in washing anymore.[4]

The princely prophet Isaiah reminds us to do this very thing when he says: ". . . Look to the rock from which you were hewn, And to the quarry from which you were dug" (Isa. 51:1).

That sounds much more noble and respectable than its literal meaning. In the Hebrew text, the word *quarry* actually refers to "a hole." The old King James Version doesn't miss it far: "the hole of the pit whence ye are digged." Never forget "the hole of the pit."

What excellent advice! Before we get all enamored with our high-and-mighty importance, it's a good idea to take a backward glance at the "hole of the pit" from which Christ lifted us. And let's not just *think* about it; let's admit it. Our "hole of the pit" has a way of keeping us all on the same level—recipients of grace. And don't kid yourself, even those who are extolled and admired have "holes" from which they were dug.

With Moses, it was murder.

With Elijah, it was deep depression.

With Peter, it was public denial.

With Samson, it was recurring lust.

With Thomas, it was cynical doubting.

With Jacob, it was deception.

With Rahab, it was prostitution.

With Jephthah, it was his illegitimate birth.

Marian Anderson has never forgotten that her roots reach back into poverty. No amount of public acclaim will ever cause her to forget that her mama took in washing to put food in little Marian's tummy. I have the feeling that every time she starts to get exaggerated ideas of her own importance, a quick backward glance at her humble beginnings is all it takes to conquer conceit. And the best part of all is that she doesn't hide her humble roots.

The next time we're tempted to become puffed up by our own importance, let's just look back to the pit from which we were dug. It has a way of deflating our pride.

Second, Don't Trust in Your Wealth for Security

Earlier in the chapter, we looked at the proverb that talks about riches sprouting wings and flying away. How true! Foolish indeed is the person who considers himself safe and sound because he has money. Part of the reason it is foolish is because the value of our money is decreasing at a frightening rate of speed. As the verse states, money is "uncertain."

In an article that was released at the end of 1980 dealing with the changes ahead of us for the next twenty years, the accelerating prices of new homes were mentioned. Today's average was quoted to be $77,600. By 1985, the same basic dwelling will cost $121,000 if 10 percent inflation continues. I gulped when I read that the same place by 1995 would sell for $314,000.[5]

And another reason it's foolish to trust in riches for security is that money, in the final analysis, brings no lasting satisfaction, certainly not in the area of things that really matter. There are many things that no amount of money can buy. Think of it this way:

Money can buy medicine, but not health.

Money can buy a house, but not a home.

Money can buy companionship, but not friends.
Money can buy entertainment, but not happiness.
Money can buy food, but not an appetite.
Money can buy a bed, but not sleep.
Money can buy a crucifix, but not a Savior.
Money can buy the good life, but not eternal life.

That explains why we are told in this section of the Scriptures that it is God (alone) who is able to supply us "with all things to enjoy." As Seneca, the Roman statesman once said: "Money has never yet made anyone rich."

Third, Become a Generous Person

Look at 1 Timothy 6:18–19 one more time:

Command them to do good, to be rich in good deeds, and to be generous and willing to share. In this way they will lay up treasures for themselves as a firm foundation for the coming age, so that they may take hold of the life that is truly life (NIV).

It is so clear it hardly needs an explanation. Woven through the fabric of these words is the same term: give, give, give, give, give.

You have money? Release it, don't hoard it. Be a great-hearted person of wealth. Let generosity become your trademark. Be generous with your time, your efforts, your energy, your encouragement, and, yes, your money.

Do you know what will happen? Along with being enriched, knowing that you are investing in eternity, you will "take hold of the life that is truly life." You will go beyond "the good life" and enter into "the *true* life." There is a vast difference between the two.

REVIEW AND REMINDER

We haven't exhausted the subject of money, but we have addressed several critical issues. To those who struggle to make ends meet, guard against being envious of the wealthy and work on being contented with life as it is.

To those who would have to admit that the pursuit of money is now a passionate drive, hear the warning again: If you don't come to terms with yourself, it's only a matter of time before you'll find yourself ensnared and miserable. In the process, you'll lose the very things you think money will buy—peace, happiness, love, and satisfaction.

And to those who are rich? Put away conceit, forget about finding ultimate security in your money, and cultivate generosity . . . tap into "the true life."

During His life on earth, Jesus frequently talked about those things that kept people from a meaningful relationship with God. One of the barriers, according to His teaching, is money. It need not be, but it often is.

• He taught that "the deceitfulness of riches" has a way of choking the truth of Scripture, making it unfruitful in a life (Mark 4:19).

• He also taught that we need to "be on guard against every form of greed," since life really doesn't consist of the things we possess (Luke 12:15).

• He even went so far as to say "for where your treasure is, there will your heart be also" (Luke 12:34).

• But the punch line in all His teaching on this subject says it all: "You cannot serve both God and Money" (Matt. 6:24, NIV).

Straight talk, but that's what it takes to strengthen our grip on money. Tell me, are you gripping it or is it gripping you?

DISCUSSION QUESTIONS AND IDEAS TO HELP YOU STRENGTHEN YOUR GRIP ON MONEY

• What one idea stands out in your mind as the single most helpful thought in this chapter? See if you can state it in your own sentence.

• Turning back to the 1 Timothy 6 passage, review the three categories of people. Any trouble spots?

• Heavy artillery from our world pounds away on our eyes and ears. The media pulsates with a constant message. What is it? Be specific. The next few times you watch television, pay close attention to the commercials. Behind the beautiful camera shots and clever script is a powerful pitch. Discuss it out loud as it happens. Talk about what that pitch does to you as you enter into the commercial.

• Be extremely honest with your answers. Are you caught up in the syndrome of living beyond your means? Are you taking steps to change those habits? Name a few. Are you any further along toward financial stability than you were, say, one year ago? Two years ago? Define your number one weakness in handling your money.

• Finally, is your giving what it ought to be? Is it proportionate to the size of your income, for example? Would you be viewed by others (if they knew your giving habits) as a generous, cheerful giver? Talk briefly about generosity. Pray specifically that the Lord Jesus Christ might be the Master of your money . . . the Master of how you earn it, where you spend it, when and to what you give it, why you save and invest it. End these moments in prayer by making Christ the Lord of your treasure.

CHAPTER SIX

Strengthening Your Grip on Integrity

DR. EVAN O'NEILL KANE, the sixty-two-year-old chief surgeon of Kane Summit Hospital in New York City, was convinced that most major operations could be performed while patients were under local anethesia and thereby avoid the risks of general anesthesia. To prove his point, on February 15, 1921, Dr. Kane *operated on himself* and removed his appendix while under local anesthesia. The operation was a success, and his recovery progressed faster than that usually expected of patients who were given general anesthesia.... Another medical breakthrough!

I would like you to operate on yourself as you read this chapter. Not physically, of course, but spiritually. Let's call it "self-exploratory surgery of the soul." While you are fully conscious, fully aware, I invite you to allow the Spirit of God to assist you, handing you the only instrument you need to do soul surgery—the germ-free scalpel of Scripture. Hebrews 4:12 tells us that God's Word is...

... living and active and sharper than any two-edged sword, and piercing as far as the division of soul and spirit, of both joints and marrow, and able to judge the thoughts and intentions of the heart.

With this reliable instrument in your hand, take a hard, honest look deeper into your inner man and see if you can determine and evaluate the condition of your integrity. For some, it will be your first-ever glance; for others, not the first, but one long overdue. Whatever, I can assure you that it is a necessary (though rare) procedure.

TWO TESTS, EACH REVEALING AND EFFECTIVE

As is true in the physical realm, so it is in the spiritual that certain preliminary tests must precede surgery. To determine the inner condition of our souls, we must analyze our response to these tests.

The Test of Adversity

When we encounter trouble, calamity, loss, all kinds of adversity, we quickly learn the depth of our stability. Solomon of old tells us this. "If you falter in times of trouble, how small is your strength!" (Prov. 24:10, NIV).

There is nothing like adversity to show us how strong (or weak) we really are. People in Balvano, Italy, who endured that massive earthquake in November of 1980 had a test of strength far more revealing than those of us in Los Angeles who get nervous with a tremor every now and then. And how about those overnight guests at the MGM Hotel in Las Vegas when it became a towering inferno? Or the law-abiding citizens of Afghanistan who watched as their country was swallowed up by Soviet rule? Or Mary Enterline, the mother of a two-year-old son in Middletown, Pennsylvania, who lives within blocks of a nuclear reactor? Talk about a test of strength! Mrs. Enterline admits:

> I am scared to death... every night when I pull his shade down at bedtime and look out the window and see the cooling towers, I nearly cry. I am in a panic. I have never considered myself a violent person, but I am beginning to think I am going crazy—I do believe I am.[1]

What's happening? The test of adversity is at work... the ultimate limits of our stability. Add double-digit inflation, cancer scares, unemployment, smog, wayward kids, and racial flare-ups, and lots of things come to the surface. I agree with the wag who shrugged: "Anybody who isn't schizophrenic these days just isn't thinking clearly."

Take time to look inside. How are you holding up? Did you think you were stronger than you actually are? Has adversity surprised you with unexpected test results? It has a way of doing that!

But there is a second pre-op test that is equally revealing, perhaps even tougher, yet much more subtle.

The Test of Prosperity

Adversity is a test of our stability—our ability to endure, to survive. But prosperity is a test of our *integrity*. Like nothing else, it reveals the honest-to-goodness truth regarding our most basic value system. Difficult though it may be to grasp this fact, integrity is hammered out on the anvil of prosperity... *or* it fails the test completely. Again, let's look at what Solomon says: "The crucible for silver and the furnace for gold, but man is tested by the praise he receives" (Prov. 27:21, NIV).

The path of prosperity is strewn with the litter of its victims. But on a more positive note, those who have integrity possess one of the most respected virtues in all of life. Furthermore, they stand out in any office or school or community. If you can be trusted, whether alone or in a crowd ... if you are truly a person of your word and convictions, you are fast becoming an extinct species. And the test of prosperity will help reveal the truth.

DANIEL: A BIBLICAL EXAMPLE

Because the Bible contains such a wealth of information on this subject and because all of us have an easier time getting a hold on abstract truth when it is fleshed out in a person's life, I'd like us to strengthen our grip on integrity by seeing it in the life of a man in the Old Testament. He is one of those people we usually associate with just one event (the lions' den) instead of knowing the bottom-line message of his life. For Daniel, it was integrity. He overflowed with it. It was his middle name. In fact, it was the reason he was thrown into the lion's den in the first place.

But enough preliminaries. Let's get into the story.[2] I'll begin by going back to the familiar account of the events leading up to the lions' den and then move into the man's character. Because the background is significant, please take the time to read each line of Scripture.

It seemed good to Darius to appoint 120 satraps over the kingdom, that they should be in charge of the whole kingdom, and over them three commissioners (of whom Daniel was one), that these satraps might be accountable to them, and that the king might not suffer loss.

Then this Daniel began distinguishing himself among the commissioners and satraps because he possessed an extraordinary spirit, and the king planned to appoint him over the entire kingdom.

Then the commissioners and satraps began trying to find a ground of accusation against Daniel in regard to government officials; but they could find no ground of accusation or evidence of corruption, inasmuch as he was faithful, and no negligence or corruption was to be found in him.

Then these men said, "We shall not find any ground of accusation against this Daniel unless we find it against him with regard to the law of his God."

Then these commissioners and satraps came by agreement to the king and spoke to him as follows: "King Darius, live forever!

"All the commissioners of the kingdom, the prefects and the satraps, the high officials and the governors have consulted together that the king should establish a statute and enforce an injunction that anyone who makes a petition to any god or man besides you, O king, for thirty days, shall be cast into the lions' den.

"Now, O king, establish the injunction and sign the document so that it may not be changed, according to the law of the Medes and Persians, which may not be revoked."

Therefore King Darius signed the document, that is, the injunction.

Now when Daniel knew that the document was signed, he entered his house (now in his roof chamber he had windows open toward Jerusalem); and he continued kneeling on his knees three times a day, praying and giving thanks before his God, as he had been doing previously.

Then these men came by agreement and found Daniel making petition and supplication before his God.

Then they approached and spoke before the king about the king's injunction, "Did you not sign an injunction that any man who makes a petition to any god or man besides you, O king, for thirty days, is to be cast into the lions' den?" The king answered and said, "The statement is true, according to the law of the Medes and Persians, which may not be revoked."

Then they answered and spoke before the king, "Daniel, who is one of the exiles from Judah, pays no attention to you, O king, or to the injunction which you signed, but keeps making his petition three times a day."

Then, as soon as the king heard this statement, he was deeply distressed and set his mind on delivering Daniel; and even until sunset he kept exerting himself to rescue him.

Then these men came by agreement to the king and said to the king, "Recognize, O king, that it is a law of Medes and Persians that no injunction or statute which the king establishes may be changed."

Then the king gave orders, and Daniel was brought in and cast into the lions' den. The king spoke and said to Daniel, "Your God whom you constantly serve will Himself deliver you" (Dan. 6:1–16).

The book of Daniel has twelve good-sized chapters filled with events, stories, and vast prophetic scenes. But, to the public, the most familiar topic in all the book is "Daniel and the Lions' Den."

Doing Right, Suffering Wrong

I remember, as a little boy in Sunday school (when they kept me quiet enough to listen), hearing the story of "Daniel and the Lions' Den." Two things always bothered me. First, who threw old Daniel in a dangerous place like that, and second, what had he done that was so bad that they put him in a dungeon where the king of the jungle lived? One of the reasons I was curious about all that was because I did not want to wind up there myself!

As I got older and began to study the story for myself, I was surprised. I found out that Daniel was not in the lions' den because he had done something *wrong*, but because he had done something *right*. That confused me all the more! As a matter of fact, it still confuses many Christians today. We are under the impression that when we do what is wrong, we will be punished for it; but, when we do what is *right*, we will be rewarded for it soon afterwards. Now that makes good, logical, common sense . . . but, it *isn't always true*. Sometimes, when you do things wrong, you are rewarded for it (as far as this world is concerned); and occasionally, when you do what is *right*, you pay a terrible price for it. Invariably, that throws us a curve.

I had a man come to me following a morning worship service in our church in Fullerton, California, and share with me how he had done what was right on his job. He had diligently done his work. As a man of strong conviction, he stood by his guns, believing what he was doing was right. He had been both careful and consistent to do all this with wisdom. But, the very next Monday morning, he faced the threat of losing his job because of doing what was right. As a matter of fact, the following day he *did* lose his job.

That was his "lions' den," so to speak. Daniel was certainly not the last man to suffer for doing what was right.

Promotion and Prosperity

Let's turn to Daniel 6 . . . the lions'-den chapter. But our interest will be on what happened *before* Daniel was dumped into the dungeon.

This chapter revolves around the decision of an exceedingly powerful man named Darius, the sixty-two-year-old king, the man to whom Daniel answered. Notice the first verse of Daniel 6: "It seemed good to Darius to appoint 120 satraps. . . ."

We don't know what *satraps* means, because we do not use the term today. Some translations have rendered it "overseers." These were 120 men who shared Darius' delegation of authority over his kingdom. They were governmental officials serving under the king who were in charge of large sections of the kingdom. Darius set up 120 "overseers" to whom he delegated some of the authority of his responsibility. However, as soon as authority is delegated, a king runs the risk of corruption, and that's exactly what Darius feared, so he placed over those "satraps" an upper echelon. They were called "commissioners." Look at the verses with me.

It seemed good to Darius to appoint 120 satraps over the kingdom, that they should be in charge of the whole kingdom, and over them three commissioners (of whom Daniel was one), that these satraps might be accountable to them, and that the king might not suffer loss (Dan. 6:1–2).

The commissioners were responsible for the activity of the overseers. Daniel was one of the three commissioners (v. 2). This accountability arrangement was set up so the king would not suffer loss. The second verse clearly states that fact. It was to guard against financial rip-offs, quite frankly. Those 120 overseers or governors could otherwise make off with a lot of illegal revenue and get away with all sorts of illegal acts if they were not kept accountable.

And so these three men, who were apparently the most trusted in the kingdom, were given authority over the whole kingdom. What a responsible position Daniel held! He was, by this time, in his eighties. Even though in his eighties, Daniel wasn't shelved. He wasn't a useless, retired, dust-collecting, rocking-chair type. He was involved. (Was he ever!) He not only had seniority, he had superiority over many others. Look at verse 3.

Then this Daniel began distinguishing himself among the commissioners and satraps because he possessed an extraordinary spirit, and the king planned to appoint him over the entire kingdom (Dan. 6:3).

INTEGRITY ON DISPLAY

Now, I want you to study verse 3 very carefully. In our world, it's not what you know, it's who you know that usually brings about a promotion. But in God's world, it's what you *are*, not who you know. It's what you are in your character. God saw fit, because of the integrity in Daniel's life, to move in the heart of King Darius to plan a promotion. Notice his extraordinary spirit. The Berkeley Version of the Bible calls it a "surpassing spirit."

Our tendency is to think in terms of the spiritual life—that he was a spirit-filled man. That's true, but I don't take it to mean just that here in verse 3. I take it to refer to his attitude.

An Excellent Attitude

The first sign of integrity in the life of Daniel was his excellent attitude. Now, if we want to be a person of integrity, we must begin down deep within. We must begin with our attitude. It's so easy to mask our lives and look as though our attitude is good when in reality it isn't. One of the first places it shows up is in the realm of our employment.

It's significant that there was no jealousy in Daniel's heart against those other two men who were appointed as commissioners. He could have been threatened, he could have been competitive, he could have been rather nasty and ugly in his responsibilities, because he had the longest time in the kingdom. Long before those men had even come upon the scene, he had been in authority under previous monarchs. But, because he possessed that "extraordinary spirit," the king planned to appoint him over the entire kingdom.

Let me pause right here and ask you about your attitude. How is it? Perhaps it's good right now, but what about tomorrow morning when you punch in on the time clock? Or what about by the end of the day tomorrow evening? How will your eight to ten hours have been? As you work shoulder to shoulder with people in your shop, in your office, or among the sales force where you are employed, or in the secretarial pool, what kind of attitude will you have? An excellent attitude means much! It is so important that I have written an entire chapter on attitudes later in this book.

You might wonder, "Will my boss notice if I have a good attitude?" Don't worry about that. He'll stumble all over it! He'll be amazed by it. In fact, he'll be terribly impressed. Maybe I should warn you ahead of time—your problem won't be with your employer. Your main troubles will come from your fellow workers, who are often lazy and dishonest and bothered that you're not like them. And because you won't be like they are, you will discover they will become envious and jealous and so petty that you might even begin to endure what Daniel experienced.

Read on and you'll see that's exactly what happened. Look at the plot that took place against our eighty-year-old friend. First, there were attempted accusations:

> Then the commissioners [that is, the other two—Daniel's peers] and satraps began trying to find a ground of accusation against Daniel in regard to government affairs... (Dan. 6:4).

Now, isn't that significant? Here's a man who was doing a splendid job, who had an excellent attitude, and who was working diligently for his superior and among his peers. And yet those who were working around him and under him set up a spying program against him. They began to search for some things they could use as accusations against him. It says they searched in the realm of "government affairs." And what did they find? Well, verse 4 continues: "... they could find no ground of accusation or evidence of corruption...."

Wow! How would you like *your* work to come under that kind of close scrutiny? I mean, out there where you make a living—not the way you are on Sunday, but the way you are where you earn your living. How would you make out if for some reason a group of secret investigators began to examine your work? What would they find? Would it make you nervous? Would you have to destroy some evidence? Or hide some of the skeletons you have tucked away in the closet? Daniel was investigated to see if they could find anything amiss with regard to his work—the governmental affairs—his occupational realm. And the remarkable thing is that they could not find one ground of accusation. They could not find one shred of damaging evidence... no corruption! That's not only remarkable, today it seems impossible.

Some of us are going through a time of real re-thinking about our total trust in government. We who love this country and love it dearly (and would fight to the last day to preserve it) are becoming increasingly more concerned about integrity at the higher levels of our government. I think it speaks with immediate relevance when it says that Daniel was not found guilty of any accusation or corruption.

Faithful in His Work

Here is the second mark of integrity: Daniel was faithful on the job. Now, be careful here. We often use the word "faithful" only as it relates to the spiritual life, the religious life. But it's not talking about faithfulness at church or in the temple, as if referring to worship. They are investigating his occupation. They are looking for something they could criticize in his faithfulness at work. This passage says that when Daniel was investigated, he was found to be faithful in his work. There was an absence of negligence. The Berkeley Version of the Bible says he was faithful "in the discharge of his official duties" (Dan. 6:40). The New International Version says he was ". . . neither corrupt nor negligent."

Look at Proverbs 20:6–7. Verse 6 reads: "Many a man proclaims his own loyalty, but who can find a trustworthy man?"

Superb question! Trustworthy people are rare, I remind you. Only on very few occasions will you find an individual who is completely trustworthy. I had a man tell me recently that in his business it isn't the public that gives him trouble; it's his employees. It isn't just the public that steals his goods, it's more often those who work for him. It has come to the place where many an employer will no longer hire a Christian! As a matter of fact, when we were living in Texas, we were close friends with the president of a bank, and the highest risk for bank loans were preachers! Isn't that significant? Those who gave him the most grief were those who were engaged continually in the ministry of God's Word.

It's time again to appraise our personal lives. Are we trustworthy? Can others count on us to get the job done when the boss isn't around? Are we faithful employees? Can we be trusted with money? An expense account? The privilege of a company car?

Verse 7 goes on to say: "A righteous man who walks in his integrity—How blessed are his sons after him."

A righteous man walks where? He walks in his *integrity*. Now, that's what Daniel 6 is talking about. Daniel was faithful in his work. There was no negligence, no corruption found in him. What a man! Faithful in his work.

Personal Purity

I find in the last part of verse 4 yet another mark of integrity: personal purity. A life of purity that can stand up under the most intense scrutiny. Today, we would say that they "tailed" him. They followed him, spied on him, searched through his personal effects, and they discovered after that examination that there was nothing lacking. No hanky-panky. No hidden dirt. Zero! He was a man of personal purity. They could dig all they wished and Daniel came out smelling like a rose.

Wouldn't you love to hire a person like that? Wouldn't that be great? I am continually hearing from employers that their number one problem is personnel; that is, finding trustworthy personnel. I mean through and through.

Some time ago, I heard about a fellow in Long Beach who went into a fried chicken franchise to get some chicken for himself and the young lady with him. She waited in the car while he went in to pick up the chicken. Inadvertently, the manager of the store handed the guy the box in which he had placed the financial proceeds of the day instead of the box of chicken. You see, he was going to make a deposit and had camouflaged it by putting the money in a fried chicken box.

The fellow took his box, went back to the car, and the two of them drove away. When they got to the park and opened the box, they discovered they had a box full of money. Now that's a very vulnerable moment for the average individual. He realized there must have been a mistake, so he got back in his car and returned to the place and gave the money back to the manager. Well, the manager was elated! He was so pleased that he told the young man, "Stick around, I want to call the newspaper and have them take your picture. You're the most honest guy in town."

"Oh, no, don't do that!" said the fellow.

"Why not?" asked the manager.

"Well," he said, "you see, I'm married, and the woman I'm with is not my wife!"

Now, I think that is a perfect illustration of how on the surface we may look like people of honesty and great integrity—people so thoroughly honest they'd give the dime back at the phone booth . . . but underneath, it isn't unusual to find a lot of corruption there. Look far enough, search deep enough, and we can usually find some dirt.

Not in Daniel! They found him to be incredible—a man with an excellent attitude, faithfully doing his job at work, an honest man who was personally pure. No hypocrisy. Nothing to hide.

Now, that so frustrated those who were investigating him that, as verse 5 tells us, they set up a devastating plan. After their earlier plot began to run its course and they couldn't find an accusation, they then determined to do something worse. They would have an injunction written against him. Maybe Daniel wasn't corrupt, but it was obvious those men were.

> Then these men said, "We shall not find any ground of accusation against this Daniel unless we find it against him with regard to the law of his God" (Dan. 6:5).

One thing they had discovered about Daniel when they investigated him was that he was a man of God. They said, "Look, this man is so consistent in his walk that the only place we're going to trip him up is to use his faith in God against him." Go on to the next verse: "Then these commissioners and satraps came by agreement to the king..." (Dan. 6:6).

Interesting, "by agreement." It was all a conspiracy. It was a well-planned program to sell Daniel down the river. Then they appealed to the vanity of the king. "'King Darius, live forever! All the commissioners of the kingdom ... have consulted together....'"

Wait a minute! That's a lie! All the commissioners had not participated in that decision. Daniel didn't know anything about it, but they acted as though Daniel was part of this plan. Here's the way it reads:

> All the commissioners of the kingdom, the prefects and the satraps, the high officials and the governors have consulted together that the king should establish a statute and enforce an injunction that anyone who makes a petition to any god or man besides you, O king, for thirty days, shall be cast into the lions' den (Dan. 6:7).

Now, *that* is the reason for the lions' den. By the way, they didn't want to throw Daniel in a fiery furnace because they were Zoroastrians by faith. That religion believed fire to be sacred, and to have cremated him would have been to make a god out of him. So many who dedicated themselves to fire did it as a worship to the gods. They didn't want to put him into a fire, because that would be worshiping their god through a sacrifice. So they said, "Let's put into a den of lions anyone who doesn't worship Darius for thirty days." How interesting.

Many years ago, there was a program on television entitled, "Queen for a Day." You may remember that the lady who won got top treatment for that entire day. Well, in this case, they were suggesting that Darius be made "God of the

Month"! That's exactly what they said, "For these thirty days, if anybody worships anyone else but you, O king, they will be thrown into the lions' den." How flatteringly cruel! How deceitful!

> "Now, O king, establish the injunction and sign the document so that it may not be changed, according to the law of the Medes and Persians..." (Dan. 6:8).

Some people use that same phrase today: "the law of the Medes and Persians"—it will never be changed. But let's look again at verses 8 and 9·

> ". . which may not be revoked." Therefore King Darius signed the document, that is, the injunction.

Darius thought it was a great idea. Naturally, he would. Now what happens? Don't forget that our man Daniel isn't deserving of *any* of this. This sneaky conspiracy against him was because he had done what was right, remember? Verse 10: "Now when Daniel knew that the document was signed...."

That's significant. He knew nothing of it until the document was signed. Dirty deal! Not only had they tried raking through his life to find some slip-up in his service record, but they concocted a law that Daniel's honest and pure lifestyle would automatically violate. And they did it behind his back. Some reward for having nothing to hide!

Consistent Walk with God

But then we learn what Daniel did when he heard that the document was signed.

> Now when Daniel knew that the document was signed, he entered his house (now in his roof chamber he had windows open toward Jerusalem); and he continued kneeling on his

knees three times a day, praying and giving thanks before his God, as he had been doing previously (Dan. 6:10).

I submit to you, that's an incredible response to one's own death warrant. I find here his fourth mark of integrity—his consistent walk with God.

I think the last part of that verse is the most remarkable. He came before his God "... as he had been doing previously."

Daniel did not turn to prayer in panic. He had been consistently on his knees three times a day before his God, day in, day out, year after year. By the way, remember, he was one of the top officials in the land, yet he had time with God regularly. The psalmist writes: "Evening, and morning, and at noon, will I pray, and cry aloud: and he shall hear my voice" (Ps. 55:17, KJV).

Isn't that a great verse? Evening, morning, noon, I will pray. Daniel was no stranger to prayer. But still he didn't flaunt the fact that he was a man of prayer. Notice his windows were *already* open. He didn't suddenly bang them open so that everyone would know he was praying and be impressed with his piety.

There was an advertisement some time ago from one of the airlines. It said, "When you've got it, flaunt it." That may work for an airline, but it doesn't work for an authentic man or woman of God. When you've got it, you *don't* flaunt it. Why? Because when you flaunt it, you really don't have it.

Daniel just quietly walked to a room in his home and poured out his fear, his concern, his future, his life. Daniel is phenomenal. Just very nearly unreal. We Christians have a low threshold of pain, don't we? When things run along pretty well, we can stay fairly consistent; but a little ripple comes in the water, and we plunge! We pray at those times, but they are usually panic prayers, "Help-me-out-of-this-mess" prayers. Not Daniel! The remarkable thing about him is that he simply went back to God as before. I think if he had had the opportunity to take regular electrocardiograms, the one on this day would read just the same as always, as has been the case with our modern astronauts just before blast off. Scientists and medical specialists doing this test on them found that the results were just like the morning before when they were having breakfast. "What else is new? Going around the earth, ho hum." And off they went.

And Daniel? When he heard the news of the document, he just went right back to God and told God about it. He had a place to meet. By the way, will you observe that he got on his knees. I want to suggest that kneeling is a good way to pray, because it's *uncomfortable*. Our problem is that we pray in such a comfortable position that we just sort of drift off after a few sentences. Try that. Jim Elliot, a missionary slain by the Auca Indians in the 1950s, once said:

> God is still on His throne and man is still on his footstool. There's only a knee's distance in between.

How is *your* time in prayer? What does it take to get you on your knees? A tragedy? A real emergency? This man had been doing this as a habit of his life. He had a place to meet with God and he met. He consistently kept his life and his burdens at the throne. Please don't excuse yourself because you're too busy. Not a person reading this page is busier than Daniel could have been as one of the three top men in the country. You can't get busier than that. But somehow, his consistent walk with God was so important, he simply stayed before His presence. I don't think he spent hours there, but I think he spent significant periods of time, week in and week out, just communicating his needs of the day.

If the truth were known, this is not a priority in many of our lives. And I freely confess that it has not been on a number of occasions in my own life. At one of those "low tide" experiences in my life, I saw this quotation hanging on a wall:

When you're faced with a busy day, save precious time by skipping your devotions.

Signed, Satan.

The public arrest came as a direct result of Daniel's godly life. "Then these men came by agreement and found Daniel making petition and supplication before his God" (Dan. 6:11).

Isn't that significant? They interrupted him in prayer. That's where they found him "doing wrong." And the final result? The lions' den.

Then the king gave orders, and Daniel was brought in and cast into the lions' den (Dan. 6:16).

How about that? A more godly influence could not be found in the entire kingdom of Persia, and yet he was the man who was thrown into the lions' den. The only man with real, unvarnished integrity was dumped into the dungeon.

INTEGRITY: PASS IN REVIEW

Thanks to the reliable Book of God's Truth, this episode out of the life of Daniel has been preserved for all to read and admire *and appropriate*. Remember those marks of integrity?

• An excellent attitude
• Faithfulness and diligence at work
• Personal purity of the highest caliber
• Consistency in his walk with God.

You have the scalpel in your hand. Self-examination is now up to you. It is not only a good idea, it's a biblical imperative, "But let a man examine himself . . . if we judged ourselves rightly, we should not be judged" (1 Cor. 11:28, 31).

One final reminder: Only *you* can do the surgery on your soul, only you. No one else can know the truth. You can cover up, twist the facts in your mind, rationalize, and ignore... and no one will know the difference—no one except you. But if you really want to strengthen your grip on integrity, you will come to terms with the *whole* truth, regardless of the consequences.

Chuck Colson, ex-Marine captain and former confidant of the President of the United States, was once described as "tough, wily, nasty, and tenaciously loyal to Richard Nixon" by *Time* magazine. Colson's conversion and subsequent announcement of his faith in Christ jarred Washington. There was laughter from some, bewilderment from a few, and suspicion on the part of many. But it proved to be real. The middle-aged "hatchet man" was genuinely born again, and as a result, the Spirit of God enabled him to do soul surgery on himself. Before long, he was forced to face the truth. Was he innocent of *all* the charges brought against him... or *many* of those charges? As he spoke to a group of people at a prayer breakfast, he concluded his talk with:

> No one else seemed to have noticed my slip. There was nothing about it in the press. But the words *many of the charges* throbbed with the pulse of the jet engines flying me back to Washington. Was it a Freudian slip? Or was it God using my voice? "Many, *but not all* the charges, Chuck."

> My own words had clinched it. My conversion would remain incomplete so long as I was a criminal defendant, tangled in the Watergate quagmire. I had to put the past behind me completely. If it meant going to prison, so be it!

> In his book *The Cost of Discipleship* Dietrich Bonhoeffer wrote of what he called the Great Divide: "The first step which follows Christ's call cuts the disciple off from his previous existence. The call to follow at once produces a new situation. To stay in the old situation makes discipleship impossible."

> It had all looked so simple once, just getting in tune with God, finding out who Christ was and believing in Him. But

whether I was ready for discipleship or not, here I was and there was no turning back.[3]

The ultimate result is now history. Because Chuck Colson told the truth, he went to prison. He was finally released a free man. Free within. Clean. Able to live without guilt. True to his word. Christ gave him the courage to face the truth, the whole truth. To become a disciple with integrity.

Does it pay? Is it worth it? Ask Chuck Colson.

DISCUSSION QUESTIONS AND IDEAS TO HELP YOU STRENGTHEN YOUR GRIP ON INTEGRITY

• In your own words, define integrity. See if you can remember the two tests that reveal our character. Why, in your opinion, is the test of our integrity more complicated than the test of our stability?

• Turn in your Bible to Psalm 75:4–7. Compare those verses with Proverbs 27:21. Any significant observations?

• We thought a lot about Daniel's integrity. Of the four marks that characterized his life, which one seems most important to you? Why?

• A couple or three questions need to be answered if we plan to get serious and strengthen our grip on integrity:

1. What things do I allow to occur that hinder me from becoming a person with integrity?

2. Why do I allow them to persist if I know they hinder me from becoming all God wants me to be?

3. How and when shall I face this squarely and begin the process of change?

• Pray. Pray specifically about your own integrity. Ask the Lord to show you ways to implement your desires. Become accountable to at least one other person. Make plans to meet again, soon.

CHAPTER SEVEN

Strengthening Your Grip on Discipleship

A BUZZ WORD IN CHRISTIAN circles during the 1970s was discipleship. Everybody, it seemed, got on the bandwagon. I didn't keep a written record, but during that decade I doubt that I read a dozen books or magazine articles on the church or some specific area of ministry that did *not* mention discipleship.

In a way, one might think that is unfortunate, since overexposure tends to take the punch out of any subject. What else can be said about discipleship that hasn't already been said? But in another sense, it was a refreshing change from years past when much of the emphasis was on big, impersonal, mass gatherings. The shift from simply attending church meetings and evangelistic crusades to "body life" (another buzz word) and discipleship involvements was long overdue. I'll always cast my vote for anything that helps personalize one's faith, moving people out of the spectator realm and onto the playing field. Discipleship certainly does that . . . therefore, it deserves some space in a book that claims to address many of the essentials in today's Christianity. Overused or not, discipleship is indeed an essential. One thing is for sure, everybody may be talking about it, but everybody is certainly *not* doing it.

ORIGIN: WHO THOUGHT UP THE IDEA?

Was discipleship a Dawson Trotman original? Were The Navigators, an organization he founded, the ones who blazed the first trail through the ecclesiastical wilderness? No, not hardly. Well, how about Bill Bright? Since his international organization, Campus Crusade for Christ, claims to place as much emphasis (some say *more*) on follow-up as on evangelism, was it he who got the concept going? Again, the answer is no. How about Inter-Varsity? Or Campus Life? Or some missionary organization? Or what about one of the theological seminaries that trains its students to disciple those with whom they minister?

Obviously, none of these fine parachurch ministries originated the idea. God has used many organizations to fine tune the mechanics of discipleship, but He alone holds the original patent. That's important to remember. If it had been conceived in a human heart, we would have reason to question its validity. We could opt for a better way. We might even call it a fad. But since Christ Himself cut the first record, the concept deserves our full attention and calls for our involvement.

Think back to Jesus' earthly life and ministry. Unlike the "professional clergy" of His generation, He did not fall into the mold of formal religion. His ministry didn't fit the standard scene of first-century rabbis. It started so differently— He simply called a few men to follow Him. No high-powered programs to reach multitudes, no big-time campaigns, not even a strategy to start a school to teach people how to preach. No, He just got close to a handful of men and made them the focal point of His teaching, of His philosophy of life, and of His entire ministry.

And what about later? Did things change by the time He concluded His earthly life and went back to the Father? Hardly. Listen to the words that describe that last scene before His ascension:

But the eleven disciples proceeded to Galilee, to the mountain which Jesus had designated.

And when they saw Him, they worshiped Him; but some were doubtful.

And Jesus came up and spoke to them, saying, "All authority has been given to Me in heaven and on earth.

"Go therefore and make disciples of all the nations, baptizing them in the name of the Father and the Son and the Holy Spirit, teaching them to observe all that I commanded you; and lo, I am with you always, even to the end of the age" (Matt. 28:16–20).

Those are the closing words in Matthew's Gospel. The last part is familiar to many Christians. We call it "the Great Commission." Look back at those final verses. To what great goal did Christ commission us? To win converts? He doesn't say that. To hold city-wide rallies... to give out tracts... to study theology so we can defend our faith? Well, as important as those things may be, they do not appear in this commission. One thing stands out—only one: "Make disciples"... the heart and center of His command. Three other action words surround this main directive ("go," "baptize," "teach"), but the core assignment is clearly disciple-making.

TECHNIQUE: HOW DOES IT WORK?

To understand what discipleship is all about, one needs merely to examine the technique Jesus employed with the training of His disciples. Since it originated with Him and since He modeled the method, it makes good sense to study His style and reproduce it. Space does not allow me to present this in sufficient detail, but perhaps a brief survey will help. If you wish to get serious about disciple-making, I'd suggest you purchase a copy of *The Master Plan of Evangelism* and thoroughly digest it. It is a concise yet reliable volume that describes the process without a lot of double-talk. I am indebted to its author, Robert Coleman, for some of the insights I want to share with you.

Mark 3:13–14 reads:

> And He went up to the mountain and summoned those whom He Himself wanted, and they came to Him.
>
> And He appointed twelve, that they might be with Him, and that He might send them out to preach.

Although brief, these two verses bulge with significance. Jesus is beginning His ministry, He's laying the groundwork for His strategy. Interestingly, He starts quietly and carefully. He gets alone, thinks through His plan, and determines whom He would choose to train, and then He makes His *announcement*. This is followed by an *appointment*. The selection was definite and sure. Apparently, there were many available, but He limited the group to twelve. Afterwards there was *involvement*. The verse not only gives us the facts, it also includes the order. Those men were to be "with Him"—association was the curriculum. Nothing flashy or catchy or clever. Just time spent *with* Him. Finally, there was the *assignment* as He sent them "out to preach."

Selection *then* association. Long before they got involved in the activities of ministering to others, they spent time with the Master. They watched Him, asked Him questions, listened as He taught, caught His vision, absorbed His ideas and philosophy. That's what Mark means when he says they were "with Him." We never read in the New Testament that the twelve were instructed to write something down or to memorize a series of lines He gave them to repeat back to Him or to rehearse with each other some method they would later employ. No, none of that . . . but those men *did* spend time with Him. And finally they did succeed in turning the world upside down.

"Well," you may be thinking, "they were exceptionally bright men . . . sensitive, well-educated, and creative enough to make it work." No, quite the contrary. One authority writes:

> What is more revealing about these men is that at first they do not impress us as being key men. None of them oc-

cupied prominent places in the Synagogue, nor did any of them belong to the Levitical priesthood. For the most part they were common laboring men, probably having no professional training beyond the rudiments of knowledge necessary for their vocation. Perhaps a few of them came from families of some considerable means, such as the sons of Zebedee, but none of them could have been considered wealthy. They had no academic degrees in the arts and philosophies of their day. Like their Master, their formal education likely consisted only of the Synagogue schools. Most of them were raised in the poor section of the country around Galilee. Apparently the only one of the twelve who came from the more refined region of Judea was Judas Iscariot. By any standard of sophisticated culture then and now they would surely be considered as a rather ragged aggregation of souls. One might wonder how Jesus could ever use them. They were impulsive, temperamental, easily offended, and had all the prejudices of their environment. In short, these men selected by the Lord to be His assistants represented an average cross section of the lot of society in their day. Not the kind of group one would expect to win the world for Christ.[1]

I'd suggest that neither you nor I would have chosen any one of those men as a partner in a business venture... with the possible exception of Judas Iscariot, no doubt the brightest of the bunch. Do you think that is too strong a statement? Let me remind you that this was the opinion of their contemporaries. That's what made Jesus' ministry so amazing— He pulled it off with that "ragged aggregation of souls."

On one occasion several years later Peter and John were arrested and stood trial for actions that the religious officials resented. According to the biblical account, these two disciples impressed their critics.

"And there is salvation in no one else; for there is no other name under heaven that has been given among men, by which we must be saved."

Now as they observed the confidence of Peter and John, and understood that they were uneducated and untrained men, they were marveling, and began to recognize them as having been with Jesus (Acts 4:12–13).

Even though they were without notable pedigree, lacking in higher education, and unpolished men, one thing was undeniable. They had been "with Jesus." Not shallow converts. Not spiritual babies. They were distinctly "Jesus men." They were different. The time they had spent with the Savior paid off. They were disciples... and they were now in the business of making disciples, just as Jesus had done with them. During those years they had spent with Him truth had been carefully transferred, deep convictions replaced superficial belief, and a growing consecration and commitment to the eternal dimension of life emerged slowly yet firmly. Ultimately, they personified Christ's teachings and they qualified as men who could carry on His work without His needing to be present. They had been made into true disciples.

COMMITMENT: WHAT DOES IT MEAN?

Maybe this isn't clear in your mind. You understand that Jesus said we are to "make disciples," but all that that means is still confusing. You are a Christian, but you may not be a disciple—and that bothers you. I mentioned earlier that the original disciples grew in their commitment and consecration and therefore they became "disciples" (in the true sense of the term) not merely casual followers. That needs to be explained, lest it sound spooky and unattainable. After all, how much commitment is enough commitment? And who tells whom, "Ah, you are *now* a disciple"?

To solve that dilemma, we need to look at another section of Scripture, this time from Luke's Gospel.

Now great multitudes were going along with Him; and He turned and said to them, "If anyone comes to Me, and does not hate his own father and mother and wife and children and brothers and sisters, yes, and even his own life, he cannot be My disciple.

"Whoever does not carry his own cross and come after Me cannot be My disciple.

"For which one of you, when he wants to build a tower, does not first sit down and calculate the cost, to see if he has enough to complete it?

"Otherwise, when he had laid a foundation, and is not able to finish, all who observe it begin to ridicule him, saying, 'This man began to build and was not able to finish.'

"Or what king, when he sets out to meet another king in battle, will not first sit down and take counsel whether he is strong enough with ten thousand men to encounter the one coming against him with twenty thousand?

"Or else, while the other is still far away, he sends a delegation and asks terms of peace.

"So therefore, no one of you can be My disciple who does not give up all his own possessions" (Luke 14:25–33).

Go back to the beginning of the account and read again that opening line. It is strategic to an understanding of Jesus' reaction. Big crowd. Lots of skin-deep attraction. The "Miracle-Maker" was being followed by folks who wanted to see His show. As Dr. Luke put it, they were merely "going along with Him." No depth of commitment, just "going along." Seeing this and no doubt feeling some tension because of the apparent ho-hum attitude of the crowd, Jesus abruptly turned around and said some extremely potent words.

If you study His remarks with an eye for detail, you will observe that no less than three times He told them they could not be His disciples (vv. 26, 27, 33). Why would He say such strong things? Obviously, to thin the ranks. Keep in mind that Jesus was never interested in attracting big crowds. Numbers never turned Him on. I told you He was different! As a matter of fact, He was turned *off* by the large number of those who casually hung around, waiting for the show to start. He was interested in making disciples, not increasing last year's attendance. The best way to get the message across would be to tell the people the level of commitment He was looking for. And so, without hedging a bit, He picked three sensitive areas and announced the nonnegotiable terms of in-depth discipleship. Hold on to your hat.

Personal Relationships

"If anyone comes to Me, and does not hate his own father and mother and wife and children and brothers and sisters, yes, and even his own life, he cannot be My disciple" (Luke 14:26).

How's that for starters? Talk about a statement to thin the ranks! Now, let's be careful how we interpret Jesus' words. He would be contradicting other statements made in the Scriptures if He were telling us to treat our parents and family members hatefully. Obviously, that is not what He meant.

I believe He is talking about the very real possibility of competition in loyalty between the Lord and other close personal relationships. At such times those who are truly His disciples will choose Him rather than them. At those times we follow our Lord, it may appear that we "hate" those whom we seemingly turn away from, out of a greater loyalty to the Lord God. Here's the point: Disciples have no higher priority in their lives than Christ—not even their love for their own family members.

Jim Hutchens, a friend of mine in seminary, comes to my mind. Jim was a chaplain among the paratroopers in the Viet Nam War. His ministry was exceedingly effective as he served his Lord during those dark days of combat in Southeast Asia. When his tour of duty came to an end, he was free to leave and return to his loving wife Patty and their children back in the United States. Because he believed the Lord was not through with him among the troops, he chose *not* to return, but rather to stay in the combat zone and continue to minister to those battle-weary fighting men. Chaplain Hutchens dearly loved his wife and family... but because he was, in every sense of the word, a disciple, he placed a higher priority on God's will than his own feelings. To use the words of Jesus, he "hated... wife and children."

Stop a moment and take an honest look at your priorities as they relate to *your* personal relationships. Can you say that, first and foremost, Jesus Christ is number one in your life? If so, you pass the first of three tests of discipleship. You are well on your way.

Personal Goals and Desires

"Whoever does not carry his own cross and come after Me cannot be My disciple" (v. 27).

The crowd that surrounded Jesus understood exactly what he meant. They were familiar with the scene he referred to. They had often seen criminals carrying their crosses to the place of their execution. In those days carrying one's own cross meant the same as a person in our day walking to the gas chamber or the electric chair. It meant death—sure, absolute death.

But again, to take Jesus' words literally is to confuse His point. He is not saying that *all* His true disciples take their own lives. Notice the sentence includes the fact that those same disciples "... come after Me," which removes the idea of literal death.

The subject is commitment, a high level of consecration on the part of those who wish to become disciples. He seems to have in mind our goals in life, our ultimate desires. Those who wish to be His disciples replace their selfish goals and desires with God's desire for them. They sacrifice their way for His way. The New Testament frequently refers to this issue:

I urge you therefore, brethren, by the mercies of God, to present your bodies a living and holy sacrifice, acceptable to God, which is your spiritual service of worship.

And do not be conformed to this world, but be transformed by the renewing of your mind, that you may prove what the will of God is, that which is good and acceptable and perfect (Rom. 12:1–2).

Do nothing from selfishness or empty conceit, but with humility of mind let each of you regard one another as more important than himself; do not merely look out for your own personal interests, but also for the interests of others (Phil. 2:3–4).

Jesus himself modeled this truth the night He was arrested in the Garden of Gethsemane. Luke tells us that prior to his arrest, Jesus "withdrew from them about a stone's throw, and He knelt down and began to pray, saying, 'Father, if Thou art willing, remove this cup from Me; yet not My will, but Thine be done'" (Luke 22:41–42).

On another occasion Jesus openly admitted that He did not come to earth to do His will, but rather the will of the Father. He even said He did nothing on His own initiative (John 8:28) nor did He seek glory for Himself (John 8:50). He openly declared:

"For I have come down from heaven, not to do My own will, but the will of Him who sent Me" (John 6:38).

The point is clear. A genuine disciple embraces that philosophy of life. He or she comes to that place where no major decision is made without a serious consideration of the question, "What would the Lord want me to do?" as opposed to, "How will this benefit me?" That kind of thinking is rare these days. Driven by our pride and stroked by the endless flow of books (not to mention the media blitz) urging us on to find ourselves and please ourselves and satisfy ourselves and "be our own persons," we tend to recoil when we run upon advice like "Take up your cross and follow Me" or "Present your body a living sacrifice" or "Do nothing from selfishness or empty conceit."

That helps explain why discipleship never fails to thin the ranks. Christians all around the globe will line up to listen to somebody talk on prophecy. Our curiosity knows no bounds when it comes to future events. But instruction on discipleship—on giving up my goals and desires if God so leads—well, that will empty the room fast! I have the distinct impression that a few of my readers are also beginning to squirm right now. This teaching has a way of peeling off the veneer and getting down to the nerve endings, doesn't it? If it is any help, that same reaction occurred among people in Christ's day.

> Many therefore of His disciples, when they heard this said, "This is a difficult statement; who can listen to it?"
>
> As a result of this many of His disciples withdrew, and were not walking with Him any more (John 6:60,66).

You see, even back then many (yes, the verse says "many") withdrew when the Master pressed the issue of commitment. At the risk of overkill, I want to ask three questions before we turn to the third test of discipleship:

1. As you think through the major decisions you have recently made (during the past six to eight months), have they pleased the Lord or fed your ego?

2. Have you begun to take your personal goals and desires before the Lord for His final approval?

3. Are you really willing to change those goals if, while praying about them, the Lord should lead you to do so?

Discipleship refuses to let us skate through life tossing around a few religious comments while we live as we please. It says, "There can be no more important relationship to you than the one you have with Jesus Christ." And it also says, "When you set forth your goals and desires in life, say no to the things that will only stroke your ego, and yes to the things that will deepen your commitment to Christ."

There is one more test of discipleship.

Personal Possessions

"So therefore, no one of you can be My disciple who does not give up all his own possessions" (Luke 14:33).

Here is another of those extreme statements designed to get us off the fence and into the action. It deals with something that occupies a big chunk of our time and energy—*things*. Jesus' words are neither complicated nor vague. He simply says, "If you are going to call yourself one of My disciples, you must release your grip on materialism." To keep all this in proper perspective, think of it this way. He is not saying that we cannot possess anything, but things must not be allowed to possess us. To use His words, we must "give up" our possessions.

Corrie ten Boom, that saintly lady who endured such brutality from the Nazis in Ravensbruck during World War II, once said that she had learned to hold everything loosely in her hand. She said she discovered, in her years of walking with Him, that when she grasped things tightly, it would hurt when the Lord would have to pry her fingers loose. Disciples hold all "things" loosely.

Do you? Can you think of *anything* that has a tap root to your heart? Let go! Give it up to Him! Yes, it may be painful . . . but how essential! Listen to the wise, tough counsel of the late A. W. Tozer, author of *The Pursuit of God*:

There can be no doubt that this possessive clinging to things is one of the most harmful habits in the life. Because it is so natural it is rarely recognized for the evil that it is; but its outworkings are tragic.

We are often hindered from giving up our treasures to the Lord out of fear for their safety; this is especially true when those treasures are loved relatives and friends. But we need have no such fears. Our Lord came not to destroy but to save. Everything is safe which we commit to Him, and nothing is really safe which is not so committed. . . .

Let us never forget that such a truth as this cannot be learned by rote as one would learn the facts of physical science. They must be *experienced* before we can really know them. . . .

The ancient curse will not go out painlessly; the tough old miser within us will not lie down and die obedient to our command. He must be torn out of our heart like a plant from the soil; he must be extracted in agony and blood like a tooth from the jaw. He must be expelled from our soul by violence as Christ expelled the money changers from the temple. And we shall need to steel ourselves against his piteous begging, and to recognize it as springing out of self-pity, one of the most reprehensible sins of the human heart. . . .

Father, I want to know Thee, but my coward heart fears to give up its toys. I cannot part with them without inward bleeding, and I do not try to hide from Thee the terror of the parting. I come trembling, but I do come. Please root from my heart all those things which I have cherished so long and which have become a very part of my living self, so that Thou mayest enter and dwell there without a rival. Then shalt Thou make the place of Thy feet glorious. Then shall my heart have no need of the sun to shine in it, for Thyself wilt be the light of it, and there shall be no night there.

In Jesus' Name, Amen.[2]

I haven't the slightest idea what you need to release, but *you* know. As difficult as it may be for you to turn it loose, it will be worth it. You will then (and only then) be free, truly free to serve your Lord.

Go back for a moment to that time when Jesus walked the shores of Galilee. He came upon two brothers, Simon and Andrew, casting nets into the sea. As He called to them and invited them to follow Him, do you remember what they did? They—". . . immediately left the nets, and followed Him",

(Matt. 4:20). Shortly thereafter He saw two other brothers, James and John, mending their nets. Do you recall their response when He called them? They—"... immediately left the boat and their father..." (Matt. 4:22).

Those four men did more than walk away; they abandoned themselves to Him. They got their first taste of consecration to His cause. Unlike the shallow, "whatever you like is fine" kind of accommodating Christianity being marketed today by smooth-talking pushers of religious mediocrity, Jesus was ever firm and strong on the cost of discipleship. And so must we be as well.

There can be no dilly-dallying around with the commands of Christ. We are engaged in a warfare, the issues of which are life and death, and every day that we are indifferent to our responsibilities is a day lost to the cause of Christ. If we have learned even the most elemental truth of discipleship, we must know that we are called to be servants of our Lord and to obey His Word. It is not our duty to reason why He speaks as He does, but only to carry out His orders. Unless there is this dedication to all that we know He wants us to do now, however immature our understanding may be, it is doubtful if we will ever progress further in His life and mission. . . .

One must ask, why are so many professed Christians today stunted in their growth and ineffectual in their witness? Or to put the question in its larger context, why is the contemporary church so frustrated in its witness to the world? Is it not because among the clergy and laity alike there is a general indifference to the commands of God, or at least, a kind of contented complacency with mediocrity? Where is the obedience of the cross? Indeed, it would appear that the teachings of Christ upon self-denial and dedication have been replaced by a sort of respectable "do-as-you-please" philosophy of expediency.

The great tragedy is that little is being done to correct the situation, even by those who realize what is happening. Certainly the need of the hour is not for despair, but for action. It is high time that the requirements for membership in the church be interpreted and enforced in terms of true Christian discipleship. But this action alone will not be enough. Followers must have leaders, and this means that before much can be done with the church membership, something will have to be done with the church officials. If this task seems to be too great, then we will have to start like Jesus did by getting with a few chosen ones and instilling into them the meaning of obedience.[3]

Evaluation: Why So Costly?

I must confess that I misunderstood the teaching of Jesus in Luke 14 for many years. Within the context of declaring the extreme terms of discipleship, He slips in two stories that explain why the terms are so costly.

> "For which one of you, when he wants to build a tower, does not first sit down and calculate the cost, to see if he has enough to complete it?
>
> "Otherwise, when he has laid a foundation, and is not able to finish, all who observe it begin to ridicule him, saying, 'This man began to build and was not able to finish.'
>
> "Or what king, when he sets out to meet another king in battle, will not first sit down and take counsel whether he is strong enough with ten thousand men to encounter the one coming against him with twenty thousand?
>
> "Or else, while the other is still far away, he sends a delegation and asks terms of peace.
>
> "So therefore, no one of you can be My disciples who does not give up all his own possessions" (Luke 14:28–33).

The first study has to do with building and the second has to do with fighting. Both emphasize the high cost of doing each correctly... the importance of counting the cost. But be careful how you read these words. We are not told to count the cost. Look again at the verses and see it for yourself. Who, in the two stories, counts the cost? Well, the one in charge of the building project does that. And the king, who is responsible for the outcome of the battle, does that. Not the construction crews, not the fighting men. No, it's the one in charge.

Obviously, it is the Lord Himself whom Jesus has in mind. He has designed the kind of "spiritual building" that will best display His glory ... He is also fully aware of the battle that must be fought to get the job done. Having that perspective, He *Himself* has counted the cost and determined the quality of workmanship His "building" requires. And He *Himself* has counted the cost and determined the characteristics His soldiers must have to win the battle which will inevitably be waged against His plan. He (not *we*) has counted the cost.

Doesn't that make better sense? I recall, many years ago, preaching strong sermons on counting the cost. I even sang songs with the same idea in mind. But after looking deeply into the whole scene, I really believe it is not the Christian who determines the cost; it's our Lord. After all, the whole arrangement is His entirely.

Why are the qualifications so high? Why are the terms so costly? Stop and think about that. The "building" He has designed cannot be erected correctly without skilled, committed laborers. To lower His standards would lessen the quality of His ultimate product. He isn't willing to do that. And the kind of battle that must be fought cannot be handled by weary, ill-trained, noncommitted, half-hearted troops. That explains why the terms of discipleship must remain top-level ... and why the ranks will always be thinned when the general, run-of-the-mill crowd of Christians is faced with Christ's no-nonsense call for committed disciples.

I want to close this chapter by sharing with you a slice out of my life you probably don't know about. It will help you understand why I now take these things so seriously.

For a number of years after I became a Christian, I messed around with spiritual things. Just messed around. I ran around with church folks, I learned the God-talk, I sang the hymns, I even memorized the verses. I prayed pretty good prayers, I carried my Bible to church Sunday after Sunday, I sang in the choir, and I added to my schedule a Bible class or two every now and then. But my life was *my* life. I did not let all that religious stuff interfere with things like my career, my home, my strong will, my pursuit of things, my determination to go my own way, or my own personal plans. I wasn't a wife-beater, or a criminal, or an alcoholic, or some awful, notorious sinner. No, I was just a selfish man. I knew how to get what I wanted and nothing was going to stand in my way. Stubborn and opinion- ated, I rolled up my sleeves and was ready to slug it out with whoever stood in my way... including God. I was a Christian, but certainly *not* a disciple.

And then shortly after joining the Marines (an- other evidence of my determination to be tough and self- assured), I was transferred overseas, as I mentioned in the chap- ter on purity. For once I was faced with a major decision I could not change. Alone and lonely, I was forced to entrust my wife to the Lord, since she couldn't go to the Orient with me, and to lean on Him for numerous things I had always been able to handle myself.

While overseas I met a man who saw behind my tough mask and was determined to help me come to terms with the Christ I claimed as my Savior. In the words of this chapter, he "discipled" me. Month after month, we met together, talked together, played ball together, laughed together, wept and prayed together, studied the Scriptures and witnessed for Christ together. Like Jesus with His men, this man took the time to help me peel off my mask of religion and absorb the authentic message of Christ. I found myself slowly changing down deep inside. I got to the place where I hated the hypocrisy of my former religious lifestyle. I got into the Scriptures *on my own* and they became my bread and meat. I even addressed the priorities, the goals, and the objectives of my life. I opened each door of my inner house to let Christ in, room after room after room. Not suddenly, but slowly. Quietly. "Things" became less and less important to me. My stubborn will came under the scrutinizing eye of the Spirit of God. And I began to meet each day with my Lord, asking Him to deal with my ugly selfishness . . . and did He ever!

Looking back, I realize now I was in the process of becoming a disciple. Does that mean I have now arrived? Am I suggesting I have a handle on the whole thing? Absolutely not. But in spite of all my humanity (and there is tons of it still with me!), God has really gotten my attention. He has taken me to task about my stubborn will. I humbly praise Him for His patience and mercy as He faithfully stayed on the job and wouldn't let me go until I surrendered. He replaced a "me-only" mentality with a much broader view of the importance of others. He has tempered my opinionated dogmatism and given me a tolerance that is altogether unlike the me of yesteryear.

It is a little difficult sharing this in such detail lest I come off as some superpious saint with wings starting to sprout. Nothing could be further from the truth! I still blow it. I still fight the urge to have my own way. I still have those desires to please only myself. But the big difference between now and years ago is that I no longer defend those urges. I really don't want them to control me, whereas before I rationalized around it. I want my Lord in control, and I find myself increasingly more embarrassed when those fleshly drives express themselves. The difference occurred in my life when I turned the corner in my spiritual growth and decided I had had enough of the game-playing with God.

I have a feeling that many of you who read these words identify with my pilgrimage. The details may be different, but the overall scene is similar, right? For some of you, this represents a risk you want to take, but you're afraid of the cost. Take it from me, it's worth it! The Lord God will see you through. All you need to do is get alone with the Master, pour out your fears and your failures, then tell Him you are ready to take that first step away from a world that centers on you and into a new life that focuses on Him. That's when you'll begin to strengthen your grip on discipleship and loosen your grip on mere religion.

> I had walked life's path with an easy tread,
> Had followed where comfort and pleasure led;
> And then by chance in a quiet place—
> I met my Master face to face.
>
> With station and rank and wealth for goal,
> Much thought for body but none for soul,
> I had entered to win this life's mad race—
> When I met my Master face to face.
>
> I had built my castles, reared them high,
> Till their towers had pierced the blue of the sky;
> I had sworn to rule with an iron mace—
> When I met my Master face to face.
>
> I met Him and knew Him, and blushed to see
> That His eyes full of sorrow were fixed on me;
> And I faltered, and fell at His feet that day
> While my castles vanished and melted away.
>
> Melted and vanished; and in their place
> I saw naught else but my Master's face;
> And I cried aloud: "Oh, make me meet
> To follow the marks of Thy wounded feet."
>
> My thought is now for the souls of men;
> I have lost my life to find it again
> Ever since alone in that holy place
> My Master and I stood face to face.[4]

> Author Unknown

Discussion Questions and Ideas to Help You Strengthen Your Grip on Discipleship

• The "in word" for the seventies was discipleship. We tossed it around the church, mission organizations used it often, and books included long chapters on the subject. But what does it mean? Can you *describe* discipleship? Try to do so in two or three sentences.

• In this chapter we probed into Luke 14:25–33. We first learned that Jesus spoke these words to "thin the ranks" of His followers. Why would He want to do that? How does that relate to discipleship? And while discussing that subject, answer this: Are all believers automatically *disciples?* Explain your answer.

• While developing the whole idea of becoming His disciple, Jesus addressed three particular areas that often give us trouble. Looking back over verses 26 through 33 of Luke 14, see if you can name those three areas. Talk about each briefly. Does one give you more problems than another? Discuss why.

• In Luke 14:28–33 (please take the time to read), Jesus gave a couple of illustrations that were designed to clarify the issue of becoming His disciple. As you look over these verses, see if you can explain how they relate to the subject. In both cases, someone sits down and thinks through the involvement (verses 28, 31). Talk about the importance of what this implies.

• Finally, think seriously about being a part of someone else's spiritual growth. In our age of distance and isolation, the most natural thing is to operate at arm's length . . . to maintain an "aloofness" from one another. Talk about the value of coming in closer. Name two or three specific benefits connected with small-group ministries and even one-on-one relationships. Ask God to lead you into this type of ministry during this year.

CHAPTER EIGHT

Strengthening Your Grip on Aging

NUMEROUS POSSIBILITIES, FEW INEVITABILITIES—that's life. The sky's the limit, but in that journey there are a few inescapable realities. Growing older is one of them. Aging not only happens, it happens *fast*.

I turned forty-seven this week. Three years shy of half a century! That's enough to make a guy want to lie down and take a nap... especially after I looked at myself in our double-width mirror this morning. While I studied my reflection, I immediately remembered a little sign I'd seen in a local gift shop:

> When you get too old for pimples
> you go right into wrinkles.

You know you're getting older when...

... most of your dreams are reruns,

... the airline attendant offers you "coffee, tea, or Milk of Magnesia,"

. . . you sit down in a rocking chair and you can't
    get it started,

. . . your mind makes commitments your body can't keep,

. . . the little grey-haired lady you help across the
    street is your wife!

. . . reading *The Total Woman* makes you sleepy,

. . . everything hurts, and what doesn't hurt doesn't work,

. . . you sink your teeth into a juicy steak
    and they stay there,

. . . you watch a pretty girl go by and your pacemaker
    makes the garage door open.

Those who are retired begin to get the message.
They find themselves falling into the rut of inactivity if they're
not careful. Like the gentleman who admitted:

> I get up each morning, dust off my wits,
>   Pick up the paper and read the obits.
> If my name is missing, I know I'm not dead
>   So I eat a good breakfast—and go back to bed.

Although I'm a long way from retirement, I must
confess that sounds like a marvelous schedule these days!

But not everyone is smiling. For many, growing
older represents a grim reality, a lonely and frightening journey
that seems overwhelming . . . at times unbearable.

HUMAN ATTITUDES ON AGING

The more I talk with and listen to older people, the
more I sense a growing discontentment rather than acceptance. I
witnessed it in my own father during the last decade of his life.
My mother died in 1971, but he (although fifteen years older

than she) lived on into 1980. He lived a number of those years in our home with us, allowing us a never-to-be-forgotten occasion to observe first-hand the agony of aging alone, even though he was surrounded by our family of six who wanted to relate to him, express our love, and include him in the mainstream of our world. We detected that "Pee-Po" had adopted a series of attitudes that made a close relationship extremely difficult, if not impossible.

Because they are not unique to him, I share them openly. Without wanting to sound critical, I believe it is correct to say that these attitudes come from our humanity . . . not from the Lord. They are therefore terribly demoralizing.

Uselessness

This feeling says, "I'm over the hill" . . . "I get in the way" . . . "I really don't have much to contribute anymore, so I'll just back off from life." This frequently emerges from those who were once resourceful, competent persons. In fact, it isn't uncommon to find that those who once played an extremely significant role in life feel the most useless as the sands of time cover their past achievements.

Guilt

What an awful companion to journey with during our later years! And yet guilt has a way of hijacking our minds as age slows our steps and sensitizes our memories. "I blew it" . . . "If only I had a second chance, I'd rear my family differently" . . . "I'd handle my money more wisely" . . . "I was too this—not enough that." On and on. With more time on our hands, we yield to guilt's finger of blame and to the frowns of "Shame on you!" Inevitably, feelings of dissatisfaction growl and churn within. Like the anonymous verse I learned years ago:

Across the fields of yesterday he sometimes comes to me,
A little lad just back from play, the boy I used to be.
He smiles at me so wistfully when once he's crept within,
It is as though he'd hoped to see the man I might have been.

Such imaginary visits never fail to grab hold and slam us to the mat. Guilt is a coward and bully, forever picking fights we can't seem to win.

Self-Pity

There's yet another attitude that plagues the aging, that old nemesis, self-pity... the woe-is-me syndrome convincing us that no man's land is our own island. "Nobody cares, so why should I? Nobody cares if I live or die!" Self-pity spans the extremes of blame and bitterness. And it often takes us under the proverbial juniper tree with the prophet Elijah as we join in the familiar chorus, "It is enough; now, O Lord, take my life..." (1 Kings 19:4).

Fear

Perhaps more than any other attitude, the feelings of fear are most common among those who are getting on in years... economic fears, fear of losing health or mind, mate or friends. "The world is spinning by me at a terribly fast clip—I'm afraid I can't stay up with it." Couple this with the impatience of youth, the rising crime rate where senior citizens are victimized by violence and fraud, add hearing loss and crippling disease... and it isn't difficult to understand why fear attaches itself to the aged.

I do not want to seem without compassion when I write this next sentence, but it needs to be said right up front. As natural and understandable as feelings of uselessness, guilt, self-pity, and fear may be, *they do not come from God*. The Lord does not prompt those feelings—we do. They are strictly and completely human in their source, leaving us caught in their undertow. To strengthen our grip on aging, these feelings must somehow be counteracted. For the rest of the chapter, let's consider how we might do that.

A Psalm with a Principle

God's Word never fails to guide us into the right perspective on life. Psalm 90 is no exception. Written by an older gentleman (Moses) in his eighties—perhaps even older than that—the psalm takes a brief, but accurate look at life. It begins by reminding us that God is ageless:

> Lord, you have been our dwelling place
> > throughout all generations.
> Before the mountains were born
> > or you brought forth the earth and the world,
> > from everlasting to everlasting you are God.
> > > (Ps. 90:1–2, NIV)

Once that is settled, the writer then turns his attention to humanity, choosing several different word pictures to paint the brevity and pain of life in vivid color. See if you can locate three or four of those illustrations:

> You turn men back to dust,
> > saying, "Return to dust, O sons of men."
> For a thousand years in your sight
> > are like a day that has just gone by,
> > or like a watch in the night.
> You sweep men away in the sleep of death;
> > they are like the new grass of the morning—
> though in the morning it springs up new,
> > by evening it is dry and withered.

We are consumed by your anger
  and terrified by your indignation
You have set our iniquities before you,
  our secret sins in the light of your presence.
All our days pass away under your wrath;
  we finish our years with a moan.
The length of our days is seventy years—
  or eighty, if we have the strength;
yet their span is but trouble and sorrow,
  for they quickly pass, and we fly away.

(Ps. 90:3–10, NIV)

Life? It is "like a day gone by."
Like "a watch in the night."
Like "new grass."

We finish our years with "a moan," sometimes living seventy years, sometimes eighty. No matter, "they quickly pass, and we fly away."

So? So how do we make heads or tails of it? Is there some guideline, some piece of advice, some divine principle to follow that will help us strengthen our grip on aging? Yes!

Teach us to number our days aright, that we may gain a heart of wisdom (Ps. 90:12, NIV).

The Hebrew text suggests that we correctly "account" for our days. I find it interesting that we are to view life by the days, not *the years*. We are to live those days in such a way that when they draw to a close, we have gained "a heart of wisdom." With the Lord God occupying first place in our lives (we're back to *priorities*, chapter 1) we accept and live each day enthusiastically for Him. The result will be that "heart of wisdom" the psalmist mentions.

I'm forty-seven this week. Forty-seven years, when multiplied by 365 days each year, tallies up to be 17,155 days. I cannot identify with a huge chunk of days that equal one year, but I can certainly bite off a nibble that represents one day. When I live it God's way, as prescribed here in Psalm 90:12, I take that day as His gift to me, which I live under His control and for His glory.

Here, then, is the principle:

> SINCE EVERY DAY IS A GIFT FROM GOD,
> I LIVE EACH ONE ENTHUSIASTICALLY FOR HIM.

"Aw, come on, Chuck, how idealistic can you get?" I can hear those words bouncing from your mind to mine right now. "If you only knew my situation, you'd have to rework that principle!"

No, I seriously doubt that I would back down, even though you may be in a situation right now that seems somewhere between terrible and impossible.

What might help is seeing this abstract, theoretical principle fleshed out in the life of a person in his eighties. If we can see the truth incarnated, I'm convinced it will help all of us get a tighter grip on aging. The person I have in mind lived a rugged life, experienced his share of disappointments, approached his twilight years with no easy chair in sight—and *loved* the challenge of it all. He's a character in the Bible named Caleb.

A MAN WHO STAYED OUT OF MOTH BALLS

I really do not know of a Bible character in the Old Testament I admire more than Caleb, whose life is beautifully summed up in several verses of Joshua 14. Everything about the man is concentrated into a nutshell, but the tentacles of his biography stretch back forty-five years earlier. You'll see why I say this as you read his story.

Then the sons of Judah drew near to Joshua in Gilgal, and Caleb the son of Jephunneh the Kenizzite said to him, "You know the word which the Lord spoke to Moses the man of God concerning you and me in Kadesh-barnea.

"I was forty years old when Moses the servant of the Lord sent me from Kadesh-barnea to spy out the land, and I brought word back to him as it was in my heart.

"Nevertheless my brethren who went up with me made the heart of the people melt with fear; but I followed the Lord my God fully.

"So Moses swore on that day, saying, 'Surely the land on which your foot has trodden shall be an inheritance to you and to your children forever, because you have followed the Lord my God fully.'

"And now behold, the Lord has let me live, just as He spoke, these forty-five years, from the time that the Lord spoke this word to Moses, when Israel walked in the wilderness; and now behold, I am eighty-five years old today.

"I am still as strong today as I was in the day Moses sent me; as my strength was then, so my strength is now, for war and for going out and coming in.

"Now then, give me this hill country about which the Lord spoke on that day, for you heard on that day that Anakim were there, with great fortified cities; perhaps the Lord will be with me, and I shall drive them out as the Lord has spoken."

So Joshua blessed him, and gave Hebron to Caleb the son of Jephunneh for an inheritance.

Therefore, Hebron became the inheritance of Caleb the son of Jephunneh the Kenizzite until this day, because he followed the Lord God of Israel fully (Josh. 14:6–14).

Before we get neck deep into Caleb's life, I want to mention two very obvious truths that emerge from his example. They perfectly apply to all who are aging and are beginning to feel the hot breath of that old dragon, Time, on the back of their neck:

1. It is possible for life's greatest achievements to occur in old age.

2. There is no retirement from the Christian life. Before going any further, we need to understand

those two facts. And we also need to realize they apply to you and me just as much as they apply to a man named Caleb. His story is not to be viewed as unique.

Earlier Years

Caleb begins by reflecting on those days forty-five years earlier when he, Joshua, and ten other Israeli spies slipped into Canaan before the Jews invaded and conquered the land. Caleb says he was forty years old at the time. He also remembers that the report he gave back then was a minority report. Ten of the twelve spies were afraid, absolutely convinced there was no way they could occupy the territory.

Numbers 13:25–33 gives us the account Caleb refers to in his words to Joshua.

> When they returned from spying out the land, at the end of forty days, they proceeded to come to Moses and Aaron and to all the congregation of the sons of Israel in the wilderness of Paran, at Kadesh; and they brought back word to them and to all the congregation and showed them the fruit of the land.
>
> Thus they told him, and said, "We went in to the land where you sent us; and it certainly does flow with milk and honey, and this is its fruit.
>
> "Nevertheless, the people who live in the land are strong, and the cities are fortified and very large; and moreover, we saw the descendants of Anak there.
>
> "Amalek is living in the land of the Negev and the Hittites and the Jebusites and the Amorites are living in the hill country, and the Canaanites are living by the sea and by the side of the Jordan."
>
> Then Caleb quieted the people before Moses, and said, "We should by all means go up and take possession of it, for we shall surely overcome it."
>
> But the men who had gone up with him said, "We are not able to go up against the people, for they are too strong for us."

So they gave out to the sons of Israel a bad report of the land which they had spied out, saying, "The land through which we have gone, in spying it out, is a land that devours its inhabitants; and all the people whom we saw in it are men of great size.

"There also we saw the Nephilim (the sons of Anak are part of the Nephilim); and we became like grasshoppers in our own sight, and so we were in their sight."

Caleb recalls that neither he nor Joshua ever doubted. Forty-five years ago he stood alone, he trusted God, he publicly announced his confident opinion that they could overcome those "giants" of Canaan. But because the people chose not to believe God, they wandered forty long years in the wilderness. Only he and Joshua—now the oldest in the camp—survived that death march. With younger men and women all around them, they continued to fight, to work, and finally to conquer the land of Canaan. Look again at Caleb's words:

"I was forty years old when Moses the servant of the Lord sent me from Kadesh-barnea to spy out the land, and I brought word back to him as it was in my heart.

"Nevertheless my brethren who went up with me made the heart of the people melt with fear; but I followed the Lord my God fully.

"So Moses swore on that day, saying, 'Surely the land on which your foot has trodden shall be an inheritance to you and to your children forever, because you have followed the Lord my God fully" (Josh. 14:7–9).

Caleb is getting excited again. Don't forget, he's eighty-five years young. Maybe it was actually his birthday. Whatever, the man has lost none of his enthusiastic zest for life.

Middle Years

I love these next two verses!

"And now behold, the Lord has let me live, just as He spoke, these forty-five years, from the time that the Lord spoke this word to Moses, when Israel walked in the wilderness; and now behold, I am eighty-five years old today.

"I am still as strong today as I was in the day Moses sent me; as my strength was then, so my strength is now, for war and for going out and coming in" (Josh. 14:10–11).

Notice, please, I'm referring to this eighty-five-year-old man as being in his "middle years." That way we don't offend anybody!

What does this man say of himself? How does he view the person inside his own skin? Struggling with fear or self-pity or uselessness or guilt? Hardly. He sees himself strong as ever. Capable and qualified to fight or give counsel, use a weapon or use his mind. It is so encouraging to read this man's opinion of himself. Although up in years, he was anything but over the hill! And speaking of the hill, read on:

"Now then, give me this hill country about which the Lord spoke on that day, for you heard on that day that Anakim were there, with great fortified cities; perhaps the Lord will be with me, and I shall drive them out as the Lord has spoken."

So Joshua blessed him, and gave Hebron to Caleb the son of Jephunneh for an inheritance (Josh. 14:12–13).

Later Years

As Caleb peered into the future, his eyes sparkled with enthusiasm, optimism, hope, and faith.

Not: "Leave me alone, I'm tired."

"I deserve a comfortable, shady spot."

"You owe me some benefits for all those years I've worked and fought."

"I've done my part, now it's *their* turn!"

But: "See that range of mountains—gimme that to conquer."

"Bring on those ugly giants."

"Lemme at those fortified cities."

"Here, you take these bedroom slippers, Joshua. I'm puttin' on the waffle stompers!"

I suggest we start a new club. How about "The Caleb Climbers" or "Sons of Caleb." We could call it "SOC" for short. And you'd have to be sixty-five or older to join! I firmly believe we would have thousands in that club in a matter of hours, once they read these words of Caleb.

You see, age isn't our problem. A traditional attitude is. We suffer from an invisible media fallout. We've been programmed to believe that at sixty-five we turn into an occupational pumpkin. Some kind of black magic has put a hex on our motivation, making us think we need to shuffle, stoop, sneer, and snore our way through the rest of life.

Nonsense!

The real giants are those kinds of thoughts. They growl and roar like a forest full of Big Feet ... but who says, "SOC" needs to listen? Caleb didn't. He rolled up his sleeves and dared those giants to put up a fight. He *refused* to be intimidated or discouraged. Larry Olsen, author of *Outdoor Survival Skills*, illustrates beautifully the importance of a positive attitude as he describes a man lost in the desert. His attitude is the only thing that enabled him to survive:

> "He has been out of food and water for days. His lips are swollen, his tongue is swollen, he's all beat up and bloody. Some of his bones are almost peeking through. He has been just scraped and beat up by the cactus and sand and sun. He's blistered. As he is crawling over this little hill he comes across this little plant and he props himself up on one bloody elbow and looks down at this plant and he says, 'You know, if things keep going like this I might get discouraged!'"[1]

Sounds a lot like something old Caleb might have said. And the good news is this: He doesn't have a corner on the market.

RESPONDING CORRECTLY TO AGING

Can you recall the principle from Psalm 90? I'll repeat it once again.

**SINCE EVERY DAY IS A GIFT FROM GOD
I LIVE EACH ONE ENTHUSIASTICALLY FOR HIM.**

Because we cannot alter the inevitable, we adjust to it. And we do that not a year at a time, but a day at a time. Instead of eating our heart out because a few more aches and pains have attached themselves to our bodies, we determine to celebrate life rather than endure it. Aging isn't a choice. But our response to it is. In so many ways we ourselves determine how we shall grow old.

I'd like to talk about that before drawing this chapter to a close. I want you to give serious thought to staying out of moth balls. Really, the choice is yours. The late General Douglas MacArthur realized this on his seventy-fifth birthday.

In the central place of every heart there is a recording chamber; so long as it receives messages of beauty, hope, cheer, and courage, so long are you young. When the wires are all down and your heart is covered with the snows of pessimism and the ice of cynicism, then, and then only are you grown old.[2]

Realizing the truth of all that, let's consider a couple of alternate responses to aging.

First, *view life as a challenge not a threat.* You've been around long enough to know that nobody can predict our tomorrows. So, obviously the answer is that we adopt Caleb's mentality and refuse all temptations to hibernate, to worry, to curl up, fold up, and dry up. Grab each day (remember, the secret is handling each *day*) and accept each hour as a challenge. Here's how one man suggests that we do it:

HOW TO LIVE

Don't be bashful.
    Bite in.
Pick it up with your fingers and
    let the juice that may
    run down your chin.

Life is ready and ripe
    NOW
        whenever you are.

You don't need a knife or fork
or spoon or napkin or tablecloth

For there is no core
    or stem
    or rind
    or pit
    or seed
    or skin
        to throw away.[3]

If viewing life as a challenge were an unachievable goal, it would be mockery for me to hold it out as a carrot. But it is definitely attainable. I see older men and women all the time refusing to sink into the swamp of depression. We have recently begun an exciting program in our church here in Fullerton, California, for our older adults. They call themselves the *Forever Young* group, and they mean business! They enjoy a meal together once or twice a week, they travel to various places of interest together, they do projects together, but most of all they are *together*. It's thrilling to see some who once were alone, discouraged, and failing mentally coming out of their shell and enjoying life.

Every once in a while certain American athletes emerge as models of this contagious lifestyle. Ball players like Pete Rose and George Blanda and Alan Page and John Havlicek are only a few of those we could name. Even some coaches seem to be timeless models of enthusiasm—like John Wooden with UCLA for so many years and George Halas with the Chicago Bears and Paul "Bear" Bryant with the Crimson Tide of Alabama. Have you gotten a close look at the old Bear lately? He has more than a wrinkle or two! But don't you think for a minute that he's backing away from the challenge. This tough-minded, continually creative coach has just become the winningest college football coach in the land, passing up Amos Alonzo Stagg (314 wins) and even Pop Warner (313).

And he's definitely still alert. I love the story Frank Broyles, the athletic director at the University of Arkansas, tells on Bear. He says that whenever you see Bear standing around the sidelines, he's always so grave and dignified, almost like he's about to say, "Let us pray." But he doesn't. He's thinking. Planning. Always several plays ahead of the game. Broyles testifies there's another side of Bryant many people don't know. When he learns of a good prospect at a little town, no matter what it takes, he pursues!

Like that kid named Gene Donaldson, an offensive guard from a tiny town in Texas. The kid was great, naturally the object of many college coaches' attention. But Broyles says Bear was the only one who found out the boy was Catholic. So what was his strategy? Well, Bryant dressed up one of his assistant coaches as a priest—black suit, white collar, beads, the works—and dispatched him to Donaldson's home town. The youngster had just about decided to go to Notre Dame, but Bear wanted him at Kentucky, where he was coaching at the time. He told his assistant exactly what to say to the wide-eyed kid:

"Young man, the Pope wants you to go to Kentucky."

That did it. A few weeks later he enrolled and became one of Bear's first All-Americans!

Although the Bear's approach here seems rather extreme, it does illustrate how this wrinkled old coach refuses to put his head in neutral. It's the challenge of it all that keeps him interested. He may look old, but age is only skin deep, you know.

The second alternate response to aging is to *follow the Lord fully, not halfheartedly.* That's exactly what Caleb did.

> Therefore, Hebron became the inheritance of Caleb the son of Jephunneh the Kenizzite until this day, because he followed the Lord God of Israel fully (Josh. 14:14).

I'm certain that was a major factor in his youthful response to life. In fact, a close look at this biography will reveal that on two other occasions the same thing is said of Caleb, he "... followed the Lord God fully" (vv. 8–9). In other words, Caleb's walk of faith was constant, a regular part of his day. The man determined that the Lord his God would be his life's Partner, regardless.

I want to encourage you to make that same commitment, starting today. Yes, you can! The only thing standing in your way is that decision to turn your life over to Him. When (and *only* when) you do that will you begin to realize that no amount of clouds will dim the Son from your life. Become a part of the Sons of Caleb. Join the club. As soon as you do, you will be amazed at the difference in your outlook on life.

Several years ago an older couple attended a Bible conference in Colorado. Their children were raised and they were facing the sunset years of their lives. Both were Christians, but neither had ever come out of the closet spiritually. The conference theme was "Looking Unto Jesus" and that became the emphasis of the week. While attending the conference and coming to grips with the message of wholesale commitment to Christ, each one decided to place Him on the throne of his or her life. No matter what, they would follow the Lord fully, not halfheartedly. They prayed before starting that long drive back to their home:

> "Lord, we give you first place. We have lived too many years for ourselves. No longer. We have decided to spend the balance of our lives for You. No matter what happens, the rest of our days are in Your hands."

En route to their destination late that evening a car swerved over onto their side of the highway, heading straight toward them. The man jerked the steering wheel to the right, slammed on his brakes, and skidded down into a ditch, finally coming to a stop in the middle of a shallow ravine. As water began to pour into their car, she pulled herself out of the window on her side and he did the same on his. They stood on top of their car as the water passed by beneath them. They were stunned, but so grateful to be alive that they embraced tightly then began to sing, spontaneously and softly:

"Praise God from whom all blessings flow;
   Praise Him, all creatures here below;
Praise Him above, ye heavenly host;
   Praise Father, Son, and Holy Ghost. Amen."[4]

As their voices trailed off, they looked up on the narrow bridge above them and saw a large number of people staring down in silent disbelief. A highway patrolman was there, they said later, who had placed his hat over his heart. Nobody knew what to say.

Suddenly the elderly husband was seized with the realization that even *this* could be used as a testimony to the glory of God. With a twinkle in his eye, a smile on his lips, and with a trembling voice he began, "You might have wondered why we called this meeting today. . . ." And he then proceeded to tell the onlookers about their decision to "look unto Jesus" no matter what. And instead of complaining and succumbing to fear, the two of them spoke openly of the Lord their God, whom they now followed fully, not halfheartedly.

Are you getting older? Yes, we all are. Are you interested in strengthening your grip on that inevitable aging process? I'm sure you are. Don't postpone it any longer. Regardless of your age, your circumstance, your past, or your feelings, be a modern-day Caleb. Give in no longer to feelings of uselessness, guilt, self-pity, or fear.

View life as a challenge, not a threat.
Follow the Lord fully, not halfheartedly.
And one more thing, start today, not later.

DISCUSSION QUESTIONS AND SUGGESTIONS TO HELP YOU STRENGTHEN YOUR GRIP ON AGING

• See if you can recall some of the common attitudes found among those who are aging. In your opinion, why would these feelings be so strong? Can you think of an example of someone you know who is currently caught in the grip of one or more of these attitudes?

• As we looked at Psalm 90 in this chapter, we observed several word pictures that describe the brevity of life. Then we suggested a principle that grew out of Psalm 90:12. Can you state that principle? Talk about what helps you the most. Try to be specific.

• Caleb, the eighty-five-year-old warrior, determined not to be covered over with moth balls. Call to mind one of two reasons he stayed young at heart. How does that apply to you?

• Toward the end of this chapter, we thought about a couple of ways to respond correctly to aging. Name them, then discuss their significance in your own, personal situation.

• Perhaps it's a good time to pray about your major struggle with aging. In an honest, simple manner, express yourself to God and ask for His assistance. Is there something you need to do to help relieve that struggle?

CHAPTER NINE

Strengthening Your Grip on Prayer

I SHOULD TELL YOU UP FRONT that this is not going to be your basic religious-sounding chapter on prayer. Sorry, I just don't have it in me.

No, I'm not sorry.

To be painfully honest with you, most of the stuff I have ever read or heard said about prayer has either left me under a ton-and-a-half truckload of guilt or wearied me with pious-sounding cliches and meaningless God-talk. Without trying to sound ultra cynical, I frequently have walked away thinking, "Who needs it?" Because I didn't spend two or three grueling hours a day on my knees as dear Dr. So-and-So did... or because I failed to say it just the "right way" (whatever that means)... or because I wasn't able to weave several Scripture verses through my prayer... or because I had not been successful in moving mountains, I picked up the distinct impression that I was out to lunch when it came to this part of the Christian life. It seemed almost spooky, mystical, and (dare I say it) even a little superstitious. A lot of verbal mumbo-jumbo laced with a secret jargon some people had and others didn't. And I definitely *didn't*.

If you had asked me twenty or more years ago if prayer was one of the essentials in an aimless world like ours, I would surely have said, "No." At least, not the brand of prayer I had been exposed to. It wasn't that I was unaware of the high-profile prayer plays in the Bible. I was simply turned off by the exposure I had had. So I pretty well tuned it out.

Maybe you have too. It is quite possible, therefore, that you have put off reading this chapter for awhile. I fully understand. And I do not blame you. On the contrary, I admire you for plunging in! Let's see if there is something I can say that will help put prayer in a better light for you. Hopefully, you will see rather soon that it isn't *authentic* prayer you've been struggling with, but rather a caricature, a distortion, a pitiful imitation of the genuine item.

PERSPECTIVE FROM PAUL

In the fourth chapter of Philippians, a small first-century letter Paul wrote that found its way into the New Testament, he mentions a series of things all of us want:

- We all *want* to stand firm in our faith (v. 1).
- We all *want* to have a joyful attitude through the day (v. 4).
- We all *want* to have minds that dwell on beneficial things (v. 8).
- We all *want* to apply God's principles so completely that we are flooded with His peace (v. 9).
- For sure, we all *want* contentment and satisfaction (vv. 10–12).

Yes, we all *want* these things, but few of us experience them on a regular basis.

So? Our anxiety level rises higher and higher. Worries multiply. Cares increase. Irritation often invades, making us feel resentful and confused. We can't even crank it out. We struggle with thoughts like, "I'm a hypocrite, I'm a poor Chris-

tian example." What's most interesting is this: The first and
only thing that will work is the last thing we
try... prayer. Take a look at this:

> Be anxious for nothing, but in everything by prayer
> and supplication with thanksgiving let your requests be made known
> to God.
> And the peace of God, which surpasses all com-
> prehension, shall guard your hearts and your minds in Christ Jesus
> (Phil. 4:6–7).

Most Christians are so familiar with those words, I
fear they may have lost their punch. To guard against that, let's
read them from another translation—The Amplified Bible:

> Do not fret or have any anxiety about anything, but
> in every circumstance and in everything by prayer and petition
> [definite requests] with thanksgiving continue to make your wants
> known to God.
> And God's peace [be yours, that tranquil state of a
> soul assured of its salvation through Christ, and so fearing nothing
> from God and content with its earthly lot of whatever sort that is,
> that peace] which transcends all understanding, shall garrison and
> mount guard over your hearts and minds in Christ Jesus (Phil.
> 4:6–7, Amplified).

Now *that's* a mouthful! If I understand this correctly, the anxiety that mounts up inside me, the growing irritation and the struggles that make me churn, will be dissipated—
and, in fact, replaced with inner peace plus all those other
qualities I want so much—if I will simply talk to my God. Prayer
is the single most significant thing that will help turn inner
turmoil into peace. Prayer is the answer.

But, wait! Why, then, is it such a struggle? What is
it about prayer that makes even the great and the godly (those we
admire so much) so guilty? So dissatisfied? So unhappy with their
own prayer life?

In no way do I wish to be disrespectful by saying the following things, but I believe it's time somebody declared them to help clarify the barrier that keeps us from entering into authentic prayer. That barrier is the traditional wrappings that have been placed around prayer. Not even the grand models of church history admitted to much joy or peace or satisfaction in their prayer life!

Dietrich Bonhoeffer, for example, once admitted that his prayer experience was something to be ashamed of. The German reformer, Martin Luther, anguished in prayer, saving three of the best hours of the day to pray... yet he seldom seemed satisfied. Go down through the list and we find one after another working hard at prayer, but frequently we'll find they're dissatisfied, some of them even *woefully* unhappy about their prayer life.

E. M. Bounds, Alexander Maclaren, Samuel Rutherford, Hudson Taylor, John Henry Jowett, G. Campbell Morgan, Joseph Parker, Charles Haddon Spurgeon, F. B. Meyer, A. W. Tozer, H. A. Ironside, V. Raymond Edman, William Culbertson, and on and on. Great men, strong Christian examples, magnificent models, yet you can hardly find one of that number who was satisfied with his prayer life. Oh, they labored in prayer, they believed in prayer, they taught and preached prayer ... but why the dissatisfaction? Why the guilt? Or disappointment? Or, for some, embarrassment? I ask you—why?

At the risk of sounding downright heretical, I'm convinced that for centuries Christians have forced prayer into a role it was never designed to play. I would suggest we have *made* it difficult, hard, even painful. The caricature that has emerged through years of traditional (not biblical) modeling is now a guilt-giving discipline, not an anxiety-relieving practice. It is self-imposed. It doesn't come from God.

Remember Philippians 4:6–7? Paul's perspective on prayer was this: It *results* in peace, it doesn't take it away. It *alleviates* anxiety, it isn't designed to create it! But, you see, we have been led to believe that in order for prayer to be effective, it must be arduous, lengthy, even painful. And we must stay at it for hours on end... pleading, longing, waiting, hurting.

Are you ready for a shocker? You don't find any of that in the Scriptures. Except in very few and extreme cases, prayer is neither long nor hard to bear. And I cannot find any biblical characters who struggled with guilt because they didn't pray long enough or because they weren't in enough pain or because they failed to plead and beg sufficiently. Check it for yourself. It isn't there.

During my years in seminary, there was an upper-classman who believed God was calling him to the mission field. He was a sincere, careful student who read numerous biographies of great men and women who served Christ throughout their lives. The more he read, the more convinced he became that commitment required an infliction of bodily pain, sleepless nights spent in prayer. He even slept on the floor instead of his bed. He became increasingly more masochistic in his pietism, firmly dedicated to his self-imposed lifestyle of rigorous denial. A marked fanaticism characterized the man's attitude. He became more distant and defensive, less tolerant and balanced in his whole view of life. He was a driven man who, by the way, often spoke of his lack of enough time spent in prayer and his need for greater devotion to Christ. I recall, on one occasion, asking him to show me the biblical basis of his enough-is-never-enough mentality. I'm still waiting for his answer.

A warning: Let's be careful about making the extreme our standard. When it comes to prayer, let's get rid of all the traditional garbage and come back to the original model our Savior gave to us when He walked and talked among us.

Instruction from Jesus

Religious people in Jesus' day took their cues from the leaders of the synagogue—the Pharisees, the Sadducees, and the scribes. Didn't *they* believe in prayer? Yes, indeed. They had a saying, "He who prays within his house surrounds it with a wall that is stronger than iron." They only regretted they couldn't pray all day long. And it was this intensity that caused prayer to degenerate from a flowing spontaneity to a rigid, packaged plan, dispensed routinely by the religious leaders. Prayer changed from a privilege to an obligation. From pleasure in God's presence to man-made requirements. To help us understand what Jesus had to face, let's examine for a few minutes the impact of tradition on first-century Judaism.

How Prayer Had Degenerated

Anyone who makes a serious study of the life of Christ in the first four books of the New Testament (Matthew, Mark, Luke, John) quickly picks up the idea that Jesus' teachings were different from the official leaders of Judaism. He was, in every sense of the term, a radical revolutionary in their eyes, ultimately a threat to their system. In other words, He blew them away! This is evident when we read His now-famous "Sermon on the Mount" which is punctuated with a repeating of the same statement: "You have heard... but I say to you...." Time after time He addressed the teaching they had received from the Pharisees and then offered a fresh and much-needed alternative. Take, for example, prayer.

In those days prayer had degenerated in five specific areas.

1. Prayer became a formal exercise rather than free expression. There were stated prayers for all occasions. Prayer was liturgical, standardized, a cut-and-dried routine.

... certain faults had crept into the Jewish habits of prayer. It is to be noted that these faults are by no means peculiar to Jewish ideas of prayer; they can and do occur anywhere. And it is to be noted that they could only occur in a community where prayer was taken with the greatest seriousness. They are not the faults of neglect; they are the faults of misguided devotion. ...

. . . Jewish liturgy supplied stated prayers for all occasions. There was hardly an event or a sight in life which had not its stated formula of prayer. There was prayer before and after each meal; there were prayers in connection with the light, the fire, the lightning, on seeing the new moon, comets, rain, tempest, at the sight of the sea, lakes, rivers, on receiving good news, on using new furniture, on entering or leaving a city. Everything had its prayer. Clearly there is something infinitely lovely here. It was the intention that every happening in life should be brought into the presence of God. But just because the prayers were so meticulously prescribed and stated, the whole system lent itself to formalism, and the tendency was for the prayers to slip off the tongue with very little meaning.[1]

2. Prayer was ritualistic, not spontaneous. There were set times to pray, much like the Muslims of today who bow toward Mecca at specific times daily. In Jesus' day the "required" hours were 9:00 A.M., 12 noon, and 3:00 P.M. There were certain places to pray as well; the most preferred were the synagogues.

3. Prayers were long, filled with verbiage. It was actually believed that whoever was long in prayer was heard more readily by God. And the more flowery, the better. One well-known prayer had no less than sixteen adjectives preceding the name of God! There was this strange subconscious idea that whoever banged long and hard enough on the doors of heaven was granted God's attention.

4. There were repetitious words and phrases. We remember reading about this among Gentile idol-worshipers ("O Baal, hear us! O Baal, hear us!" in 1 Kings 18, for example), but by the first century the same tendency crept into the synagogue. Prayer led to an almost intoxication with words as those engaged in the practice fell under the spell of meaningless repetition.

5. Praying became a cause for pride rather than the humble expressions of one in need. It was a legalistic "status symbol" to pray well. The religious system, when followed to the letter, led to an ostentatious public display with hands out-

stretched, palms up, head bowed, three times a day . . . out on a public street corner!

Is it any wonder prayer had lost its value? As it degenerated into an insignificant routine marked by overt hypocrisy and meaningless terms, coupled with a judgmental spirit, prayer hit the skids. Such high expectations that became impossible for the common person to achieve resulted in the entire act becoming a fleshly display proudly performed by the religious hot shots. This explains why our Lord took them to task in His immortal sermon. It also helps us understand why He says what He does about prayer and other religious attitudes in Matthew 6.

How Prayer Can Be Effective

Jesus makes three strong statements (all of them negative) as He suggests a plan to follow if we want a satisfying and God-honoring prayer life.

1. Don't be hypocritical.

"Beware of practicing your righteousness before men to be noticed by them; otherwise you have no reward with your Father who is in heaven.

"When therefore you give alms, do not sound a trumpet before you, as the hypocrites do in the synagogues and in the streets, that they may be honored by men. Truly I say to you, they have their reward in full.

"And when you pray, you are not to be as the hypocrites; for they love to stand and pray in the synagogues and on the street corners, in order to be seen by men. Truly I say to you, they have their reward in full.

"And whenever you fast, do not put on a gloomy face as the hypocrites do; for they neglect their appearance in order to be seen fasting by men. Truly I say to you, they have their reward in full" (Matt. 6:1–2, 5, 16).

Jesus reserved some of His strongest comments for hypocrisy. It is safe to say He *despised* it. The comment He repeats (for the sake of emphasis) is that those who do their thing to be seen get all the reward they will ever get *now*. He makes it clear there will be nothing gained later. Rather than making a cheap show of it, Jesus says:

> "But you, when you pray, GO INTO YOUR INNER ROOM, AND WHEN YOU HAVE SHUT YOUR DOOR, pray to your Father who is in secret, and your Father who sees in secret will repay you" (Matt. 6:6).

Prayer is never something we do to be seen. It loses its whole purpose if it becomes a platform to impress others. It is a private act of devotion, not a public demonstration of piety. According to Jesus, it belongs in the closet of our lives, an act done in secret.

We looked previously at Daniel in the chapter on integrity. Remember the decision of the king and how Daniel continued to pray three times a day? Do you recall where he went to pray?

> Now when Daniel knew that the document was signed, he entered his house (now in his roof chamber he had windows open toward Jerusalem); and he continued kneeling on his knees three times a day, praying and giving thanks before His God, as he had been doing previously (Dan. 6:10).

No big public demonstration, just a quiet retreat to his room where he met, in secret, with his Lord. And you'll note he had done it many times before. This was a regular habit with Daniel. The absence of hypocrisy impresses us.

2. Don't use a lot of repetition.

> "And when you are praying, do not use meaningless repetition, as the Gentiles do, for they suppose that they will be heard for their many words.
>
> "Therefore do not be like them; for your Father knows what you need, before you ask Him" (Matt. 6:7–8).

Even a casual reading of these words will lead us to realize that Christ never saw prayer as pleading or begging or hammering away at the throne of God. No, the Father knows His children, He knows what we need. Therefore, there is no reason to think that connecting with Him requires special words excessively repeated.

Now, let me be even more specific. Today, just as in that day, there is no part of the Christian life more in need of freshness and spontaneity than prayer. Whether it is prayer from a pulpit or a church group meeting for prayer or prayer before meals or before a meeting gets started, meaningless repetition abounds! Tired, overworked words and phrases keep returning. Break loose from those old bromides! For starters, I dare you to pray without using "*bless*" or "*lead, guide, and direct*" or "*help so-and-so*" or "*Thy will*" or "*each and every*" or any number of those institutionalized, galvanized terms. I dare you!

On one occasion, evangelist Dwight L. Moody had been the recipient of numerous benefits from the Lord. In his abundance, he was suddenly seized with the realization that his heavenly Father was showering on him almost more than he could take. Encouraged and overwhelmed, he paused to pray. With great volume he simply stated, "Stop, God!" Now *that's* spontaneous. It is also a beautiful change from, "Eternal, almighty, gracious Father of all good things, Thy hand hath abundantly and gloriously supplied our deepest needs. How blessed and thankful we are to come to Thee and declare unto Thee . . . ," and on and on and on, grinding into snore city. Can you imagine one of your kids approaching you like that? I'll tell you, if one of mine did, I would stare directly at him and wonder, "What in the world is wrong?"

Listen to brand new Christians pray. You know, those who are fresh from birth who haven't learned "how to do it" yet, thank goodness. They talk to God like He's their friend, they use street terms anybody can understand, and they occasionally laugh or cry. It's just beautiful. Another tip that may add a new dimension to your prayer is the use of music. Sing to your

God. We've started doing more and more of that in our church family... even the pastoral prayer often includes a chorus of worship. Or when you have prayer before your meals, have each person pray for one thing or pray for the specific food, naming the vegetables or the meat dish. Occasionally, our family will spend a few minutes before supper telling one thing that happened that day, then the one who prays mentions two or three of those matters before God. The point is clear: Guard against meaningless verbiage.

3. Don't harbor anything against another.

> "For if you forgive men for their transgressions, your heavenly Father will also forgive you.
> "But if you do not forgive men, then your Father will not forgive your transgressions" (Matt. 6:14–15).

Before God will forgive us, we must be certain that our conscience is clear. A familiar verse from the Psalms frequently pops into my mind when I begin to pray: "If I regard wickedness in my heart, The Lord will not hear" (Ps. 66:18). If I want cleansing, I must be certain things are right between myself and others.

Prayer includes praise and thanksgiving, intercession and petition, meditation, and confession. In prayer we focus fully on our God, we capture renewed zeal to continue, a wider view of life, increased determination to endure. As we strengthen our grip on prayer, it is amazing how it alters our whole perspective.

The late Dr. Donald Barnhouse, greatly admired American pastor and author of the last generation, once came to the pulpit and made a statement that stunned his congregation: "*Prayer changes nothing!*" You could've heard a pin drop in that packed Sunday worship service in Philadelphia. His comment, of course, was designed to make Christians realize that God is sovereignly in charge of everything. Our times are literally in His hands. No puny human being by uttering a few words in prayer takes charge of events and changes them. God does the shaping, the changing, it is He who is in control. Barnhouse was correct... except in one minor detail. Prayer changes *me*. When you and I pray, *we* change, and that is one of the major reasons prayer is such a therapy that counteracts anxiety.

A FINAL ENCOURAGEMENT

Prayer was never intended to make us feel guilty. It was never intended to be a verbal marathon for only the initiated... no secret-code talk for the clergy or a public display of piety. None of that. Real prayer—the kind of prayer Jesus mentioned and modeled—is realistic, spontaneous, down-to-earth communication with the living Lord that results in a relief of personal anxiety and a calm assurance that our God is in full control of our circumstances.

I encourage you to start over. Form some brand new habits as you fight off the old tendency to slump back into meaningless jargon. Get a fresh, new grip on prayer. It is essential for survival.

Many years ago I decided to do that very thing. I was fed up with empty words and pharisaical phrases. In my search for new meaning, I came across this brief description of prayer, which I set on my desk and carried in the front of my Bible for years. I cannot locate the book from which it was taken, but I do know the author, a seventeenth-century Roman Catholic Frenchman named François Fenelon. Although written centuries ago, it has an undeniable ring of relevance:

Tell God all that is in your heart, as one unloads one's heart, its pleasures and its pains, to a dear friend. Tell Him your troubles, that He may comfort you; tell Him your joys, that He may sober them; tell Him your longings, that he may purify them; tell Him your dislikes, that He may help you to conquer them; talk to Him of your temptations, that He may shield you from them; show Him the wounds of your heart, that He may heal them; lay bare your indifference to good, your depraved tastes for evil, your instability. Tell Him how self-love makes you unjust to others, how vanity tempts you to be insincere, how pride disguises you to yourself and to others.

If you thus pour out all your weaknesses, needs, troubles, there will be no lack of what to say. You will never exhaust the subject. It is continually being renewed. People who have no secrets from each other never want for subjects of conversation. They do not weigh their words, for there is nothing to be held back; neither do they seek for something to say. They talk out of the abundance of the heart, without consideration they say just what they think. Blessed are they who attain to such familiar, unreserved intercourse with God.

DISCUSSION QUESTIONS AND SUGGESTIONS TO HELP YOU STRENGTHEN YOUR GRIP ON PRAYER

• Give your own definition of prayer... without the aid of a dictionary. Describe the things that come to your mind as you think of the struggles *you* have with prayer. Try to be very candid and open.

• We looked into several scriptures in this chapter. Can you recall one or two passages that "came alive" for you? What stands out as one of the most helpful insights you received in dealing with prayer? Explain why it was important to you.

• This may take some time, so before you bite into it, make sure you have more than a few minutes. Does prayer itself actually change anything? Try to be biblical in your answer. If "yes" is your answer, describe how you arrived at that response. If "no," then *why pray?* Think hard.

• How can a person break the habit of using meaningless words and phrases in prayer? Why do we cling to these so tightly?

• Let's do some honest evaluation of our own prayer lives. Share a few of the things that have helped you overcome the tendency to put off prayer. Talk also about a recent difficulty you were facing in which prayer helped you through. Take the time to describe how the burden was shifted from your shoulders to the Lord's. Describe the difference in your emotions once the anxiety was shifted from your shoulders to the Lord's.

      • Finally, give some thought and time to the value of praise and thanksgiving. How can these two expressions become a part of your day on a regular basis? Before ending this discussion, spend some time in prayer. Make it more meaningful by speaking in conversational tones and by talking with God as with a close, personal friend... something like Fenelon mentions in his piece on prayer.

CHAPTER TEN

Strengthening Your Grip on Leisure

THIS CHAPTER BUILDS UPON THE principles I have dealt with in the booklet *Leisure*[1] and has one major objective: to help you enjoy yourself, your life, and your Lord more than ever without feeling guilty or unspiritual. Yes, you read correctly . . . *enjoy* is the word I used.

In our work-worshiping world, learning to enjoy life is no small task. Many have cultivated such an unrealistic standard of high-level achievement that a neurotic compulsion to perform, to compete, to produce, to accomplish the maximum has taken control of their lives. Getting with it twelve to fifteen hours a day is now the rule rather than the exception. Enough is no longer enough.

And I'll be honest with you, those who need to strengthen their grip on leisure as much as anyone I come into contact with are Christians—especially vocational Christian workers. I often think of this segment of society when I see the familiar Datsun commercials that shout, "We are driven!"

How many Christian leaders can you name who really take sufficient time to relax? More often than not, we hear them boast about not having vacationed for several years. Or being too busy to take time to get away to rest and repair, even for a day or two.

The Christian's primary source of identity is fast becoming his or her work. Soon after giving someone our name, we describe what we "do for a living." And to add the ultimate pressure, we operate under the old banner, "You aren't really serving the Lord unless you consistently push yourself to the point of fatigue." It's the tired yet proud-sounding *burn-out-rather-than-rust-out* line. Either way we're "out," which never has made much sense to me.

Let's face it, as essential as leisure is to our physical, emotional, and mental health, we are strangers to it. We would rather hear our family members and other people tell us we shouldn't work so hard than face the possibility of someone thinking we lacked diligence. For many of us raised under the work ethic of our parents, fatigue and burn-out are proofs of the deepest level of commitment, to which I say—*hogwash!*

This chapter offers a different rationale. It says not only, "It's okay to relax," but also, "It's absolutely essential." Without encouraging laziness or irresponsibility, I want to open your eyes to the fact that you can enjoy times of leisure and still be efficient. In fact, you'll be *more* efficient.

And so to all workaholics and churchaholics... overcommitted, hassled, grim-faced, tight-lipped believers... plowing through responsibilities like an overloaded freight train under a full head of steam, I invite you to slow down, find a siding, and take a break. Pour yourself a refreshing glass of iced tea or a cup of coffee, kick off your shoes, prop your feet up, and take time to digest these pages slowly, quietly. If you are in a hurry to get somewhere, close the book and come back to it later. The counsel you're about to receive is too important to glance over on the run.

Is Fatigue Next to Godliness?

Strangely, the one thing we need is often the last thing we consider. We've been programmed to think that fatigue is next to godliness. That the more exhausted we are (and look!), the more committed we are to spiritual things and the more we earn God's smile of approval. We bury all thoughts of enjoying life... for those who are genuinely dedicated Christians are those who work, work, work. And preferably, with great intensity. As a result, we have become a generation of people who worship our work... who work at our play... and who play at our worship.

Hold it! Who wrote that rule? Why have we bought that philosophy? Whatever possessed someone to make such a statement? How did we ever get caught in that maddening undertow?

I challenge you to support it from the Scriptures. Start with the life (and *lifestyle*) of Jesus Christ and try to find a trace of corroborating evidence that He embraced that theory. Some will be surprised to know that there is not one reference in the entire New Testament saying (or even implying) that Jesus intensely worked and labored in an occupation to the point of emotional exhaustion. No, but there are several times when we are told he deliberately took a break. He got away from the demands of the public and enjoyed periods of relaxation with His disciples. I'm not saying He rambled through His ministry in an aimless, halfhearted fashion. Not at all! But neither did He come anywhere near an ulcer. Never once do we find Him in a frenzy.

According to Mark 6:30–34, Jesus purposely sought relief from the hurried pace of ministering to others and advised his apostles to do the same.

> The apostles gathered around Jesus and reported to him all they had done and taught. Then, because so many people were coming and going that they did not even have a chance to eat, he said to them, "Come with me by yourselves to a quiet place and get some rest."
>
> So they went away by themselves in a boat to a solitary place (Mark 6:30–32, NIV).

His was a life of beautiful balance. He accomplished everything the Father sent Him to do. Everything. And He did it without ignoring those essential times of restful leisure. If that is the way *He* lived, then it makes good sense that that is the way we, too, must learn to live. If you have formed the habit of overwork and you haven't cultivated the ability to take a break and relax, these things may appear difficult to you, but they are not impossible.

THE PLACE TO START: GOD

Since most humans suffer from a lack of balance in their lives, our best counsel on this subject comes from God's Word, the Bible. In that Book, there appears a most unusual command: "Be imitators of God, therefore, as dearly loved children... " (Eph. 5:1, NIV). Maybe you never realized such a statement was in the Bible. What a strange command: "Be imitators of God"!

The Greek term translated "be imitators" is *mimeomai*, from which we get the English word *mimic*. One reliable scholar, W. E. Vine, says that this verb "is always used in exhortations, and always in the continuous tense, suggesting a constant habit or practice."[2]

In other words, this is neither a passing thought nor a once-in-a-blue-moon experience. The practice of our being people who "mimic God" is to become our daily habit. We are to do what He does. Respond to life as He responds. Emulate similar traits. Model His style.

But to do that, to be an imitator of God, requires that we come to terms with the value of quietness, slowing down, coming apart from the noise and speed of today's pace and broadening our lives with a view of the eternal reach of time. It means saying no to more and more activities that increase the speed of our squirrel cage. Knowing God *requires* that we "be still" (Ps. 46:10).

It means if I'm a pastor, I do more than tend the sheep. I must, or I ultimately begin to walk dangerously near the ragged edge of emotional disintegration. The same applies if I'm a businessman or a homemaker. It means I refuse to be driven by guilt and unrealistic demands (mine or others). To be God-mimics, we must begin to realize that leisure is not a take-it-or-leave-it luxury. It is necessary for survival.

Please understand that leisure is more than idle free time not devoted to paid occupations. Some of the most valuable work done in the world has been done at leisure... and never paid for in cash. Leisure is free activity. Labor is compulsory activity. In leisure, we do what we like, but in labor we do what we must. In our labor we meet the objective needs and demands of others—our employer, the public, people who are impacted by and through our work. But in leisure we scratch the subjective itches within ourselves. In leisure our minds are liberated from the immediate, the necessary. As we incorporate leisure into the mainstream of our world, we gain perspective. We lift ourselves above the grit and grind of mere existence.

Interestingly, *leisure* comes from the Latin word *licere*, which means "to be permitted." If we are ever going to inculcate leisure into our otherwise utilitarian routine, we must give ourselves permission to do so. God did (as we shall see) and so must we if we intend to mimic Him.

But this calls for a closer look. We need some specific guidelines on which to focus that will help us imitate God and at the same time "permit" us to cultivate leisure in our lives.

FOUR GUIDELINES FROM GENESIS

If we are to imitate God as a daily habit of life, we need to nail down some specific guidelines. It occurred to me recently that an excellent place to locate those specifics in the Scriptures would be the first place He reveals Himself to us—the book of Genesis, especially the first two chapters.

I want to encourage you to read this familiar section. You will discover that God is involved in four activities:
- He creates
- He communicates
- He rests
- He relates

Let's limit our thoughts to those four specifics. Each one fits perfectly into the cultivation of leisure. They form some excellent guidelines to follow as we begin to develop an accurate concept of leisure.

Creativity

First and foremost, God is engaged in the act of creation, according to Genesis 1 and 2. He begins with that which is "formless and void" (1:2), lacking meaning, beauty, and purpose.

He takes time to create with His own hands. In His mind are thoughts of a universe, indescribably beautiful. He mentally pictures vast expanses of land masses, deep oceans, colorful vegetation, an almost endless variety of living creatures ... not to mention the stars, the planets, and the perfect motion and rhythm of all those celestial bodies. Finally, He creates mankind with a body and mind that still amaze students of physiology and psychology.

As He created He added the music, harmony, and coordination of movement—the miracle of birth and growth, the full spectrum of colors, sights, and sounds. He cared about details—from snowflakes to butterfly wings, from pansy petals to the bones of bodies, from the microscopic world of biology to the telescopic world of astronomy.

In doing all this, He set the pace. He, the first to create, announced its significance.

If I may suddenly jump forward to today, let me ask a penetrating question: *Are you taking time to create?* Obviously, you cannot create a solar system or bring forth an ocean from nothing, but you *can* make things with your hands. You can write things with your pen... or paint things with your brush... or compose things, using your piano or guitar or harmonica. You can dream things with your mind and then try to invent them or draw them or, in other ways, bring them to reality through some creative process.

You hold in your hand a book. In the book are numerous chapters filled with thousands of words. There was a time when none of these things existed. It all began as a dream, an idea that was mine which, by the way, occurred in one of my leisure moments. I gave myself permission to relax for several days on vacation, and the idea of this book emerged and began to take shape. There was no required or forced structure. It has been almost entirely a creative experience. One of my most enjoyable leisure activities is writing... something I would never have thought possible twenty years ago. But now I realize I've had this itch inside me most of my life. It wasn't until I began to let it out freely and fully that a whole new dimension of my life was added. And it is *such* fun!

All children have built-in creativity. Just look at the things they make and do (and say!) on their own. There is an enormous wealth of creative powers in the mind of a child. Walt Disney believed that and often spoke of it. But if we aren't careful, we adults will squelch it. We'll fail to encourage it or cultivate it or even let it out of its cage. Why? Well, it takes a little extra time and it often costs some money. I should add that it tends to be messy. Not many really creative people—in the process of creating—keep everything neat, picked up, and in its place.

There's a good motto to remember if you're determined to encourage and cultivate creativity:

A CREATIVE MESS
... IS BETTER THAN TIDY IDLENESS.

If we are going to imitate God, we will need to find creative outlets in times of leisure. Yours may be music or one of the arts. It may be in the area of interior design. My wife enjoys house plants and quilting. Yours may be gardening or landscaping projects, woodworking or brick and stone work around the house. We had our patio enclosed during the remodeling of our house. Both the bricklayer and the carpenter who did the work employed a great deal of creativity in their skills. It's an added plus when we can create and even get paid for it! But regardless, our creativity needs expression.

If you intend to strengthen your grip on leisure, give some thought to how you might utilize your creativity in the process. God did and so can we.

Communication

If you read the Genesis account of creation rather carefully, you'll see that interspersed within the creative week were times of communication. He made things, then said, "That's good." After the sixth day, His evaluation increased to, "That's *very* good."

The Godhead communicated prior to the creation of man, you may recall:

> Then God said, "Let us make man in our image, according to our likeness; and let them rule over the fish of the sea and over the birds of the sky and over the cattle and over all the earth, and over every creeping thing that creeps on the earth" (Gen. 1:26).

And after God created man, the highest form of life on earth, He communicated with him.

> And God blessed them; and God said to them, "Be fruitful and multiply, and fill the earth, and subdue it; and rule over the fish of the sea and over the birds of the sky, and over every living thing that moves on the earth."
> Then God said, "Behold, I have given you every plant yielding seed that is on the surface of all the earth, and every tree which has fruit yielding seed; it shall be food for you;

and to every beast of the earth and to every bird of the sky and to every thing that moves on the earth which has life, I have given green plant for food"; and it was so (Gen. 1:28–30).

Again, I'd like to apply this to our times. Initially, in leisure, we take time to communicate with ourselves (as God did) and affirm ourselves, "That's good . . . that's *very* good." Do you do that? Most of us are good at criticizing ourselves and finding fault with what we have done or failed to do. I'd like to suggest an alternate plan—spend some of your leisure time finding pleasure and satisfaction in what you have done as well as in who and what you are. Sound too liberal? Why? Since when is a good self-esteem liberal?

There are times we need to tell ourselves, "Good job!" when we know that is true. I smile as I write this to you, but I must confess that occasionally I even say to myself, "That's *very* good, Swindoll," when I am pleased with something I've done. That isn't conceited pride, my friend. It's acknowledging in words the feelings of the heart. The Lord knows that we hear more than enough internal put-downs! Communicating in times of leisure includes self-affirmation, acknowledging, of course, that God ultimately gets the glory. After all, He's the One who makes the whole experience possible.

Alan McGinnis, in his fine book *The Friendship Factor*, views affirmation so significant he devotes an entire chapter to the subject. Appropriately, he entitles it "The Art of Affirmation,"[3] for it is indeed an art practiced by few and mastered by even fewer.

Leisure also includes times of communicating with others who are important to us, just as God the Creator did with man the creature. Unless we are careful, the speed of our lives will reduce our communication to gutteral grunts, frowns, stares, and unspoken assumptions. Be honest. Has that begun to happen? Sometimes our children mirror the truth of our pace.

I vividly remember several years ago being caught in the backwash of too many commitments in too few days. It wasn't long before I was snapping at my wife and our children, choking down my food at mealtimes, and feeling irritated at those unexpected interruptions through the day. Before long, things around our home started reflecting the pattern of my hurry-up style. It was becoming unbearable. I distinctly recall after supper one evening the words of our younger daughter Colleen. She wanted to tell me about something important that had happened to her at school that day. She hurriedly began, "Daddy, I wanna tell you somethin' andIwilltellyoureallyfast."

Suddenly realizing her frustration, I answered in a rather deliberate manner, "Honey, you can tell me . . . and you don't have to tell me *really fast*. Say it slowly."

I'll never forget her answer: "Then *listen* slowly."

I had taken no time for leisure. Not even at meals with my family. Everything was up tight. I hit the floor running at breakneck speed. And guess what began to break down? You're right, those all-important communication lines.

God not only made man, He talked with him, He listened to him. He considered His creature valuable enough to spend time with, to respond to. It took time, but He believed it was justified. As we mimic Him, we must do the same.

There are entire books written on communication, so I'll not be so foolish as to think I can develop the subject adequately here. I only want to emphasize its importance. It is *imperative* that we understand that without adding sufficient leisure time to our schedule for meaningful communication, a relationship with those who are important to us will disintegrate faster than we can keep it in repair.

Take time to listen, to feel, to respond. In doing so, we "imitate God" in our leisure. And the rewards are far reaching, so very satisfying.

Rest

Following the sixth day of creation, the Lord God deliberately stopped working. Do you remember the Genesis account?

Thus the heavens and the earth were completed, and all their hosts.

And by the seventh day God completed His work which He had done; and He rested on the seventh day from all His work which He had done.

Then God blessed the seventh day and sanctified it, because in it He rested from all His work which God had created and made (Gen. 2:1–3).

He rested. Take special note of that. It wasn't that there was nothing else He could have done. It certainly wasn't because He was exhausted—omnipotence never gets tired! He hadn't run out of ideas, for omniscience knows no mental limitations. He could easily have made many more worlds, created an infinite number of other forms of life, and provided multiple millions of galaxies beyond what He did.

But He didn't. He stopped.

He spent an entire day resting. In fact, He "blessed the seventh day and sanctified it," something He did not do on the other six days. He marked this one day off as extremely special. It was like no other. Sounds to me like He made the day on which He rested a "priority" period of time.

If we intend to imitate God, we, too, will need to make rest a priority.

- A good night's rest on a regular basis;
- A full day's rest at least once a week;
- Moments of rest snatched here and there during the week;
- Vacation times of rest for the refreshment and repair of both body and soul;
- A release from the fierce grip of intense stress brought on by daily hassles.

I feel so strongly about declaring war on personal anxiety that I have written an entire booklet dealing specifically with stress[4] and the toll it can take on our lives. Several things contribute to our lack of inner rest:

- A poorly developed sense of humor;
- Focusing more on what we don't have rather than on what we *do* have;
- Failure to give play, fun, rest, and leisure a proper place of dignity;
- Our strong tendency to compete and compare, leading to a wholesale dissatisfaction with things as they are;
- Our continual preoccupation with getting more;
- Self-imposed guilt... unrealistic expectations;
- An "all-work-and-no-play-will-make-me-happy" philosophy of life.

And the result? Look around. Stretched across most faces of Americans driving to and from work is boredom. Not fulfillment. Not a deep sense of satisfaction. Not even a smile of quiet contentment.

Even though our work-week is decreasing and our weekend time is increasing, our country lacks inner peace. External leisure does not guarantee internal rest, does it?

For sure, our nation believes in the *theory* of leisure. I heard over a television documentary that we spend more on recreation each year than we do on education, construction of new homes, or national defense. The latest figures I've read show that Americans will spend more than $300 billion on leisure products and activities by 1985. But I question the chewing gum ads that tell us that if we double our pleasure, we'll automatically double our fun. Mental hospitals remain overcrowded... and most of the patients are not what we would call senior citizens.

Time on our hands, we have. But we don't have meaningful "rest" in the biblical sense of the term.

I suggest that you and I do more than cluck our tongues and wag our heads at the problem. That helps nobody! Our greatest contribution to the answer is a radical break with the rut of normal living. My good friend, Tim Hansel of Summit Expedition, suggests taking different kinds of vacations: midget vacations or mini-vacations (two minutes or more!) or, if you're able, maxi-vacations... or even, if possible, *super*-maxi-vacations where you take time to enjoy extended lesiure. He calls it the "Year of Adventure" where we try our hand at sailing or rock climbing, skydiving, or learning karate. Or whatever.

Change your routine, my friend. Blow the dust of boredom off your schedule. Shake yourself loose and get a taste of fresh life. Here are several suggestions for adding "zip" to your leisure:

- Begin jogging and/or an exercise program.
- Buy a bicycle and start pedaling two to three miles each day.
- Get an album or two of your favorite music and drink in the sounds as you lie flat on your back.
- Enroll in a local art class and try your hand at painting.
- If you have the money, travel abroad.
- Build a small sailboat with a friend.
- Take up a new hobby, like photography or ceramics or making artificial floral arrangements.
- Start writing letters of encouragement to people you appreciate.
- Make something out of wood with your own hands.
- Dig around in the soil, plant a small garden, and watch God cooperate with your efforts.
- Take a gourmet cooking class.
- Spend some time at the library and pick up several good books on subjects or people of interest to you... then sit back, munch on an apple, and read, read, read.
- Plan a camping or backpacking trip soon with one of your children, your mate, or your friend and spend a night or two out under the stars.
- Pull out all those old snapshots, sort them, and put them into albums.
- Write some poetry

- Visit a museum or zoo in your area.
- By the way, don't forget the simple pleasures of life. Take time to enjoy the beauty of a sunrise or sunset... smell the roses along the way.

Broaden your world. Kick away the thick, brick walls of tradition. Silence the old enemy Guilt, who will sing his same old tune in your ears. And work on that deep crease between your eyes. Look for things to laugh at... and *laugh out loud*. It's biblical! "A joyful heart is good medicine, But a broken spirit dries up the bones" (Prov. 17:22).

Comedian Bill Cosby is right. There's a smile down inside of you that is just dying to come out! It won't until you give yourself permission. Take time to smile. Rest releases humor.

One more glance at the Genesis passage will be worth our effort. Remember where we've been?

- God created... in leisure; so do *we*.
- God communicated... in leisure; so must *we*.
- God rested... in leisure; so will *we*.

But He also *related* with the man and woman He made.

Relating

The passage in Genesis 2 is so familiar. After God made man, He observed a need inside that life, a nagging loneliness that Adam couldn't shake. "Then the Lord God said, 'It is not good for the man to be alone; I will make him a helper suitable for him'" (Gen. 2:18). As a fulfillment to the promise to help Adam with his need for companionship, God got involved.

So the Lord God caused a deep sleep to fall upon the man, and he slept; then He took one of his ribs, and closed up the flesh at that place.

And the Lord God fashioned into a woman the rib which He had taken from the man, and brought her to the man (Gen. 2:21–22).

Later we read that the Lord came to relate to His creatures "in the cool of the day" (Gen. 3:8). I take it that such a time must have been a common practice between the Lord God and His friends, Adam and Eve.

He considered them valuable, so the infinite Creator-God took time to relate to the couple in the Garden of Eden. He got personally involved. He observed their needs. He carved out time and went to the trouble to do *whatever* was necessary to help them. He cultivated that friendship. He saw it as a worthwhile activity.

I was amused at a cartoon that appeared in a magazine. It was the picture of a thief wearing one of those "Lone Ranger" masks. His gun was pointed toward his frightened victim as he yelled: "Okay, gimme all your valuables!"

The victim began stuffing into the sack all his *friends*.

How valuable to *you* are relationships? If you have trouble answering that, I'll help you decide. Stop and think back over the past month or two. How much of your leisure have you spent developing and enjoying relationships?

Jesus, God's Son, certainly considered the relationship He had with His disciples worth His time. They spent literally *hours* together. They ate together and wept together, and I'm sure they must have laughed together as well. Being God, He really didn't "need" those men. He certainly did not need the hassle they created on occasion. But He loved those twelve men. He believed in them. They had a special relationship—a lot like Paul, Silas, and Timothy; David and Jonathan; Barnabas and John Mark; Elijah and Elisha.

As the poet Samuel Taylor Coleridge once put it, "Friendship is a sheltering tree."[5] How very true! Whatever leisure time we are able to invest in relationships is time well spent. And when we do, let's keep in mind we are "imitating God," for His Son certainly did.

How to Implement Leisure

The bottom line of all this, of course, is actually *doing* it. We can nod in agreement until we get a whiplash, but our greatest need is not inclination; it's demonstration.

Here are two suggestions that will help.

1. *Deliberately stop being absorbed with the endless details of life.* Our Savior said it straight when He declared that we cannot, at the same time, serve both God *and* man. But we try so hard! If Jesus' words from Matthew 6 are saying anything, they are saying, "Don't sweat the things only God can handle." Each morning, deliberately decide not to allow worry to steal your time and block your leisure.

2. *Consciously start taking time for leisure.* After God put the world together, He rested. We are commanded to imitate Him.

For rest to occur in *our* lives, Christ Jesus must be in proper focus. He must be in His rightful place before we can ever expect to get *our* world to fall in place.

A bone-weary father dragged into his home dog tired late one evening. It had been one of those unbelievable days of pressure, deadlines, and demands. He looked forward to a time of relaxation and quietness. Exhausted, he picked up the evening paper and headed for his favorite easy chair by the fireplace. About the time he got his shoes untied, *plop!* into his lap dropped his five-year-old son with an excited grin on his face.

"Hi, Dad, . . . let's play!"

He loved his boy dearly, but his need for a little time all alone to repair and think was, for the moment, a greater need than time with Junior. But how could he maneuver it?

There had been a recent moon probe and the newspaper carried a huge picture of earth. With a flash of much-needed insight, the dad asked his boy to bring a pair of scissors and some transparent tape. Quickly, he cut the picture of earth into various shapes and sizes, then handed the pile of homemade jigsaw puzzle pieces to him.

"You tape it all back together, Danny, then come on back and we'll play, okay?"

Off scampered the child to his room as dad breathed a sigh of relief. But in less than ten minutes the boy bounded back with everything taped perfectly in place. Stunned, the father asked: "How'd you do it so fast, Son?"

"Aw, it was easy, Daddy. You see, there is this picture of a man on the back of the sheet... and when you put the man together, the world comes together."

And so it is in life. When we put the Man in His rightful place, it's amazing what happens to our world. And, more importantly, what happens to us. I can assure you that in the final analysis of your life—when you stop some day and look back on the way you spent your time—your use of leisure will be far more important than those hours you spent with your nose to the grindstone. Don't wait until it's too late to enjoy life.

Live it up now. Throw yourself into it with abandonment. Get up out of the rut of work long enough to see that there is more to life than a job and a paycheck. You'll never be the same!

Maybe it would help to pray right now. Allow me to express the feelings of my heart, which may reflect many of your own thoughts.

Lord, our God:

It is true that we are spending our entire life preparing to live indefinitely. Habits and fears, guilt and discontentment have teamed up against us and pinned us to the mat of monotony.

We find ourselves running in a tight radius, like a rat in a sewer pipe. Our world has become too small, too routine, too grim. Although busy, we have to confess that a nagging sense of boredom has now boarded our ship in this journey of life. We are enduring the scenery instead of enjoying it. We have really begun to take ourselves too seriously.

We desire change . . . a cure from this terminal illness of dullness and routine.

We are sheep, not rats. You have made us whole people who are free to think and relax in leisure, not slaves chained to a schedule. Enable us to break loose! Show us ways to do that. Give us the courage to start today and the hope we need to stay fresh tomorrow . . . and the next day and the next.

Bring the child out from within us. Introduce us again to the sounds and smells and sights of this beautiful world you wrapped around us. Convince us of the importance of friendships and laughter and wonder. Put our world back together.

May we become people like Your Son, committed to the highest standard of excellence and devotion to Your will, yet easy to live with, at peace within, taking time for leisure.

In His strong name we pray,
Amen.

DISCUSSION QUESTIONS AND SUGGESTIONS TO HELP YOU STRENGTHEN YOUR GRIP ON LEISURE

• Without the aid of a dictionary, define *leisure*. Afterwards, discuss what there is about our culture that makes us view leisure as either an enemy of the diligent or a luxury reserved especially for the rich. Why is that false?

• Do a little scriptural survey. Locate three or four verses or passages that lend support to the need for leisure. After reading each one, personalize it by relating it to something occurring today—preferably either in your own life or in your home situation.

• Think deeply about this before answering. What is the reason for leisure? Is it true that its basic purpose, its most primary function, is to provide relief from work? Is the point of leisure restoration . . . a pick-me-up time of relaxation?

• Do you agree with this statement?

Most middle-class Americans tend to worship their work, to work at their play, and to play at their worship. As a result, their meanings and values are distorted. Their relationships disintegrate faster than they can keep them in repair and their lifestyles resemble a cast of characters in search of a plot" (Gordon Dahl).

If you do agree, express your reaction. If not, why not?

• Leisure, stillness, silence, and rest go together. They belong to one another. They fit. In light of this, substitute the words *Have leisure* for *Be still* in Psalm 46:10. And in place of the repeated term *rest* in Hebrews 4:1–11, try using the word *leisure*. Talk about how this broadens the concept of leisure.

• Finally, sit quietly and evaluate the normal level of your intensity. Are you "always on the go"? Does it give you strokes to have people say you're a workaholic? Is it hard for you to be quiet, to be at ease, to be alone and still? Pray about this.

CHAPTER ELEVEN

Strengthening Your Grip on Missions

MY FIRST SERIOUS ENCOUNTER with God's world program occurred a few miles from Alcatraz.

No, I wasn't at church or in a seminary chapel surrounded by moving, melodic strains of Bach on an enormous pipe organ. I did not feel lifted up to glory by huge heavenly arms, giving me a panoramic view of this planet, nor was there a strange cloud formation, like divine skywriting, spelling out "Go overseas. Be a missionary!" I never saw an angel pointing at me like the old patriotic image of Uncle Sam, saying, "I want you." No, none of that. From start to finish, there was absolutely *nothing* religious about the entire episode. To be candid with you, I didn't like God very much at the time. I felt He had let me down after I had counted on Him to help me out.

This needs a little explanation. It was back in the latter half of the 1950s—1957 to be exact. I had been married for less than two years. I had been deferred from military service while I finished my schooling, but time was up. The hot breath of the United States Defense Department was hitting the back of my neck, and it wasn't going to be long before my exemption card would be replaced with a 1-A draft card. The question was not would I go, but which branch would I choose. In those days, one's military service was not an option.

All those Navy posters "Join the Navy and See the World" had no appeal. Being married, I had no interest in seeing the world. I just wanted to do my duty, have my wife with me throughout the time, and get it over with. Because the Marine Corps recruiting officer promised me that I would have nothing to worry about ("No chance you'll go abroad, young man") and because he assured me when it was all behind me I'd have something to look back on with pride, I enlisted in the Corps. Some of you veterans are smiling right now.

Throughout boot camp, before I knew where my wife and I would be stationed, I prayed that God would fulfill my desire that I'd be in a stateside area. By the way, I also prayed that I would survive boot camp. Both seemed pretty shaky at the time. Well, less than six months later both prayers were granted... initially, that is.

We set up housekeeping in a quaint little apartment in Daly City, California. My first (I hoped my *only*) military assignment was 100 Harrison Street, downtown San Francisco. Great duty! I had been the envy of my entire company in our Advanced Infantry Regiment at Camp Pendleton a few weeks earlier when all of us received our orders. Some guys were sent to Barstow, others to Twenty-Nine Palms—both lovely, picturesque spots in the middle of the Mohave Desert. A few were shipped immediately overseas to an infantry or tank outfit (ugh!) in some jungle or wilderness region. Not me, pal. "Open up those golden gates, San Francisco, here I come." And there we stayed. It was just delightful... for a few months.

And then one foggy afternoon as I was checking out for the day, a letter was pressed into my hand. Because it looked like another governmental form letter, I never bothered to open it until I parked my car on a hill across the street from the place where my wife was employed. I slit open the envelope, unfolded the letter, *and had my first serious encounter with world missions.* It was from Washington, D.C., alerting me to the fact that I was being transferred to Okinawa... and that it would not be possible for me to bring my wife—"Against Marine Corps policy." I sat there, stunned. An enormous knot in my throat made me gag.

One word burned itself into the pit of my stomach—Okinawa—"The Rock." Ironically, I looked up through tears and in the distance I saw Alcatraz. It was a grim yet timely reminder that I might think twice before going AWOL! There was no escape. That's why I felt let down by God. Ripped off might be a better way to put it. I was confused, resentful, disillusioned about the whole thing.

Within weeks I was back at Camp Pendleton, this time terribly despondent. I was alone in a staging regiment, being made ready for overseas duty. There were dozens of innoculations, classes, and briefing sessions, mixed with long, lonely hours of time on my hands. I visited my older brother Orville and his wife in Pasadena one weekend. As I got on the bus to return to the base one grey Sunday evening, he handed me a book that was destined to change my attitude, my future, my perspective, my career... my entire life—*Through Gates of Splendor.*[1] It was the true story of the martyrdom of five young missionaries who were attempting to reach and win the tribe of Auca Indians in the interior of Ecuador. A lady I had never heard of back then was the author, Elisabeth Elliot, one of the five widows.

As that old Greyhound bus rumbled along Highway 5 toward Oceanside and the rain blew across my window, I devoured the book, page after page. I must say, for the first time I (1) began to tolerate the possibility that my transfer overseas might have been arranged by God, and (2) that God's world program might somehow include me. *Me, of all people!* You really cannot imagine what foreign thoughts those were. Looking back, however, it is so obvious, so clear.

In my broken, desperate, lonely, inescapable situation, God showed me a world much bigger than my own. Through each one of those 256 pages, He got more and more of my attention. Chapter by chapter I released more and more of my selfish territory. He scaled the walls I had built and sealed off with the words "Private Property." As I mentioned in chapter 7 on discipleship, I was a Christian, but I had made certain that none of that would get out of hand! Little did I realize what a wedge this book would drive into my self-serving, well-sealed, do-not-disturb lifestyle. I realize now that God timed everything perfectly. Without His forceful plan to get me overseas, I would never have caught His vision of an entire world without Christ. Never!

A VISIT WITH A PROPHET IN THE TIME TUNNEL

Maybe it was a similar situation with young Isaiah. Twenty-seven centuries ago this young aristocrat was born into the home of a man named Amoz in the city of Zion. As he grew up, he was somewhat aware of his world and its troubles. The lengthening shadow of Assyria was a growing threat. Names like Tiglath-pileser III, Shalmanezer, Sargon, and Sennacherib were as familiar to the Jews as names like Fidel Castro, Mao Tse-tung, and Breshnev are to Americans today. Isaiah knew his nation was weak. He probably sighed a little over the superstition, idolatry, immorality, and heathen customs from the East that ate like bone cancer on the structure of his society. The people were drifting, eroding. Even the priests were lacking in moral and spiritual purity. Most of the prophets—those once-courageous men who served as a conscience to their nation—were equally weak. Women were coarse, sensual, shallow. The needs were acute.

But Isaiah probably had no plans to get mixed up in all that. He had his life mapped out, and he was off and running in the direction he was comfortable with ... until... until a part of his world caved in... until God got his attention and turned him around one hundred eighty degrees!

Not on a bus. Not through a book. Not because a

small band of men had been killed while attempting to reach a tribe of nameless Indians. Not while he was separated from his home, serving in the Israeli Marines, but through the death of a friend, whose name was Uzziah—a king, a good man, and one of the few people in that day who modeled a righteous life.

Isaiah, still in his twenties, was grieving the loss of Uzziah, whose death was as untimely to the nation Judah as Lincoln's death was to our nation back in 1865.

RELEVANT PRINCIPLES FROM AN ANCIENT PROPHET

Isaiah 6 includes a remarkable story some twenty-seven centuries old. I find woven through this ancient account several principles that help strengthen our grip on God's world program. But before getting into a discussion of these principles, let's take a look at what the prophet wrote:

> In the year of King Uzziah's death, I saw the Lord sitting on a throne, lofty and exalted, with the train of His robe filling the temple.
>
> Seraphim stood above Him, each having six wings; with two he covered his face, and with two he covered his feet, and with two he flew.
>
> And one called out to another and said, "Holy, Holy, Holy, is the Lord of hosts, the whole earth is full of His glory."
>
> And the foundations of the thresholds trembled at the voice of Him who called out, while the temple was filling with smoke.
>
> Then I said, "Woe is me, for I am ruined! Because I am a man of unclean lips, And I live among a people of unclean lips; For my eyes have seen the King, the Lord of hosts."
>
> Then one of the seraphim flew to me, with a burning coal in his hand which he had taken from the altar with tongs.
>
> And he touched my mouth with it and said, "Behold, this has touched your lips; and your iniquity is taken away, and your sin is forgiven."

Then I heard the voice of the Lord, saying, "Whom shall I send, and who will go for us?" Then I said, "Here am I. Send me!" (Isa. 6:1–8).

In reading these verses it is easy to become so impressed with the vision that we pass over the circumstance that brought it about. If I understand this correctly, it was a time of loss, an experience of grief for Isaiah. His friend had died. Perhaps the prophet had slipped into the house of God for some quietness and prayer. Maybe he was feeling lonely or abandoned. *The Living Bible* links the vision with the grief: "The year King Uzziah died I saw the Lord!"

Principle 1: God Uses Circumstances to Make Us Aware of His Presence

Isaiah says, "I saw the Lord!" His earthly situation turned his eyes upward. That's what happened to me back in the late 1950s. My disappointment, my loneliness and confusion, rather than hardening the soil of my soul, plowed deeply. Those things cut away at me, made me sensitive to my Lord... in a way I would otherwise *never* have been.

For you it may be a lingering illness or an unexpected move to a new location, a job change, or perhaps a sudden loss of employment entirely. I know an individual who claims that it took a divorce to bring him to his knees and (for the first time in his life) to become aware of God's presence. A couple my wife had known for fifteen years lost their eighteen-month-old baby girl. Their grief could hardly be relieved—some wondered if they would *ever* be the same. As time passed, it became obvious that her death was the turning point in their spiritual pilgrimage. That couple got off the fence and into the action. God became more real, more significant to that couple as a result of the loss of their child than He had ever been before.

It was the year his friend died that Isaiah "saw the Lord. . . ." And what was He doing? Was He frowning or pacing back and forth? No. Was He anxious or puzzled or angry? No. He was sitting down. The Lord was calmly seated on His throne. I think of majestic sovereignty when I read of Jehovah's position. He was totally in charge. He was not wringing His hands, wondering what in the world He was going to do. He was "lofty and exalted." With height comes *perspective*. And His exalted role speaks of *authority*. Isaiah saw no confused or anxious deity, but One who sat in sovereign, calm control with full perspective and in absolute authority. Interestingly, the death of Uzziah is not mentioned again. From now on it's the prophet and His God—His presence "filling the temple."

A group of multiple-winged creatures called "seraphim" (one Old Testament scholar refers to them as "flaming angels") were also present in Isaiah's vision. They formed an antiphonal choir, chanting and repeating in alternating voice: "Holy, Holy, Holy, is the Lord of hosts, the whole earth is full of His glory." It must have been some kind of sight! In *Unger's Bible Dictionary* we read, "From their antiphonal chant . . . we may conceive them to have been ranged in opposite rows on each side of the throne."[2] One group would cry out and the other would answer. And again, as the dumbfounded Isaiah stared in silence, it would happen again. Over and over. Small wonder the foundations of the earthly temple trembled. Those voices sounded like deafening thunderclaps roaring over the hillside. *It was awesome!*

Several years ago, our large chancel choir at the church I pastor in Fullerton, California, sang one of the most worshipful and beautiful musicals I have ever heard. It was entitled "Greater Is He." There is a particular part of the composition that is woven through the piece—a haunting melody with accompanying lyrics that stay with you for months afterward:

> Surely, the presence of the Lord is in this place.
> I can feel His mighty power and His grace.
> I can hear the brush of angel's wings,
> I see glory on each face,
> Surely the presence of the Lord is in this place.[3]

That's what Isaiah felt. The "brush of angels' wings" coupled with their antiphonal words of adoring praise caused the prophet to say (the NIV reads "I cried"):

Woe is me, for I am ruined!

The Berkeley Version renders his response:

Alas for me, I feel beaten!

The Living Bible says:

My doom is sealed, for I am a foul-mouthed sinner, a member of a sinful, foul-mouthed race....

Isaiah is frightened, beaten, and broken. Not only does he see the Lord sovereign, high and exalted, not only does he witness the antiphonal choir of angels swarming the heavenly throne, he also hears that God is infinitely holy. And in contrast to his own sinfulness and depravity, he feels doomed ... beaten.

Principle 2: God Reveals His Character to Make Us See Our Need.

This is a major part of the process as the Lord opens our eyes to His world program we call "missions." He shows us Himself first, not the starving millions, not the heathen in gross darkness. No, He begins with a one-on-one. He uses certain painful circumstances to make us look up, then He reveals some things about His character (theologians refer to these as God's "attributes") to make us see our need for Him. Did you catch the sharp contrast?

"Holy, Holy, Holy, is the Lord of hosts...."

"I am ruined!... I am a man of unclean lips...."

Suddenly, Isaiah is no longer viewing a vision from a safe distance, removed and out of touch. The whole scene literally comes to life as one of those seraphs steps out of the vision and flies toward our frightened friend. Without announcement, the winged creature sweeps into the prophet's presence and does something most unusual.

> Then one of the seraphim flew to me, with a burning coal in his hand which he had taken from the altar with tongs.
> And he touched my mouth with it and said, "Behold, this has touched your lips; and your iniquity is taken away, and your sin is forgiven" (Isa. 6:6–7).

The flaming angel touches Isaiah with a hot coal. Did you notice *where* he touched the prophet? On his lips. I suggest there is significance in that act. Isaiah had just admitted he was "a foul-mouthed sinner" (TLB). It shouldn't shock us, therefore, to take his confession literally. He no doubt struggled with profanity. And that is probably what the young man was using as an excuse to disqualify himself from God's service.

We all have such excuses:

"I'm not physically well. I'm sickly—not strong enough."

"I've got this temper problem."

"I can't speak very well in public."

"I don't have a lot of education."

"My past is too raunchy. If you only knew!"

"I have a prison record."

"I once had an abortion."

"I've been on drugs."

"You see, I'm a divorcee."

"I was once in a mental hospital."

And on and on and on. It's the old bird-with-the-broken-pinion routine. But God is bigger than *any* of those reasons. He specializes in taking bruised, soiled, broken, guilty, and miserable vessels and making them whole, forgiven, and useful again. Remember what the angel said to Isaiah when he touched his lips?

> ". . . your guilt is taken away and your sin atoned for"
> (NIV).

What affirmation! Where sin abounded, grace *super* abounded. The one thing Isaiah had been hiding behind, ashamed to admit but unable to conquer, God dealt with.

*Principle 3: God Gives Us Hope to Make Us
Know We Are Useful.*

You won't grasp the full impact of this principle until you read the dialogue that followed.

> Then I heard the voice of the Lord, saying, "Whom shall I send, and who will go for us?" Then I said, "Here am I. Send me!" (v. 8).

Don't miss that first word, "Then. . . ." When? After the grief that brought Isaiah to his knees. After God revealed Himself as all the things the prophet wasn't. After the seraph had touched his lips (the specific area of struggle) and assured him he was useful. After all that, God asked, "Whom shall I send?" You see, God's perspective is much broader than ours. In those days, He saw villages by the thousands, people by the millions. His heart was on a world in need. Up to that moment, Isaiah was swimming in his own tight radius, preoccupied with a limited view of his world.

Every summer I enjoy taking my family to see the Dodgers and the Angels play some of their games. Occasionally, there will be a time during each game when it gets a little slow and boring. The crowd gets unusually quiet and even the players lack spark. That happened at an Angel game last summer, and I rolled up the printed game program and looked all over the stadium through the hole at the end of the tube. We've all done this as kids. As I looked out on the field I could see only the batter and the catcher, no one else. Or I could spot only the first baseman and right fielder from where I sat. When I looked up in the stands, I could see thirty-five to forty people inside the hole, but that was all. As soon as I pulled the program away from my eye, I could immediately see thousands of heads among the baseball fans or the entire field of players.

My world back in the late 1950s was a very tight, limited radius composed of my wife, my future, my career, my desires, my perspective—almost as if I were viewing the world through a rolled-up game program. God stepped in and pushed the limitation away, exposing me to a world I had never, never considered important before. He did the very same thing with Isaiah. Anyone who makes a determined effort to strengthen his or her grip on missions will sooner or later have to toss aside the rolled-up game program and get a glimpse of God's world program, which brings us to the next principle.

Principle 4: God Expands Our Vision to Make Us Evaluate Our Availability.

I haven't words to describe the jolt I received by being exposed to that seventeen-day journey across the Pacific and then the vast numbers, cultures, and needs of people in Japan, Okinawa, Formosa, and the Philippines. An entire world literally opened up to me. Up until then I was restricted in my vision and limited in my awareness. Being from Texas, I viewed God as an American God with a Texas accent. He smiled on fried okra, sliced tomatoes, chili, red beans, cornbread, banjo pluckin', and barbeque. He liked big spreads (ranches), folk songs, family reunions, salt-water fishing. But let me tell you, when this "good ole boy" walked wide-eyed through the quaint and unusual paths of the Orient, heard the strange music from the samisen, saw those idol altars that stood several stories high, and witnessed mile after mile of rice paddies and hundreds of other foreign sights, God and His world program took on a whole new meaning. Things like personal prejudices began to fade along with my own selfish pride of my race. The determination to get my own way became increasingly less desirable. I didn't work hard to be pious or a super-spiritually minded "missionary type." No, it all just began to fall into place so naturally. I honestly found myself saying, like Isaiah, "Here am I. Send me!" I became strangely motivated to break loose from that tight little radius of my career, my future, and my plans. Without realizing it, my attention slowly shifted from my world to God's world. But before all this starts sounding like one of those cloud-nine, dreamy testimonies, let me add that the Lord kept me in constant touch with reality. Keep in mind that I was living in a Marine barracks, one of the toughest places on earth to practice authentic Christianity. This helps introduce the fifth and final principle we find interwoven in the Isaiah 6 passage.

Principle 5: God Tells Us the Truth to Make Us Focus On Reality.

A decision like the one Isaiah was considering was far too significant for it to be based on emotion alone. Lest he assume it would be a downhill slide, God hit him with the truth.

And He said, "Go, and tell this people: 'Keep on listening, but do not perceive; Keep on looking, but do not understand.'

"Render the hearts of this people insensitive, Their ears dull, and their eyes dim, Lest they see with their eyes, Hear with their ears, Understand with their hearts, And repent and be healed."

Then I said, "Lord, how long?" And He answered, "Until cities are devastated and without inhabitant, Houses are without people, And the land is utterly desolate" (vv. 9–11).

Now that's straight talk! None of this, "If you go and serve me, I'll bring untold millions into the kingdom!" business. No heavenly hype. Not even a lot of encouraging promises like, "You'll really feel good!" or "People will admire you, Isaiah." None of that. Instead, He told His man that the challenge would be gigantic, the response to his efforts would be less than exciting, and in the final analysis there wouldn't be a lot to write home about! That explains why Isaiah answered, "Lord, how long?" Strengthening one's grip on missions requires a firm handle on reality. The greatest confirmation that one needs is not the tangible results of one's labors, but the inner assurance he or she is in the nucleus of God's will.

AND WHAT ABOUT YOU AND ME . . . TODAY?

So much for that ancient scene. As valuable and important as it was, we cannot afford to stay there and live in those memories. What about all this today? Is God saying anything specific about His world program to you and me? Each one of us must answer that alone. Go back over those five principles very slowly, very carefully. Personalize them by imagining *yourself* in each one.

You may be thinking, "Hey, not me!" That's exactly what I said back in 1957 . . . until . . . until I had every crutch yanked away. Until I sat on a Greyhound bus that rainy night. Until I read about a group of men who could have been quite successful as businessmen in the States, but settled on reaching a tribe of Indians in South America. Until I was literally shipped overseas and introduced to a vast vision for the world I would never have otherwise cared to know existed. You may *think* this chapter has not been talking to you or about you, but not until you personalize these things will you know for sure.

> In some unlikely quarter, in a shepherd's hut, or in an artisan's cottage, God has his prepared and appointed instrument. As yet the shaft is hidden in his quiver, in the shadow of his hand; but at the precise moment at which it will tell with the greatest effect, it will be produced and launched on the air.[4]

Five bodies floated face down in the Curary River in the Ecuadorian interior: Jim Elliot, Nate Saint, Pete Fleming, Ed McCully, and Roger Yoderian. Five widows sat in stunned silence as the news of their husbands' heroic yet tragic deaths was announced to them. The American press either stated or implied the same verdict as the story of their martyrdom reached the States, "In vain. In vain... all in vain!" No! Tragic loss, but not "in vain."

Since that time the Auca tribe has been reached and evangelized. The dream of those five was ultimately realized. And who will ever know how many hundreds, perhaps thousands, of young men and women took up the torch of world missions?

It was not in vain. I know. I was one of them.

DISCUSSION QUESTIONS AND SUGGESTIONS TO HELP YOU STRENGTHEN YOUR GRIP ON MISSIONS

• Someone has said, "You can't take the 'go' out of the gospel." Jesus specifically commissions His followers to "Go... make disciples of all the nations...." Talk about this issue of being *personally* involved in God's world-wide program. Obviously, everybody isn't called to travel abroad and minister in another culture. How can Christians "go" yet stay here in the States?

• In this chapter, we looked closely at Isaiah's experience when the Lord revealed Himself to the prophet. Did you put yourself in the man's sandals and think, "What if that happened today?" Do so now. See if you can recall the major principles we uncovered. Are there any analogies with your life today?

• Forcing yourself to be painfully honest, try to think of some of the reasons missions turns you off. If you feel free to say so, verbalize your feelings. Remember such things as manipulation by guilt, playing on emotions, and mass exploitation.

• What stands out in your mind when you consider that God told the prophet Isaiah, in effect, that his mission would be met by insensitive people, dull ears, dim eyes, and hard hearts (Isa. 6:10)? Talk about the whole issue of success in ministry today. Don't dodge the truth that God doesn't plan for everybody to enjoy vast blessings. Discuss obedience.

• How can a Christian know *for sure* that his or her place of ministry is *not* outside the United States? How can one know it *is?* And another question: How can the person who is called to serve Christ abroad be restrained from feeling resentment toward those who stay here at home?

• Pray. If you aren't sure where God would have you serve Him, be sure to ask the Lord exactly what you can do to know His will regarding your future. Are you thoroughly willing to say, "Here am I, send me"? If so, freely say so as you pray.

CHAPTER TWELVE

Strengthening Your Grip on Godliness

FAST-LANE LIVING IN THE 1980s does not lend itself to the traits we have traditionally attached to godliness. Remember the words to the old hymn we sang in church years ago?

> Take time to be holy, speak oft with Thy Lord;
> Abide in Him always and feed on His Word.
> . . . .
> Take time to be holy, the world rushes on;
> Spend much time in secret with Jesus alone.[1]

Chances are good that we who read those words believe them and would even defend them, but we sigh as we confess that more often than not we are strangers to them. There was once a time when a stroll through the park or a quiet afternoon spent in solitude was not that uncommon. But no more. The days of sitting on the porch swing, watching the evening pass in review are relics of the past, unfortunately. We may still squeeze in an hour or so around the fireplace every now and then, but the idea of taking the kind of time "to be holy" that our grandparents once did is rather dated.

Does this mean, then, that we cannot be holy? Does an urban lifestyle force us to forfeit godliness? Must we return to the "Little House on the Prairie" in order to be godly? Obviously, the answer is "No." If godliness were linked to a certain culture or a horse-and-buggy era, then most of us are out of luck! As much as we might enjoy a slower and less pressured lifestyle, God has not called everyone to such a role, certainly not those of us who live in the Greater Los Angeles area. Yet, some of the godliest people I have ever known live in Southern California (though some of you may find that hard to believe!).

What Is Godliness, Anyway?

This brings us to a bottom-line question I seldom hear addressed these days: What exactly does it mean to be godly? Now be careful. Try hard not to link your answer with a certain geography or culture or traditional mentality. It is easy to let our prejudices seep through and erroneously define the concept on the basis of our bias.

• Does being godly mean living high up in the mountains, cutting wood to heat a log cabin, and reading the Bible under the flickering flame of a kerosene lamp?

• Or how about this? The godly person must be old, deliberate, one who prays for hours everyday, and doesn't watch much television. Is that godliness?

• Can a person be godly and yet competitive in business, keen thinking, and financially successful?

• Is it possible to be godly and drive a Porsche... and never get married and... (hold on!) not go to church every Sunday evening?

• Does being holy require that I squat on a hillside, strum a guitar with my eyes closed, eat a bagful of birdseed, and write religious music from the book of Psalms?

• Are people disqualified if they are good athletes or if they are famous entertainers (with agents!) or if they are rich or if they have champagne tastes or if they wear diamonds and furs? Can anybody in that category be a godly Christian?

• One more... and this may hurt. How about believers who still struggle, who don't have some of the theological issues settled, who don't understand many of the hymns sung in church, who don't read a lot of missionary biographies ... and who don't necessarily go along with the whole Moral Majority package?

Oh, oh... now I've done it. So far you have been willing to hang in there with me, but now you really aren't sure. Before you categorize me, tar and feather me, and toss everything out—baby and bathwater alike—please understand that I'm just asking a few questions. I'm probing, honestly trying to discover the answer to a simple question: What *is* godliness?

You'll have to agree that it can't be confused with how a person looks (hard as it is for us to get beyond that) or what a person drives or owns. As tough as it is for us to be free of envy and critical thoughts, it is imperative that we remind ourselves that "God looks on the heart" (1 Sam. 16:7); therefore, whatever we may say godliness is, it is *not* skin deep. It is something below the surface of a life, deep down in the realm of an attitude ... an attitude toward God Himself.

The longer I think about this, the more I believe that a person who is godly is one whose heart is sensitive toward God, one who takes God seriously. This evidences itself in one very obvious mannerism: the godly individual hungers and thirsts after God. In the words of the psalmist, the godly person has a soul that "pants" for the living God.

> As the deer pants for streams of water,
>   so my soul pants for you, O God.
> My soul thirsts for God, for the living
>   God.
>   (Ps. 42:1–2a, NIV)

The one who sustains this pursuit may be young or old, rich or poor, urban or rural, leader or follower, of any race or color or culture or any temperament, active or quiet, married or single; none of these things really matter. But what *does* matter is the individual's inner craving to know God, listen to Him, and walk humbly with Him. As I mentioned, the godly take Him seriously.

Don't misread this. I'm not suggesting that all godly people are themselves serious-minded folk. I *am* saying, however, that they possess an attitude of willing submission to God's will and ways. Whatever He says goes. And whatever it takes to carry it out is the very thing the godly desire to do. Remember, the soul "pants" and "thirsts" for God. There is an authentic pursuit of and delight in the Lord. Let's think about strengthening our grip on godliness. Maybe a negative example will help.

THE ANCIENT HEBREWS: RELIGIOUS, BUT NOT GODLY

I've been poring over the first thirteen verses of 1 Corinthians 10 in recent days, trying to get a handle on this matter of godliness. I was attracted to this section of Scripture because it revolves around a group of people who had every reason to be godly, but they were not. That intrigues me. Why in the world wouldn't those ancient Hebrews, who were supernaturally delivered from Egyptian bondage under Moses' leadership, model true godliness?

Paul is writing these words under the inspiration of the Holy Spirit. His thoughts in 1 Corinthians 10 are a spin-off from his closing remarks in chapter 9, where he writes:

> Do you not know that in a race all the runners run, but only one gets the prize? Run in such a way as to get the prize. Everyone who competes in the games goes into strict training. They do it to get a crown that will not last; but we do it to get a crown that will last forever. Therefore I do not run like a man running aimlessly; I do not fight like a man beating the air. No, I beat my body and make it my slave so that after I have preached to others, I myself will not be disqualified for the prize (1 Cor. 9:24–27, NIV).

Those are the words of a godly man. He wasn't playing games with his life. Therefore, he refused to let his body dictate his objectives. He "beat it black and blue" (literal rendering of the last verse) and determined to make it his slave rather than the other way around. Why? Look again at what he says. He didn't want to finish his life as a washout. Paul dreaded the thought of being disqualified. A strong preacher of righteousness who ultimately shriveled into a weak victim of his own fleshly drives. I get the distinct impression that he feared the age-old problem of trafficking in unlived truth... of not taking God seriously.

That can happen so easily in this generation of superficiality. We can run with religious people, pick up the language, learn the ropes, and never miss a lick—publicly, that is. We can even defend our lifestyle by a rather slick system of theological accommodation. The better we get at it, the easier it is to convince ourselves we are on target. All it takes is a little Scripture twisting and a fairly well-oiled system of rationalization and we are off and running. Two results begin to transpire: (1) all our desires (no matter how wrong) are fulfilled, and (2) all our guilt (no matter how justified) is erased. And if anybody attempts to call us into account, label them a legalist and plow right on! It also helps to talk a lot about grace, forgiveness, mercy, and the old nobody's-perfect song.

Paul rejected that stuff entirely. He refused to be sucked into such a system of rationalization. He panted after God. He thirsted deep within his soul for the truth of God so he might live it. He longed to take God seriously.

Suddenly Paul was seized with a classic example— the Hebrews who left Egypt at the Exodus. It's like he thought, "Now, if you need an illustration of people who had everything and yet blew it, who disqualified themselves, think about this: ..."

For I do not want you to be unaware, brethren, that our fathers were all under the cloud, and all passed through the sea;

and all were baptized into Moses in the cloud and in the sea; and all ate the same spiritual food; and all drank the same spiritual drink, for they were drinking from a spiritual rock which followed them; and the rock was Christ (1 Cor. 10:1–4).

Take a pencil and circle the frequent repetition of the little word *all*, and you'll begin to understand. They all had everything!

- Supernatural guidance: a cloud by day and a pillar of fire by night
- Supernatural deliverance: the Red Sea escape
- Supernatural leadership: God's man, Moses
- Supernatural diet: manna from heaven and water from the rock.

Get the picture? They were surrounded by unparalleled privileges. Miracles were everyday occurrences. God's presence was constant and His workings were evident. Talk about overexposure! Everywhere there was God-talk. It was like a high-level Bible conference atmosphere day in and day out, week in and week out. Surely they flourished in such a hot house, right?

Wrong!

What happens when photographic film is overexposed? Sometimes the image is lost entirely. What about a dishtowel that never dries out but rather stays wet, wadded up in a pile? It gets sour. How about a clay pot that stays only in the sun—no rain, no cool breeze, no shade? It gets hard, brittle, easily cracked.

So it was with most of the Exodus crowd. An exaggeration? No, read the facts for yourself: "Nevertheless, with most of them God was not well pleased; for they were laid low in the wilderness" (v. 5).

That ominous word, "nevertheless..." says it all. They had it ... nevertheless. They witnessed God's abundant provisions in daily doses ... nevertheless. In the process of time, miracles lost their significance. Their incessant God-talk became sour in their mouths. They turned dark in all that overexposure.

AN ANALYSIS OF CARNALITY

What exactly happened? How could that have occurred? Why wouldn't they have flourished in such a marvelous and protective bubble of blessing? In short, they failed to take God seriously. To them, the divine became commonplace. Their respect for Jehovah which caused their mouths to open in silent awe had now degenerated into a jaded yawn of disrespect.

Paul describes the sordid scene of carnal litter for all of us to read with a sigh.

> Now these things happened as examples for us, that we should not crave evil things, as they also craved. And do not be idolaters, as some of them were; as it is written, "THE PEOPLE SAT DOWN TO EAT AND DRINK, AND STOOD UP TO PLAY." Nor let us act immorally, as some of them did, and twenty-three thousand fell in one day. Nor let us try the Lord, as some of them did, and were destroyed by the serpents. Nor grumble, as some of them did, and were destroyed by the destroyer. Now these things happened to them as an example, and they were written for our instruction, upon whom the ends of the ages have come (vv. 6–11).

The grim record is punctuated with a warning on both ends: "These things happened as examples... they were written for our instruction. . . ." God takes no sadistic pleasure in recording failure just to make people of the past squirm. No, he tells us that these stand as timeless warnings—warnings for all to heed—like those huge pictures of the atrocities of World War II, exhibited outside the Dachau prison camp in West Germany.

- They craved evil things. "Don't do that!"
- They were idolatrous. "Watch out!"
- They started practicing immorality. "Stop it!"
- They became guilty of presumption. "No!"

• They were cynical and negative. "Guard against this!"

Amazing as it may seem, the people with the most ultimately appropriated the least. In the warmth of God's best blessings, they became cool, distant, indifferent. Not suddenly, but slowly, the keen edge of enthusiasm became dull. And like a snail's shell, one perilous attitude rolled into another, each increasingly more brash, until the people stood up against their God with snarling lips and tightened fists.

Wait! Who are we talking about? A body of brutal ignorant savages who never knew the name of Jehovah? No, these were those who had been relieved of the taskmaster's whip in Egypt... once for all delivered from bondage and promised a new land to inhabit. But their smile of delight became a sneer of defiance because they allowed a "business as usual" mentality to replace the fresh walk of faith. They no longer took God seriously.

APPLICATION AND WARNING

Does this still occur? Yes, the peril is always a potential ... in a Christian home where discussion of the things of God is easily taken for granted... in a Christian school or seminary where God-talk can become sterile and academic... in a Christian church where a strong pulpit becomes commonplace, where saints easily get spoiled and occasionally become sour. Even in a missionary enterprise or a Christian conference ministry, it can occur. We can slump into a tired routine if we don't stay alert to the danger of erosion.

Two reactions usually emerge as we hear such warnings from God's Word.

1. "This will never happen to me!"

If that is your response, listen to verse 12: "Therefore let him who thinks he stands take heed lest he fall."

Paul feared the age-old problem of trafficking in unlived truth... of not taking God seriously.

I never will forget the letter I received some time ago that addressed this very subject of not taking God seriously. It read:

Dear Pastor Chuck,

This past week I had a tragic illustration of the price of failure to take God seriously. Only the names have been changed. . . .

Some years ago three fresh-faced young girls came to work where I am employed.

They were quick to tell all who would listen that they were Christians, out to turn the place upside down for Christ.

Within a few months all three had decided to get a "little taste" of the world.

One is now raising an out-of-wedlock child alone.

The second came back to the Lord and has since married a keen Christian fellow who is a converted heroin addict. They have some problems from their former lifestyle, but it looks as though they might make it.

And then there was Gerry. Raised in a moral, religious home of a different faith, she rebelled in her teen years, left her faith, and was a little wild.

When she professed Christ in her late teens, her parents looked on it as part of her rebellion. It was easy to slide back into the old life. After about a year of out-of-fellowship living, Gerry began actively pursuing a married man at work. Unhappily married, he put up little resistance.

Several fellow workers, including at least one Christian, approached her about her folly. She was sure she couldn't give him up. He left his wife and moved in with her.

Gerry was disciplined at work. Her lover intervened, threatening the life of her foreman over the matter, and as a result was fired. (The discipline was unrelated to their relationship.)

When his divorce was final, they married. She dismissed his violent threats toward the foreman as "all talk," and his having beaten his former wife as the result of extreme provocation. The husband's two children came to live with them. The elder was only eight years younger than 22-year-old Gerry.

The children lacked training and discipline. They asked hard questions about their father and Gerry's relationship.

At this point Gerry confided to me that she knew she had done wrong, and had now repented. She was surprised that the repercussions of her sin continued, even after repentance.

Within a few months the marriage disintegrated into a bitter feud, each returning hurt for hurt.

Gerry filed for divorce and moved back home. Last Tuesday morning . . . as she was leaving for home after her graveyard shift, she told a fellow worker, "I've got it together now. When my divorce is final, I'm going to marry this really neat guy."

That was yesterday. Yesterday Gerry was happy. Today Gerry is dead. Shot by her estranged husband who then turned the gun on himself.

Today two broken-hearted families grieve. Two children are fatherless. All because of failure to take God seriously.

For Gerry the wages of sin was literal, physical death.[2]

Yes, I warn you, it *could* happen to you. Stay alert! Tell the Lord you *do* take Him seriously . . . you desire true godliness.

2. "I'm into the syndrome you have described. I am already too far gone to recover!"

No temptation has overtaken you but such as is common to man; and God is faithful, who will not allow you to be tempted beyond what you are able; but with the temptation will provide the way of escape also, that you may be able to endure it (v. 13).

Nothing is too hard for the Lord. No one is beyond hope. *It is never too late to start doing what is right.*

I offer a series of questions for you to answer:

• Have you begun to lose the fresh delight of your walk with the Lord?

• Is it becoming perfunctory and boring?

• Can you name a turning point or two when things began to change for the worse?

• Do you realize the extreme danger of your future if nothing changes?

• Are you willing to confess the lack of vitality in your spiritual life?

• Will you do that NOW?

I promise you this: If you will come to terms with these things and come clean before the Lord your God, the power you once knew will return. You can count on this, He will take you seriously.

DISCUSSION QUESTIONS AND SUGGESTIONS TO HELP YOU STRENGTHEN YOUR GRIP ON GODLINESS

• Define *godliness*. Using your own words, explain the difference between external religion and an internal attitude of spirituality.

• Can people who are active, on the move, living in an urban community maintain an authentic godliness? Talk about some of the perils and how they can be counteracted.

• Returning to the 1 Corinthians 10 passage of Scripture, see if you can recall several of the traps the ancient Hebrews fell into. What keeps us from blaming them?

• Share one or two techniques or habits you have begun to use that help you take God more seriously. What are two or three things that make godliness seem so far removed? Pray for one another.

• During this week, commit to memory 1 Corinthians 10:12–13. Repeat them several times a day until you can do so without looking at your Bible. See if that helps you in the weeks to come.

CHAPTER THIRTEEN

Strengthening Your Grip on Attitudes

THE COLORFUL, NINETEENTH-CENTURY showman and gifted violinist Nicolo Paganini was standing before a packed house, playing through a difficult piece of music. A full orchestra surrounded him with magnificent support. Suddenly one string on his violin snapped and hung gloriously down from his instrument. Beads of perspiration popped out on his forehead. He frowned but continued to play, improvising beautifully.

To the conductor's surprise, a second string broke. And shortly thereafter, a third. Now there were three limp strings dangling from Paganini's violin as the master performer completed the difficult composition on the one remaining string. The audience jumped to its feet and in good Italian fashion, filled the hall with shouts and screams, "Bravo! Bravo!" As the applause died down, the violinist asked the people to sit back down. Even though they knew there was no way they could expect an encore, they quietly sank back into their seats.

He held the violin high for everyone to see. He nodded at the conductor to begin the encore and then he turned back to the crowd, and with a twinkle in his eye, he smiled and shouted, "Paganini . . . and one string!" After that he placed the single-stringed Stradivarius beneath his chin and played the final piece on *one* string as the audience (and the conductor) shook their heads in silent amazement. "Paganini... and one string!" *And*, I might add, an attitude of fortitude.

Dr. Victor Frankl, the bold, courageous Jew who became a prisoner during the Holocaust, endured years of indignity and humiliation by the Nazis before he was finally liberated. At the beginning of his ordeal, he was marched into a gestapo courtroom. His captors had taken away his home and family, his cherished freedom, his possessions, even his watch and wedding ring. They had shaved his head and stripped his clothing off his body. There he stood before the German high command, under the glaring lights being interrogated and falsely accused. He was destitute, a helpless pawn in the hands of brutal, prejudiced, sadistic men. He had nothing. No, that isn't true. He suddenly realized there was one thing no one could ever take from him—just one. Do you know what it was?

Dr. Frankl realized he still had the power to choose his own attitude. No matter what anyone would ever do to him, regardless of what the future held for him, the attitude choice was his to make. Bitterness or forgiveness. To give up or to go on. Hatred or hope. Determination to endure or the paralysis of self-pity. It boiled down to "Frankl... and one string!"[1]

Words can never adequately convey the incredible impact of our attitude toward life. The longer I live the more convinced I become that life is 10 percent what happens to us and 90 percent how we respond to it.

How else can anyone explain the unbelievable feats of hurting, beat-up athletes? Take Joe Namath for instance; at age thirty he was a quarterback with sixty-five-year-old legs. Although he might have difficulty making one flight of stairs by the time he's fifty years of age, maybe before, it was attitude that kept the man in the game.

Or take Merlin Olsen and his knees. In an interview with a sports reporter, the former Los Angeles Ram all-pro defensive lineman admitted:

That year after surgery on my knee, I had to have the fluid drained weekly. Finally, the membrane got so thick they almost had to drive the needle in it with a hammer. I got to the point where I just said, "... get the needle in there, and get that stuff out."[2]

Joe Namath... Merlin Olsen... *and one string!*

ATTITUDES ARE ALL-IMPORTANT

This may shock you, but I believe the single most significant decision I can make on a day-to-day basis is my choice of attitude. It is more important than my past, my education, my bankroll, my successes or failures, fame or pain, what other people think of me or say about me, my circumstances, or my position. Attitude is that "single string" that keeps me going or cripples my progress. It alone fuels my fire or assaults my hope. When my attitudes are right, there's no barrier too high, no valley too deep, no dream too extreme, no challenge too great for me.

Yet, we must admit that we spend more of our time concentrating and fretting over the strings that snap, dangle, and pop—the things that can't be changed—than we do giving attention to the one that remains, our choice of attitude. Stop and think about some of the things that suck up our attention and energy, all of them inescapable (and occasionally demoralizing).

- The tick of the clock
- The weather... the temperature... the wind!
- People's actions and reactions, *especially* the criticisms
- Who won or lost the ball game
- Delays at airports, waiting rooms, in traffic
- Results of an X-ray
- Cost of groceries, gasoline, clothes, cars—everything!

- On-the-job irritations, disappointments, work-load.

The greatest waste of energy in our ecologically minded world of the 1980s is not electricity or natural gas or any other "product," it's the energy we waste fighting the inevitables! And to make matters worse, *we* are the ones who suffer, who grow sour, who get ulcers, who become twisted, negative and tight-fisted fighters. Some actually die because of this.

Dozens of comprehensive studies have established this fact. One famous study, called "Broken Heart," researched the mortality rate of 4,500 widowers within six months of their wives' deaths. Compared with other men the same age, the widowers had a mortality rate 40 percent higher.[3]

Major F. J. Harold Kushner, an army medical officer held by the Viet Cong for over five years, cites an example of death because of an attitudinal failure. In a fascinating article in *New York* magazine this tragic yet true account is included:

Among the prisoners in Kushner's POW camp was a tough young marine, 24 years old, who had already survived two years of prison-camp life in relatively good health. Part of the reason for this was that the camp commander had promised to release the man if he cooperated. Since this had been done before with others, the marine turned into a model POW and the leader of the camp's thought-reform group. As time passed he gradually realized that his captors had lied to him. When the full realization of this took hold he became a zombie. He refused to do all work, rejected all offers of food and encouragement, and simply lay on his cot sucking his thumb. In a matter of weeks he was dead.[4]

Caught in the vice grip of lost hope, life became too much for the once-tough marine to handle. When that last string snapped, there was nothing left.

THE VALUE OF ATTITUDES: SCRIPTURE SPEAKS

In the little letter Paul wrote to the Christians in Philippi, he didn't mince words when it came to attitudes. Although a fairly peaceful and happy flock, the Philippians had a few personality skirmishes that could have derailed them and hindered their momentum. Knowing how counterproductive that would be, he came right to the point: their attitudes.

> If therefore there is any encouragement in Christ, if there is any consolation of love, if there is any fellowship of the Spirit, if any affection and compassion, make my joy complete by being of the same mind, maintaining the same love, united in spirit, intent on one purpose (Phil. 2:1–2).

What does all this mean? Well, let's go back and take a look. There *is* encouragement in the Person of Christ. There *is* love. There is also plenty of "fellowship of the Spirit" for the Christian to enjoy. Likewise, affection and compassion. Heaven is full and running over with these things even though earth is pretty barren at times. So Paul pleads for us to tap into that positive, encouraging storehouse. How? By "being of the same mind." He's telling us to take charge of our own minds; clearly a command. We Christians have the God-given ability to put our minds on those things that build up, strengthen, encourage, and help ourselves and others. "Do that!" commands the Lord.

Attitude of Unselfish Humility

Paul gets specific at verses 3 and 4 of Philippians 2:

> Do nothing from selfishness or empty conceit, but with humility of mind let each of you regard one another as more important than himself; do not merely look out for your own personal interests, but also for the interests of others.

This is a mental choice we make, a decision not to focus on self ... me ... my ... mine, but on the other person. It's a servant mentality the Scriptures are encouraging. I have written an entire book[5] on this subject, so I'll not elaborate here except to say that few virtues are more needed today. When we strengthen our grip on attitudes, a great place to begin is with humility—authentic and gracious unselfishness.

Our example? Read on:

Have this attitude in·yourselves which was also in Christ Jesus, who, although He existed in the form of God, did not regard equality with God a thing to be grasped, but emptied Himself, taking the form of a bond-servant, and being made in the likeness of men.

And being found in appearance as a man, He humbled Himself by becoming obedient to the point of death, even death on a cross (Phil. 2:5–8).

Maybe you have never stopped to think about it, but behind the scenes, it was an attitude that brought the Savior down to us. He deliberately chose to come among us because He realized and valued our need. He placed a higher significance on it than His own comfort and prestigious position. In humility, He set aside the glory of heaven and came to be among us. He refused to let His position keep us at arm's length.

Attitude of Positive Encouragement

Listen to another verse in the same chapter: "Do all things without grumbling or disputing" (v. 14).

Ouch! If ever a generation needed that counsel, ours does! It is virtually impossible to complete a day without falling into the trap of "grumbling or disputing." It is so easy to pick up the habit of negative thinking. Why? Because there are so many things around us that prompt us to be irritable. Let's not kid ourselves, life is not a bed of roses!

On my last birthday my sister Luci gave me a large scroll-like poster. Since our humor is somewhat similar, she knew I'd get a kick out of the stuff printed on it. She suggested I tack it up on the back of my bathroom door so I could review it regularly. It's a long list of some of the inescapable "laws" of life that can make us irritable "grumblers and disputers" if we let them. They are commonly called "Murphy's Laws." Here's a sample:

- Nothing is as easy as it looks; everything takes longer than you think; if anything can go wrong it will.
- Murphy was an optimist.
- A day without a crisis is a total loss.
- The other line always moves faster.
- The chance of the bread falling with the peanut butter-and-jelly side down is directly proportional to the cost of the carpet.
- Inside every large problem is a series of small problems struggling to get out.
- 90% of everything is crud.
- Whatever hits the fan will not be evenly distributed.
- No matter how long or hard you shop for an item, after you've bought it, it will be on sale somewhere cheaper.
- Any tool dropped while repairing a car will roll underneath to the exact center.
- The repairman will never have seen a model quite like yours before.
- You will remember that you forgot to take out the trash when the garbage truck is two doors away.
- Friends come and go, but enemies accumulate.
- The light at the end of the tunnel is the headlamp of an oncoming train.
- Beauty is only skin deep, but ugly goes clear to the bone.[6]

Every item on the list is an attitude assailant! And the simple fact is they are so true, we don't even have to imagine their possibility—*they happen.* I have a sneaking suspicion they happened in Paul's day too. So when he writes about grumbling and disputing, he wasn't coming from an ivory tower. A positive, encouraging attitude is essential for survival in a world saturated with Murphy's Laws.

Attitude of Genuine Joy

Joy is really the underlying theme of Philippians—joy that isn't fickle, needing a lot of "things" to keep it smiling. . . . joy that is deep and consistent—the oil that reduces the friction of life.

Finally, my brethren, rejoice in the Lord (Phil. 3:1a).

Therefore, my beloved brethren whom I long to see, my joy and crown, so stand firm in the Lord, my beloved. . . . Rejoice in the Lord always; again I will say, rejoice! Let your forbearing spirit be known to all men. The Lord is near. Be anxious for nothing, but in everything by prayer and supplication with thanksgiving let your requests be made known to God. And the peace of God, which surpasses all comprehension, shall guard your hearts and your minds in Christ Jesus (Phil. 4:1, 4–7).

There it is again—*the mind.* Our minds can be kept free of anxiety (those strings that snap) as we dump the load of our cares on the Lord in prayer. By getting rid of the stuff that drags us down, we create space for the joy to take its place.

Think of it like this: Circumstances occur that could easily crush us. They may originate on the job or at home or even during the weekend when we are relaxing. Unexpectedly, they come. Immediately we have a choice to make . . . an attitude choice. We can hand the circumstance to God and ask Him to take control or we can roll up our mental sleeves and slug it out. Joy awaits our decision. If we do as Philippians 4:6–7 suggests, peace replaces panic and joy moves into action. It is ready, but it is not pushy.

AGGRESSIVE-PASSIVE ALTERNATIVES

Let's not kid ourselves. When we deliberately choose not to stay positive and deny joy a place in our lives, we'll usually gravitate in one of two directions, sometimes both—the direction of blame or self-pity.

Blame

The aggressive attitude reacts to circumstances with blame. We blame ourselves or someone else, or God, or if we can't find a tangible scapegoat, we blame "fate." What an absolute waste! When we blame ourselves, we multiply our guilt, we rivet ourselves to the past (another "dangling" unchangeable), and we decrease our already low self-esteem. If we choose to blame God, we cut off our single source of power. Doubt replaces trust, and we put down roots of bitterness that can make us cynical. If we blame others, we enlarge the distance between us and them. We alienate. We poison a relationship. We settle for something much less than God ever intended. And on top of all that, we do not find relief!

Blame never affirms, it assaults.
Blame never restores, it wounds.
Blame never solves, it complicates.
Blame never unites, it separates.
Blame never smiles, it frowns.
Blame never forgives, it rejects.
Blame never forgets, it remembers.
Blame never builds, it destroys.

Let's admit it—not until we stop blaming will we start enjoying health and happiness again! This was underscored as I read the following words recently:

... one of the most innovative psychologists in this half of the twentieth century ... said recently that he considers only one kind of counselee relatively hopeless: that person who blames other people for his or her problems. If you can own the mess you're in, he says, there is hope for you and help available. As long as you blame others, you will be a victim for the rest of your life.[7]

Blame backfires, hurting us more than the object of our resentment.

Self-pity

The passive attitude responds to circumstances in an opposite manner, feeling sorry for oneself. I find this just as damaging as blaming, sometimes more so. In fact, I'm ready to believe that self-pity is "Private Enemy No. 1." Things turn against us, making us recipients of unfair treatment, like innocent victims of a nuclear mishap. We neither expect it nor deserve it, and to make matters worse, it happens at the worst possible time. We're too hurt to blame.

Our natural tendency is to curl up in the fetal position and sing the silly little children's song:

> Nobody loves me, everybody hates me,
> I think I'll eat some worms.

Which helps nobody. But what else can we do when the bottom drops out? Forgive me if this sounds too simplistic, but the only thing worth doing is usually the last thing we try doing—turning it over to our God, the Specialist, who has never yet been handed an impossibility He couldn't handle. Grab that problem by the throat and thrust it skyward!

There is a familiar story in the New Testament that always makes me smile. Paul and his traveling companion Silas had been beaten and dumped in a dungeon. It was *so* unfair! But this mistreatment did not steal their joy or dampen their confidence in God. Their circumstance, however, could not have been more bleak. They were there to stay.

But about midnight Paul and Silas were praying and singing hymns of praise to God, and the prisoners were listening to them (Acts 16:25).

I would imagine! The sounds of confident praying and joyful singing are not usually heard from a stone prison. But Paul and Silas had determined they would not be paralyzed by self-pity. And as they prayed and sang, the unbelievable transpired.

And suddenly there came a great earthquake, so that the foundations of the prison-house were shaken; and immediately all the doors were opened, and everyone's chains were unfastened.

And when the jailer had been roused out of sleep and had seen the prison doors opened, he drew his sword and was about to kill himself, supposing that the prisoners had escaped.

But Paul cried out with a loud voice, saying, "Do yourself no harm, for we are all here!" (vv. 26–28).

With calm reassurance, Paul spoke words of encouragement to the jailer. He even promised there would be no attempt to escape. And if you take the time to read the full account (vv. 29–40) you will find how beautifully God used their attitude to change the entire face of their situation. I love such stories! They stand as monumental reminders that the right attitude choice can literally transform our circumstance, no matter how black and hopeless it may appear. And best of all, the right attitude becomes contagious!

I was sharing some of these thoughts at a large gathering in Chicago not long ago. It was Founders' Week at Moody Bible Institute, the annual time of celebration when Christians from all over the United States come to the school for a week of Bible teaching, singing, and interaction together. Following one of my talks, a lady I never met wrote me this letter.

Dear Chuck,

I want you to know I've been here all week and I've enjoyed every one of your talks. I know they will help me in my remaining years. . . .

I love your sense of humor. Humor has done a lot to help me in my spiritual life. How could I have raised 12 children starting at age 32 and not have had a sense of humor! I married at age 31. I didn't worry about getting married, I just left my future to God's will. But every night I hung a pair of men's pants on the bed and knelt down and prayed:

> "Father in heaven, hear my prayer
> And grant it if you can,
> I've hung a pair of trousers here,
> Please fill them with a man!"

I had a good laugh. In fact, I thought it was such a classic illustration of the right mental attitude toward life that I read it to my congregation in Fullerton, California, when I returned. In the congregation that day was half of one of our families. Mom and a sick daughter were home, but dad and an older son in his twenties were present and heard me read the letter. The mother (who knew nothing of the letter) wrote me a note a couple weeks later. She was brief and to the point. She was concerned about her older son. She said that for the last week or so he had been sleeping in his bed with a bikini draped over the footboard. She wanted to know if I might know why . . . or if this was something she needed to worry about.

FOOD FOR THE RIGHT ATTITUDE

Since our choice of attitude is so important, our minds need fuel to feed on. Philippians 4:8 gives us a good place to start:

Finally, brethren, whatever is true, whatever is honorable, whatever is right, whatever is pure, whatever is lovely, whatever is of good repute, if there is any excellence and if anything worthy of praise, let your mind dwell on these things.

Good advice: "Let your mind *dwell* on these things." Fix your attention on these six specifics in life. Not unreal far-fetched dreams, but things that are *true*, real, valid. Not cheap, flipppant, superficial stuff, but things that are *honorable*; i.e., worthy of respect. Not things that are wrong and unjust, critical and negative, but that which is *right*. Not thoughts that are carnal, smutty, and obscene, but that which is *pure* and wholesome. Not things that prompt arguments and defense in others, but those that are *lovely*, agreeable, attractive, winsome. Finally, not slander, gossip, and put-downs, but information of *good report*, the kind that builds up and causes grace to flow.

Do you do this? Is this the food you serve your mind? We are back where we started, aren't we? The choice is yours. The other discouraging strings on your instrument may snap and hang loosely—no longer available or useful, but nobody can *make* you a certain way. That is strictly up to you.

And may I take the liberty to say something very directly? Some of you who read these words are causing tremendous problems because of your attitude. You are capable. You are intelligent. You are qualified and maybe even respected for your competence. But your attitude is taking a toll on those who are near you—those you live with, those you work with, those you touch in life. For some of you, your home is a battleground, a mixture of negativism, sarcasm, pressure, cutting comments, and blame. For others, you have allowed self-pity to move in under your roof and you have foolishly surrendered mental territory that once was healthy and happy. You are laughing less and complaining more. You have to admit that the "one string" on which you can play—if you choose to do so—is out of tune.

As your friend, let me urge you to take charge of your mind and emotions today. Let your mind feast on nutritious food for a change. Refuse to grumble and criticize! Reject those alien thoughts that make you a petty, bitter person. Play that single string once again! Let it yield a sweet, winsome melody that this old world needs so desperately. Yes, you *can* if you *will*.

I was sitting at the Christian Bookseller's Association final banquet the last evening of the convention in 1981. My mind was buzzing as I was arranging my thoughts for the speech. I was a bit nervous and my attitude was somewhere between blame ("Why in the world did you say 'yes,' Swindoll?") and self-pity ("There are a dozen or more people sitting among those thousands out there who could do a lot better job than you, dummy!") when the spotlight turned from the head table to a young woman sitting in a wheelchair off to the side. She was to sing that evening.

I was greatly encouraged to see her. I was strengthened in my spirit as I thought back over Joni Eareckson's pilgrimage since 1967—broken neck; loss of feeling from her shoulders down; numerous operations; broken romance; the death of dreams; no more swimming, horseback riding, skating, running, dancing; not even an evening stroll, ever again. All those strings now dangled from her life. But there sat a radiant, remarkable, rare woman who had chosen not to quit.

I shall never forget the song she sang that quieted my nerves and put things in perspective:

When peace, like a river, attendeth my way.
When sorrows like sea billows roll;
Whatever my lot, Thou hast taught me to say,
"It is well, it is well with my soul."

Though Satan should buffet, tho' trials should come,
Let this blest assurance control,
That Christ has regarded my helpless estate,
And hath shed His own blood for my soul.[8]

Do you know what all of us witnessed that evening? More than a melody. More than grand and glorious lyrics. Much,

much more. In a very real sense, we witnessed the surpassing value of an attitude in a life that literally had nothing else to cling to. Joni Eareckson . . . and one string.

DISCUSSION QUESTIONS AND SUGGESTIONS TO HELP YOU STRENGTHEN YOUR GRIP ON ATTITUDES

• Let's begin by describing or defining *attitude*. What is it? How does it differ from things like conduct and competence? Since it *is* different from both, does one's attitude affect either one? Explain your answer.

• Biblically, we found that God says a lot about our attitudes in His Book. Can you recall one or two passages in particular that took on new meaning as a result of this chapter? Try to be specific as you state the practical significance of the scriptural references.

• Because Philippians 4:8 was a scriptural climax to the chapter, let's zero in on the six areas the verse instructs us to "let your mind dwell on." Taking each, one at a time, work your way along. Stop, think, meditate, and then talk about how each fits into some category of your life that has begun to trouble you or perhaps challenge you.

• Now let's talk about some of the darker sides of our attitudes. Risk being deeply honest as you open up and admit the battleground within. In which area(s) do you face your greatest struggles? For example, are you more often negative than positive? Or are you stubborn and closed rather than open and willing to hear? How's your attitude toward people *very* different from you? Are you prejudiced? Look over James 2:1–4.

• Compare a few verses from the book of Proverbs. Like Proverbs 4:20–23; 12:25; 15:13, 15, 30. Choose one and explain how it applies to your own personal life.

• And now—let's pray. For a change, don't pray

for yourself, but for the person sitting on your left. Call his or her name before the Lord and ask for one or two specifics on that person's behalf. Give Him thanks for the changes He will bring in your attitude and the attitudes of others. As they happen this week in your life, note the changes and give God praise in your heart.

CHAPTER FOURTEEN

Strengthening Your Grip on Evangelism

"THE EVANGELISTIC HARVEST is always urgent. The destiny of men and of nations is always being decided. Every generation is strategic. We are not responsible for the past generation, and we cannot bear the full responsibility for the next one; but we do have our generation. God will hold us responsible as to how well we fulfill our responsibilities to this age and take advantage of our opportunities."[1]

Those are the words of Billy Graham. And the man ought to know. He has spoken publicly about Christ to more people in our generation than anyone else. His evangelistic crusades have had an impact on more cities around the world and invaded more homes (thanks to television) than any other evangelistic outreach in the history of time. We cannot think of the name *Billy Graham* without attaching the word *evangelism* to it. He has a strong grip on the subject, but the question is, do we?

Probably not.

Most of us want to. We *wish* we did. We are certainly aware of the need and, if the whole truth could be told, some of us have even taken courses to help us become better at witnessing, but we still stumble. Our grip on evangelism is weak—embarrassingly weak.

A fellow pastor was honest enough to admit this in an article he wrote for a Christian magazine. Because it illustrates so well the problem all of us wrestle with, I want to share it with you. The pastor, dressed in a comfortable pair of old blue jeans, boarded a plane to return home. He settled into the last unoccupied seat next to a well-dressed businessman with the *Wall Street Journal* tucked under his arm. The minister, a little embarrassed over his casual attire, decided he'd look straight ahead and, for sure, stay out of any in-depth conversation. But the plan didn't work. The man greeted him, so, to be polite, the pastor asked about the man's work. Here's what happened:

"I'm in the figure salon business. We can change a woman's self-concept by changing her body. It's really a very profound, powerful thing."

His pride spoke between the lines.

"You look my age," I said. "Have you been at this long?"

"I just graduated from the University of Michigan's School of Business Administration. They've given me so much responsibility already, and I feel very honored. In fact, I hope to eventually manage the western part of the operation."

"So, you are a national organization?" I asked, becoming impressed despite myself.

"Oh, yes. We are the fastest growing company of our kind in the nation. It's really good to be a part of an organization like that, don't you think?"

I nodded approvingly and thought, "Impressive. Proud of his work and accomplishments.... Why can't Christians be proud like that? Why are we so often apologetic about our faith and our church?"

Looking askance at my clothing, he asked the inevitable question, "And what do you do?"...

"It's interesting that we have similar business interests," I said. "You are in the body-changing business; I'm in the personality-changing business. We apply 'basic theocratic principles to accomplish indigenous personality modification.'"

He was hooked, but I knew he would never admit it. (Pride is powerful.)

"You know, I've heard about that," he replied, hesitantly. "But do you have an office here in the city?"

"Oh, we have many offices. We have offices up and down the state. In fact, we're national: we have at least one office in every state of the union, including Alaska and Hawaii."

He had this puzzled look on his face. He was searching his mind to identify this huge company he *must* have read or heard about, perhaps in his *Wall Street Journal.*

"As a matter of fact, we've gone international. And Management has a plan to put at least one office in every country of the world by the end of this business era."

I paused.

"Do you have that in your business?" I asked.

"Well, no. Not yet." he answered. "But you mentioned management. How do they make it work?"

"It's a family concern. There's a Father and a Son. . . . And they run everything."

"It must take a lot of capital," he asked, skeptically.

"You mean money?" I asked. "Yes, I suppose so. No one knows just how much it takes, but we never worry because there's never a shortage. The Boss always seems to have enough. He's a very creative guy. . . . And the money is, well, just there. In fact those of us in the Organization have a saying about our Boss, 'He owns the cattle on a thousands hills.'"

"Oh, he's into ranching too?" asked my captive friend.

"No, it's just a saying we use to indicate his wealth."

My friend sat back in his seat, musing over our conversation. "What about with you?" he asked.

"The employees? They are something to see," I said. "They have a 'Spirit' that pervades the organization. It works like this: the Father and Son love each other so much that their love filters down through the organization so that we all find ourselves loving one another too. I know this sounds old-fashioned in a world like ours, but I know people in the organization who are willing to die for me. Do you have that in your business?" I was almost shouting now. People were starting to shift noticeably in their seats.

"Not yet," he said. Quickly changing strategies, he asked, "But do you have good benefits?"

"They're substantial," I countered, with a gleam. "I have complete life insurance, fire insurance—all the basics. You might not believe this, but it's true: I have holdings in a mansion that's being built for me right now for my retirement. Do you have that in your business?"

"Not yet," he answered, wistfully. The light was dawning.

"You know, one thing bothers me about all you're saying. I've read the journals, and if your business is all you say it is, why haven't I heard about it before now?"

"That's a good question," I said. "After all, we have a 2000-year-old tradition."

"Wait a minute!" he said.

"You're right," I interrupted. "I'm talking about the church."

"I knew it. You know, I'm Jewish."

"Want to sign up?" I asked.[2]

We've all been there, haven't we? Most of us are not as creative as the minister, however. We just stumble through a few words and hope the person soon changes the subject. We feel awkward.

FOUR HINDRANCES TO EVANGELISM

When you analyze our lack of evangelistic success and skill, it boils down to four primary reasons.

1. *Ignorance*

We just don't know how to do it. We have no method or proven "technique" that allows us to feel comfortable talking to others about Christ. We don't like a canned approach so we wind up with no approach.

2. *Fear*

Most of us are just plain scared. We're afraid the person will ask us a question we can't answer. Or he or she may become angry and tell us off.

3. *Indifference*

Hard as it is to admit it, many Christians just don't care. We think, "If that's the way the person wants to believe, that's fine. To each his own."

4. *Bad Experience*

More and more I meet believers who were turned off during their non-Christian years by some wild-eyed fanatic who pushed and embarrassed them, trying to force a decision. The result? A reluctance to say *anything* at all.

ONE MAJOR PRINCIPLE TO REMEMBER

If it's possible, let's set aside all those excuses and start from scratch. In fact, let's start *below* scratch. There is one principle that has helped me more than any other. It never fails to rescue me from dumb mistakes, and when I forget to employ it, I suffer the consequences. Here it is:

PUT YOURSELF IN THE OTHER PERSON'S PLACE.

If we can keep in mind that the person is not coming from where we are, nor does he or she understand where we are going, it will help greatly. Not infrequently will we encounter people who have an entirely different mindset or cultural background from ours, thus adding immeasurably to the complication. Jim Petersen, with The Navigators in Brazil, tells of witnessing to a well-educated industrial chemist named Osvaldo. Jim had been studying the Bible with the man's brother and

Osvaldo was curious about why his brother became so interested. Jim attempted to answer the chemist's questions by explaining the gospel to him.

I got a piece of chalk and a Bible and used the wooden floor as a chalkboard. I spent the next two hours showing him a favorite diagram I often used to explain the message. I was quite satisfied with my performance, and when I finally finished, I leaned back to observe his reaction, certain he would be on the verge of repentance.

Instead, he gazed at my illustration, then at me. He was puzzled. "Do you mean to tell me that this is why you came all the way to Brazil, to tell people that?" he said.

To Osvaldo, what I had said seemed insignificant and irrelevant. I recognized at that moment that I was facing a communication problem I had never been aware of before.[3]

Jim was wise not to argue or push. He was honest enough to realize the man wasn't being argumentative... he was just coming from another frame of reference. Those who cultivate the skill of evangelism do their best to put themselves inside the other person's skin. They do this by thinking thoughts like:

"Please think about what I'm saying. Don't just expect me to listen, you listen, too."
"If you want me to hear you, scratch my itches."
"Talk with me—don't talk down to me."
"Make sense. No riddles or secret religious code words, okay?"

Six Guidelines Worth Remembering

All of this leads us to an account in the New Testament where one man witnessed to another with remarkable success—because he did so with wisdom and skill. I never cease to marvel at the beautiful way God used him to reach out to a person (a total stranger!) from another culture and graciously guide the man to faith in Jesus Christ.

The story is found in Acts 8, a story that begins in the midst of an exciting revival, much like one that sweeps across a city during a Billy Graham Crusade. In Acts 8 the territory where revival fires are spreading is Samaria.

> And so, when they had solemnly testified and spoken the word of the Lord, they started back to Jerusalem, and were preaching the gospel to many villages of the Samaritans (Acts 8:25).

There was renewed enthusiasm. Those bold Christians were proclaiming Christ from village to village. The Spirit of God was working. The atmosphere was electric. If you've ever been a part of a scene like this, you need no further explanation. If you haven't, you cannot imagine the excitement. A contagious, authentic enthusiasm ignites the souls of men and women with such spiritual fire it's almost frightening.

Suddenly God steps in and does something strange. Without prior announcement—out of the clear blue—He dispatches an angel from heaven and redirects a man named Philip.

> But an angel of the Lord spoke to Philip saying, "Arise and go south to the road that descends from Jerusalem to Gaza." (This is a desert road.)
> And he arose and went ... (Acts 8:26–27a).

I'd like us to remember several guidelines that relate to personal evangelism. Each one will help us hurdle the barriers and become skilled in sharing our faith. The first of six is found here at the beginning of this account.

Sensitivity

How easy it would have been for Philip to be so caught up in the excitement and electricity of that Samaritan revival—where God was obviously at work—that he wasn't sensitive to a new direction. Not this man! He was alert and ready. Each day marked a new beginning. He had walked with God long enough to know that He has the right to throw a surprise curve—*and often does!*

Without stating His reason, without revealing the ultimate plan, God led Philip away from Samaria and out onto a desert road. The man was so sensitive to God's leading there was no struggle. People who become skilled in sharing their faith possess this sensitivity to God.

Availability

With sensitivity comes availability. There's no use having a sensitive spirit if we are not available and willing to go . . . wherever. Take a look at the next episode in Philip's life:

> . . . and behold, there was an Ethiopian eunuch, a court official of Candace, queen of the Ethiopians, who was in charge of all her treasure; and he had come to Jerusalem to worship.
>
> And he was returning and sitting in his chariot, and was reading the prophet Isaiah.
>
> And the Spirit said to Philip, "Go up and join this chariot" (Acts 8:27b–29).

Like our pastor friend on the plane, Philip encountered a choice opportunity. Who was riding along that desert road? A political leader from the third world. The Secretary of the Treasury of the Candace Dynasty, no less! And where had he been? To church! But the Ethiopian official had not met the Lord—he had only had his curiosity aroused. But out there in the middle of the desert is this guy in a chariot reading the Scriptures. Don't tell me God can't pull it off! And of all places to be reading, the man is reading Isaiah 53, the seed plot of the gospel in the Old Testament. God says to His servant Philip, "Go for it . . . join up with that chariot!"

Those who are available experience exciting moments like this. It's thrilling to be a part of the irresistible momentum, caught in the current of the Spirit's working. Philip's obedience pays off. His heart must have begun to beat faster.

Initiative

Look at the next move Philip made:

And when Philip had run up, he heard him reading Isaiah the prophet, and said, "Do you understand what you are reading?" (Acts 8:30).

He took the initiative. But there is not a hint of offense or put down in his approach. Just simply, "Do you know what you are reading?" He genuinely wanted to know if the stranger in the chariot understood those words.

Initiative is so important. It is the first plank in the bridge-building process. But like the cornerstone, it must be placed very carefully. And the use of questions is an excellent approach. Here are a few I have used with a good deal of success:

"Say, I've been reading a lot about our world lately. Do you have any idea what's gone wrong?"

"I'm interested in the lives of great men and women. Who, in your opinion, was the greatest person who ever lived?"

"What do you think of our President? I mean, with that former football player as his minister in California, do you think he's really a Christian?"

"With all these earthquakes and other calamities that happen so quickly, what keeps you from being afraid? Do you pray or something?"

Authoress Ann Kiemel asks, "Can I sing to you?" Now *that's* a creative starter! The late Paul Little was a master at taking the initiative. He mentions a few suggestions that I have found helpful.

After even a vague reference to "religion" in a conversation, many Christians have used this practical series of questions to draw out latent spiritual interest: First, "By the way, are you interested in spiritual things?" Many will say, "Yes." But even if the person says, "No," we can ask a second question, "What do you think a real Christian is?" Wanting to hear his opinion invariably pleases a person. From his response we'll also gain a more accurate, first-hand—if perhaps shocking—understanding of his thinking as a non-Christian; and because we have listened to him he'll be much more ready to listen to us. Answers to this question usually revolve around some external action—going to church, reading the Bible, praying, tithing, being baptized. After such an answer we can agree that a real Christian usually *does* these things, but then point out that that's not what a real Christian *is*. A real Christian is one who is personally related to Jesus Christ as a living Person. . . .

The bait can also be thrown out succinctly if we are prepared for questions we are asked frequently. Often we recognize after it is too late that we have had a wonderful opportunity to speak up but we missed it because we didn't know what to say at the moment. Sometimes we are asked questions like: "Why are you so happy?" "What makes you tick?" "You seem to have a different motivation. You're not like me and most people. Why?" "Why is it you seem to have purpose in life?" Again, we can say, "An experience I had changed my outlook on life." And then, as we are asked, we can share that experience of Christ with them.[4]

Above all, take it easy. Proceed with caution. It's like fishing. Patience, intelligence, and skill are not optional. They're *essential*. No one ever caught fish by slapping the water with an oar or by hurriedly racing through the process. Taking the initiative requires that we do so with a lot of wisdom, which brings us to the fourth guideline.

Tactfulness

There is one very obvious observation regarding Philip's method I find extremely appealing. He was completely unoffensive. It is important for Christians to remember that it is the *cross* that will be offensive, *not the one who witnesses*. Philip used tact as he became involved in a discussion with the Ethiopian official.

> And when Philip had run up, he heard him reading Isaiah the prophet, and said, "Do you understand what you are reading?"
>
> And he said, "Well, how could I, unless someone guides me?" And he invited Philip to come up and sit with him.
>
> Now the passage of Scripture which he was reading was this:
>
> > "HE WAS LED AS A SHEEP TO SLAUGHTER;
> > AND AS A LAMB BEFORE ITS SHEARER IS SILENT,
> > SO HE DOES NOT OPEN HIS MOUTH.
> > IN HUMILIATION HIS JUDGMENT WAS TAKEN AWAY;
> > WHO SHALL RELATE HIS GENERATION?
> > FOR HIS LIFE IS REMOVED FROM THE EARTH."
>
> And the eunuch answered Philip and said, "Please tell me, of whom does the prophet say this? Of himself, or of someone else?" (Acts 8:30–34).

He listened without responding as the man confessed his ignorance. He graciously awaited an invitation to climb up into the chariot before doing so. He started where the man was, rather than cranking out a canned sermon. Not once did Philip put the man down. Or pull rank. Or attempt to impress. He gave the stranger space to think it through without feeling foolish.

Rebecca Pippert, in her fine book on evangelism, *Out of the Salt Shaker and Into the World*, mentions the need for this approach:

> . . . I remember a skeptical student who said, "I could never be a Christian. My commitment to scholarship makes any consideration of Christianity impossible. It's irrational and the evidence supporting it is totally insufficient."

I answered, "I'm so glad you care so much about truth and that you really want evidence to support your beliefs. You say the evidence for Christianity is terribly insufficient. What was your conclusion after carefully investigating the primary biblical documents?"

"Ahh, well, you mean the Bible?" he asked.

"Of course," I said. "The New Testament accounts of Jesus, for example. Where did you find them lacking?"

"Oh, well, look, I remember mother reading me those stories when I was ten," he replied.

"Hmm, but what was your conclusion?" I continued and as a result discovered he had never investigated the Scriptures critically as an adult. This is all too often the case. But we can arouse curiosity in others to investigate the claims of the gospel when we help them see that their information and understanding about Christianity is lacking.

Another person who was quite hostile to what she perceived was Christianity told me in anger, "I can't stand those hypocrites who go to church every Sunday. They make me sick."

"Yes," I responded, "isn't it amazing how far they are from true Christianity? When you think of how vast the difference is between the real thing and what they do, it's like worlds apart. Ever since I've discovered what Christianity is really about, the more mystified I am."

"Ah, the real thing? Well, what do you mean by that?" she asked. We talked for an hour about faith because her hostility had been changed into curiosity.[5]

Rather than arguing, try to find a way to agree. Rather than attacking, show genuine concern. Uphold the dignity of the individual. He or she may not be a Christian, but that is no reason to think the person lacks our respect. As questions are asked (like the Ethiopian asked in verse 34), kindly offer an answer. That man was a Gentile. He had no idea of whom Isaiah, the Jewish prophet was speaking. Philip stayed calm and tactful. But when the moment was right, he came to the point.

Preciseness

In answer to the man's question, Philip spoke precisely and clearly of Jesus Christ, the Messiah:

> And the eunuch answered Philip and said, "Please tell me, of whom does the prophet say this? Of himself, or of someone else?"
>
> And Philip opened his mouth, and beginning from this Scripture he preached Jesus to him (Acts 8:34–35).

He started at square one—no mumbo-jumbo, no jargon, no double-talk, no scary charts of pyramids of multi-headed beasts or superaggressive "believe now or you'll go to hell" threats. Just *Jesus*—Jesus' person and work, Jesus' love for sinners, Jesus' perfect life and sacrificial death, Jesus' resurrection and offer of forgiveness, security, purpose, and hope. "He preached Jesus. . . ."

Stay on the issue of Christ when witnessing. Not the church or denominations or religion or theological differences or doctrinal questions. Speak precisely of Jesus, the Savior. Refuse to dart down rabbit trails. Satellite subjects are often tantalizingly tempting, but *refrain!* When self-control is applied, the other person will realize that the gospel revolves strictly around Christ and nothing else. See what happened?

> And Philip said, "If you believe with all your heart, you may." And he answered and said, "I believe that Jesus Christ is the Son of God."
>
> And he ordered the chariot to stop; and they both went down into the water, Philip as well as the eunuch; and he baptized him.
>
> And when they came up out of the water, the Spirit of the Lord snatched Philip away; and the eunuch saw him no more, but went on his way rejoicing (Acts 8:37–39).

Decisiveness

The African gentleman suggested that he be baptized. Wisely, Philip put first things first. With decisive discernment, Philip explained that faith in Jesus *precedes* baptism. That did it! The man believed and was *then* baptized. No ifs, ands, or buts. *First* there was an acceptance of the message and *after that* there was a public acknowledgment of his faith as he submitted to baptism.

Summary and Conclusion

Do you genuinely desire to strengthen your grip on evangelism? Are you honestly interested in sharing your faith with this generation of lost and confused people? Begin to cultivate these six guidelines:

- *Sensitivity.* Listen carefully. Be ready to follow God's leading.
- *Availability.* Stay flexible. If the Lord is directing you to move here or there, go.
- *Initiative.* Use an appropriate approach to break the ice.
- *Tactfulness.* With care and courtesy, with thoughtfulness, with a desire to uphold dignity, speak graciously.
- *Preciseness.* Remember the issue is Christ. Stay on that subject.
- *Decisiveness.* As the Spirit of God is evidently at work, speak of receiving Christ. Make it clear that Jesus Christ is ready to receive whomever may come to Him by faith.

I began this chapter with a statement evangelist Billy Graham once made. I close with the same question for emphasis.

The evangelistic harvest is always urgent. The destiny of men and of nations is always being decided.

Every generation is strategic. We are not responsible for the past generation, and we cannot bear the full responsibility for the next one; but we do have our generation. God will hold us responsible as to how well we fulfill our responsibilities to this age and take advantage of our opportunities.[6]

Because today's harvest is urgent, because we are held responsible to make Christ known to our generation, let's not allow our laid-back, who-really-cares society to weaken our enthusiasm or slacken our zeal.

Let's strengthen our grip on evangelism.

DISCUSSION QUESTIONS AND SUGGESTIONS TO HELP YOU STRENGTHEN YOUR GRIP ON EVANGELISM

• What do you think of when *evangelism* is mentioned? Talk about how you heard of Christ—the very first time you can remember being told of the gospel. What was the method used? Did it turn you on or off? Why? What stands out most in your mind when you recall the person who witnessed to you?

• We worked our way fairly carefully through a section of Acts 8 in this chapter. Turn to those verses (vv. 26–40) and see if you can remember a few of the guidelines. Ideally, see if all those in your group can reconstruct all six of them, in order.

• Pick one from the list and talk it over. Why is this so significant that you chose it over all the others?

• If you have a copy of *The Living Bible*, try this for a change. One of you read the part of Philip and another the part of the Ethiopian official. In this role-playing episode, imagine yourself in that person's skin. Afterwards, discuss what it was, humanly speaking, that caused the official to stay interested.

• Now then discuss ways that open the door to a meaningful witnessing experience. State (and write down) some of the verbal wedges that help you win a hearing.

• Complete the following:

Things to Guard Against (The Negative Turn-offs)	Things to Remember (The Positive Approaches)

• Here's a project for each one of you to try. During the coming week *pray* that you might be sensitive to at least one opportunity to witness. *Think* about what you want to communicate ahead of time. As the occasion occurs, *speak* graciously and carefully. Finally, be ready to *ask* the person if he or she would wish to receive the gift of eternal life. Report back and tell of your encounter.

CHAPTER FIFTEEN

Strengthening Your Grip on Authority

QUESTION AUTHORITY!—These words are not simply a bumper sticker slogan found on vans in Southern California, they're fast becoming the unwritten motto of the 1980s. Let's face it, this generation is tough, not tender.

No longer...

... is the voice of the parent respected in the home.

... is the sight of the policeman on the corner a model of courage and control.

... is the warning of the teacher in the classroom feared and obeyed.

... is the reprimand of the boss sufficient to bring about change.

... is the older person treated with dignity and honor.

... is the husband considered "the head of the home" (God help him if he even *thinks* such a thing!).

THE PROBLEM IS OBVIOUS

Not even the President of our nation carries the clout he once did. Ours is a talk-back, fight-back, get-even society that is ready to resist—and sue—at the slightest provocation. Instead of the obedient Minute Man representing our national image, a new statue with a curled upper lip, an open mouth screaming obscenities, and both fists in the air could better describe our times. Defiance, resistance, violence, and retaliation are now our "style." If you can believe it, there is even a Children's Rights Movement now established. This organization has declared its objectives in a "Child's Bill of Rights,"[1] that doesn't simply weaken parental authority, it *demolishes* it. As you would expect, it shifts the final controls from the home to the courtroom . . . making the judge the authority (what a joke!), not the parent.

Dr. James Dobson, a personal friend of mine and a man I respect for his unbending commitment to marriage and the family, addresses this whole issue quite forcefully in one of his books. He then cites a case in point:

> Only last month I received a letter from an attorney who sought my help in defending a father who was threatened with the loss of his child. The details are difficult to believe. It appears that the Department of Social Service in his community is attempting to remove a six-year-old girl from her home because her father will not permit her to attend movies, listen to rock music or watch certain television programs. This child is well adjusted emotionally and is popular with her friends in school. Her teacher reports that she ranks in the top five students in her class, academically. Nevertheless, the courts are being asked to remove her from her home because of the intolerable "abuse" she is experiencing there.[2]

We have a large number of educators in our church in Fullerton. One is a gentleman who teaches high school math in a Los Angeles public school. The man could keep all of us occupied for three hours or more relating one story after another about discipline problems in his classroom. He once told me he spends about ten minutes each class period actually teaching math and about forty minutes dealing with rebellion and related disciplinary issues.

Another teacher in her fifties informed me at a dinner party one evening that she was retiring from the classroom. Knowing her love for the profession, I asked why she was opting for an early retirement.

"I can't take the abuse another year!" she answered. Stating further, "We teachers once had the authority and (when challenged) the backing of the principal. No more." Almost with a sigh, she added, "The teachers are now afraid of the principals, the principals are afraid of the superintendents, the superintendents are afraid of the school boards, the boards are afraid of the parents, and the parents are afraid of the children . . . but the *children*? They're not afraid of anybody!"

I'll save you the dirty details, but I should mention the whole growing concern of crime, another evidence of a society in rebellion. *Newsweek* magazine dedicated an issue to this subject, calling it "The Plague of Violent Crime."[3] I thought I was ready for the facts. I wasn't. On top of that, add child and wife batterings, street demonstrations, the ever-present plague of vandalism, employer-employee squabbles, endless lawsuits of unprecedented proportions, prison riots, political blackmail kidnappings, religious in-fighting, and the abuse of many who enforce their authority without wisdom or compassion . . . and you have the makings of madness.

I fully realize there are times when resistance is needed. We would not be a free nation had we not fought for our liberty. Furthermore, the lawless would rule over the righteous if we allowed ourselves to be walked on, stolen from, and otherwise taken advantage of. There *are* times when there must be resistance and a strong determination to defend one's rights. That is not the issue I'm referring to in this chapter. My concern is the obvious erosion of respect for needed and fair authority . . . the lack of submission toward those who *should* be over us, who earn and deserve our cooperation. Instead, there is a growing independence, a stubborn defiance against *any* authority that attempts to criticize, correct, or even caution. No one can deny that this self-centered rebellion is on the rise. My desire is that we see the difference, then respond correctly to God-given authority with an attitude of true humility, the mentality mentioned in the New Testament modeled so beautifully by Jesus Christ.

Humble yourselves in the presence of the Lord, and He will exalt you (James 4:10).

Servants, be submissive to your masters with all respect, not only to those who are good and gentle, but also to those who are unreasonable.

For this finds favor, if for the sake of conscience toward God a man bears up under sorrows when suffering unjustly.

For what credit is there if, when you sin and are harshly treated, you endure it with patience? But if when you do what is right and suffer for it you patiently endure it, this finds favor with God.

For you have been called for this purpose, since Christ also suffered for you, leaving you an example for you to follow in His steps, WHO COMMITTED NO SIN, NOR WAS ANY DECEIT FOUND IN HIS MOUTH; and while being reviled, He did not revile in return; while suffering, He uttered no threats, but kept entrusting Himself to Him who judges righteously; and He Himself bore our sins in His body on the cross, that we might die to sin and live to righteousness; for by His wounds you were healed (1 Pet. 2:18–24).

You younger men, likewise, be subject to your elders; and all of you, clothe yourselves with humility toward one another, for GOD IS OPPOSED TO THE PROUD, BUT GIVES GRACE TO THE HUMBLE.

Humble yourselves, therefore, under the mighty hand of God, that He may exalt you at the proper time, casting all your anxiety upon Him, because He cares for you (1 Pet. 5:5–7).

It is easy to discount such counsel in an angry age that considers rebellion a way of life and sees resistance as a virtue. To strengthen our grip on authority, it may be helpful to expose the dark, ugly side of rebellion that never gets much press.

KING SAUL: PERSONIFICATION OF REBELLION

Back in the Old Testament we find a man who had a choice opportunity to lead the Hebrew people into victory. He was tall, strong, and capable. He had the charisma of a popular public figure and the vote of the nation. Saul had what it took to be the king. But the man had one major problem—himself. He could rule the people, but he couldn't rule himself. Deep down inside his soul was a carnal caldron that stayed on a low boil, belching up pride, selfishness, jealousy, and a stubborn streak of rebellion.

This is never more obvious than in 1 Samuel 15, the chapter that records the turning point in his reign. The chapter begins with a conversation the prophet Samuel had with King Saul.

> Then Samuel said to Saul, "The Lord sent me to anoint you as king over His people, over Israel; now therefore listen to the words of the Lord.
>
> "Thus says the Lord of hosts, 'I will punish Amalek for what he did to Israel, how he set himself against him on the way while he was coming up from Egypt.
>
> 'Now go and strike Amalek and utterly destroy all that he has, and do not spare him; but put to death both man and woman, child and infant, ox and sheep, camel and donkey'" (1 Sam. 15:1–3).

The directive was neither complicated nor vague. God had spoken through Samuel and there was to be one re-

sponse: *Obedience.* Saul was to go into battle, assault the
Amalekites, and completely annihilate the enemy, including all
living creatures in the enemy camp. Reading 1 Samuel 15:7,
you'd think that is what occurred:

> So Saul defeated the Amalekites, from Havilah as
> you go to Shur, which is east of Egypt.

But no, read on.

> And he captured Agag the king of tbe Amalekites
> alive, and utterly destroyed all the people with the edge of the
> sword.
> But Saul and the people spared Agag and the best of
> the sheep, the oxen, the fatlings, the lambs, and all that was good,
> and were not willing to destroy them utterly; but everything despised
> and worthless, that they utterly destroyed (vv. 8–9).

I find in this biblical account four characteristics of
rebellion. The first emerges from the verses we just read.

Defiance Against Authority to Accomplish One's Own Desire

The authority in this case is Almighty God. God
had said, ". . . utterly destroy all." Saul had not misunderstood.
He had willfully disobeyed. He wasn't confused, he was insubor-
dinate. He did not want to follow those directions because he
had his own desires. He thought of an alternate plan.

Recently my wife and I had the pleasure of spending an evening with former astronaut, General Charles M.
Duke. All of us in the room sat in rapt fascination as the man
told of the *Apollo 16* mission to the moon, including some interesting tidbits related to driving "Rover," the lunar vehicle,
and actually walking on the surface of the planet. We were full of
questions which General Duke patiently and carefully answered
one after another.

I asked, "Once you were there, weren't you free to make your own decisions and carry out some of your own experiments... you know, sort of do as you pleased—maybe stay a little longer if you liked?" He smiled back, "Sure, Chuck, if we didn't want to return to earth!"

He then described the intricate plan, the exact and precise instructions, the essential discipline, the instant obedience that was needed right down to the split second. By the way, he said they had landed somewhat "heavy" when they touched down on the moon. He was referring to their fuel supply. They had plenty left. Guess how much. *One minute.* They landed with sixty seconds of fuel remaining. Talk about being exact! I got the distinct impression that a rebel spirit doesn't fit inside a space suit. Whoever represents the United States in the space program must have an unconditional respect for authority.

That's what King Saul lacked. He knew the game plan. He had been briefed by Samuel. But he chose to defy authority and go with Plan "B," namely his own desire. Read on.

Then the word of the Lord came to Samuel, saying, "I regret that I have made Saul king, for he has turned back from following Me, and has not carried out My commands." And Samuel was distressed and cried out to the Lord all night.

And Samuel rose early in the morning to meet Saul; and it was told Samuel, saying, "Saul came to Carmel, and behold, he set up a monument for himself, then turned and proceeded on down to Gilgal."

And Samuel came to Saul, and Saul said to him, "Blessed are you of the Lord! I have carried out the command of the Lord" (1 Sam. 15:10–13).

God saw what had happened. He also knew why. So did Samuel. But Saul? The man was so blinded, so capable at rationalization, so quick to rewrite the rules to fit his own setup, he didn't even feel guilty. With open arms and a big smile, he welcomes Samuel to the site.

     . . . Saul greeted him cheerfully. "Hello there," he said. "Well, I have carried out the Lord's command" (v. 13, TLB).

     This brings us to the second characteristic of a rebellious spirit.

Rationalization and Coverup to Excuse Sinful Actions

     Those who resist authority become masters at this. They develop an amazing disregard for the truth. They also re-define sin. And these people, who are often Christians, are so convinced that they are right, that they are shocked when they discover otherwise. I came across an interesting statement in my reading some time ago, "Excuses are often lies packed into the skin of reason."

     To highlight the contrast, compare God's statement in 1 Samuel 15:11 with Saul's remark in verse 13.

God	Saul
". . . he has turned back . . . and has not carried out My commands. . . ."	"I have carried out the command of the Lord."

     The people who perfect resisting authority (especially God's) will not run out of ideas or ways to excuse wrong. They will search for reasons—often found in books!—that make wrong appear right. They will be ready to show how their actions make better sense. They will even explain how it is better for their health or welfare or future plans. And they will have no guilt whatever!

     Webster's dictionary defines the act of rationalization, "to provide plausible but untrue reasons for conduct . . . to attribute one's actions to rational motives without analysis of true motives." I've heard them by the dozens every year. It makes no difference whether it's rationalizing oneself out of a marriage or into another job, away from a geographical area, or back to a friendship that isn't wholesome, rationalization works.

Saul employed it, but Samuel didn't fall for it, not for a minute. In unvarnished integrity, the prophet saw through the whole mess and asked a basic empirical question: ". . . 'What then is this bleating of the sheep in my ears, and the lowing of the oxen which I hear?'" (v. 14).

There's nothing quite like being sawed off the limb by a set of hard facts! Samuel wanted to know how there could be the sounds of life if indeed Saul had silenced all life. The king looked like the cat with canary feathers all over his mouth. Whether he was willing to admit it or not, he was guilty. He had deliberately ignored God's authoritative instruction, which reveals a third characteristic that is common to a person in his rebellious condition.

Defensiveness When Confronted with the Truth

After hearing Samuel's question, the king reacted defensively. There was no vulnerability, no repentance, no admission of wrong, no humble willingness to come clean and repent. Proud, stubborn, and maybe a bit embarrassed, he said:

> . . . "They have brought them from the Amalekites,
> for the people spared the best of the sheep and oxen, to sacrifice to
> the Lord your God; but the rest we have utterly destroyed" (v. 15).

Saul is scratching around for answers. Cornered, his eyes dart in the direction of those who stood near—"They did it! It was all these people." Then to soften the blow, "We saved only a few to sacrifice to Jehovah." Now he's *really* back-pedaling. No matter how obvious it is that he failed to obey, Saul is not giving in.

I had a two-and-a-half hour layover at the Denver Airport last winter that proved to be an experience I'll never forget. I aged about ten years. It wasn't because of the delay, even though I usually hate to wait. It wasn't because of incompetent airline personnel. They were great. It was a small child—simply a preschooler—who also had to wait with her mother. But this child was not your basic little girl. She was uncontrollable. Her mother? You guessed it. Your typical, preoccupied, can't-be-bothered type... who bargains, threatens, gives in, wrings her hands, looks away, sighs, *everything but disciplines* her monster... er, *daughter.*

This child did it all. Dumped over ashtrays (I counted four), crawled over every seat (unoccupied or occupied) at least twice, screamed for something to drink or eat until she finally got both several times. The creature grabbed newspapers out of men's hands as they were reading, and finally she did the unpardonable. *She walked all over my shoes.* Now, dear hearts and gentle people, I don't have many untouchables. Having raised four busy children, having been engaged in public service for twenty years, and having been married almost twenty-seven years, I don't have many things left to call strictly my own. But my shoes have withstood the test of time. They are very carefully spit-shined (don't ask why, just accept it), placed in shoe trees each night, protected in the closet when I'm home, and covered with socks when I put them in luggage for travel. As each of my kids (and wife) will tell you, when I'm wearing my shoes, only one person walks on them, and that's me. If someone else steps on them, I have an immediate reaction. And it is not to pray for them. Or smile and say, "That's okay." Or brush the shoe across the back of my other leg and think, "I'll touch it up later." No—my instant reaction is to punch their lights out. I'm just being honest.

Well, I had a slight problem in the Denver Airport, you see. The one who stepped onto the holy of holies was a little child. Just a little girl. I rather doubt that she will do that again. I am happy to report she has fully recovered. (Just kidding.) No, I never placed a hand on her. Or a foot! With incredible and rare restraint I bit my tongue and tried to stay out of her path. Finally, when none of us could stand it any longer, the mother was given some loud and directive counsel. And guess what. She was offended. Why, the very idea that someone would even *think* of her child as being out of control! She was defensive when confronted with the truth. Even though surrounded by sand and ashes from dumped-over ashtrays, litter from several junk food-and-drink containers, irritated businessmen and women, plus one enraged minister with scuffed shoes, that mother could not imagine how rude we could be when one of us (!) finally and firmly stated, "Get control of your child!"

Samuel had heard enough. With a stern look and penetrating eyes, the exasperated prophet held up his hand and exclaimed: "Wait...."

In today's terms, "Be quiet!" or "Shut up!"

"... let me tell you what the Lord said to me last night." And he said to him, "Speak!"

And Samuel said, "Is it not true, though you were little in your own eyes, you were made the head of the tribes of Israel? And the Lord anointed you king over Israel, and the Lord sent you on a mission, and said, 'Go and utterly destroy the sinners, the Amalekites, and fight against them until they are exterminated.'

"Why then did you not obey the voice of the Lord, but rushed upon the spoil and did what was evil in the sight of the Lord?" (vv. 16b–21).

Old Saul stubbornly stood his ground. He refused to give in, illustrating the fourth characteristic of a rebel heart.

Resistance to Accountability When Wrong Has been Committed

Still passing the buck, unwilling to confess the wrong of his actions, Saul again dodges Samuel's counsel. The man *refuses* to see the error of his way. He continues to talk of offering sacrifices and using the animals they preserved for holy purposes. He mixes in a little religion to convince Samuel that a burnt offering and a sacrificial altar will make everything right.

Sound familiar?

• "I've prayed about it and I believe God led me to do it" (superpious rationalization).

• "I'm forgiven. Grace has covered it all. The Lord will use me in a greater way. He understands" (accommodating theology).

• "Even though I may have altered His plan, in the end He will be pleased" (end justifies the means).

• "Nobody's perfect" (universal generalization).

• "God wants me to be happy" (guilt-relieving excuse).

Let's take a close look at God's counsel through Samuel. Read it as though the man were saying it to us:

> And Samuel said, "Has the Lord as much delight in burnt offerings and sacrifices as in obeying the voice of the Lord? Behold, to obey is better than sacrifice, and to heed than the fat of rams (vv. 22–23).

This is one of the strongest warnings in all of Scripture. It strips away all our excuses, all our attempts at lowering His standard. It brings us back to the one thing that pleases and glorifies Him (whether or not it satisfies us!) . . . *obedience.*

Take the time to reread that last verse. God says that rebellion is not a slight misdemeanor, something we needn't fuss over. No, it is in the same category as demonic involvement. And what about insubordination? Is it just a little difficulty all of us have to get used to? No way. It is "as iniquity and idolatry." Strong, strong, strong! *The Living Bible* says:

> . . . rebellion is as bad as the sin of witchcraft, and stubbornness is as bad as worshiping idols (1 Sam. 15:23).

Stunned, Saul finally submits, "I have sinned" (v. 24).

You and Me: A Personal Application

In a world hell-bent on having its own way, it is terribly difficult to cultivate the right attitude toward authority. The "*QUESTION AUTHORITY!*" mentality is so interwoven into the fabric of our society, it seems impossible to counteract it. Realistically, about the only place we can come to terms with it is in our homes. Are you doing this? Be honest, now. Within the walls of your dwelling are you maintaining the controls? Maybe these three warnings will encourage you to stay at it . . . or start today.

1. *Childhood.* A rebellious nature is conceived in a home where parents relinquish control.

2. *Adolescence.* A rebellious spirit will be cultivated among peers who resist control. And if it isn't curbed there, it culminates at—

3. *Adulthood.* A rebellious life must be crushed by God when He regains control.

And take it from one who experienced it and deals with it week after week, nothing is more painful to endure. Some must discover the need for a submissive spirit behind bars. Others, following a divorce. Still others, through a crippling disease or a horrible automobile accident or a series of blows in life that drive us to our knees and force us to learn how to walk humbly with our God.

When Cain curled his lip and stood tight-fisted in rebellion before his Maker, he was given a sobering warning that has been preserved in Scripture for all to read and heed:

. . . if you do not do well, sin is crouching at the door; and its desire is for you, but you must master it (Gen. 4:7b).

Nothing nas changed. The mark of Cain has been branded on this generation. Resisting authority still crouches like a beast at the door, ready to spring and pounce on its prey, be it parent or policeman or teacher or employer or minister or President—whomever. Some never learn to "master it" and therefore spend their lives "under the smarting rod of God," as the old Puritans used to say. Those who question authority face a hard future.

My friend, are you in that category? Do you have a loose grip on authority? Do you think you can continue to endure God's attempts to humble you? I heard a statement many years ago that provides an appropriate ending to this chapter. If it applies to you, let its message go deep within:

> When God wants to do an impossible task,
> He takes an impossible person and crushes him.

With one word, I close—
Surrender.

Discussion Questions and Suggestions to Help You Strengthen Your Grip on Authority

• Rebellion, according to one of the scriptures we looked at toward the end of this chapter, "is as the sin of divination" (1 Sam. 15:23). What does that say to you—what does it mean? Discuss the implications of comparing rebellion with such a horrible sin. Why do you think God takes that strong a stand against it?

• No sin with the magnitude of rebellion "just happens." It is not an overnight occurrence. What prompts it? Are there hints that it is brewing before it actually comes to the surface?

• Obviously, ours is a rebellious world. Talk about this. Try to be specific as you think through the reasons for this rebellion. Can you name a few examples from recent events that illustrate rebellion? Need a few hints? How about the American home, the school, riots, Iran, and the increase in crime?

• Using Romans 1:28–32 as your guide, talk about the direct link between refusing to "acknowledge God any longer" and the scene that follows. In verse 32, there is mentioned those who "give hearty approval to those who practice" rebellious deeds. Can we be "passive rebels"?

• Discuss the difference between honest (and even humble) disagreement and overt rebellion. Can't there be a genuine, necessary resistance without the presence of sinful insubordination and rebellion? Look at Acts 5:40–42 for a scriptural case in point. Compare that with Genesis 4:6–7.

• Okay, how do we resist or disagree *without* rebelling, in the wrong sense of the term. Think of a few examples and describe both right and wrong responses. Any scriptures come to mind?

• Finally, spend some time in prayer. Before doing so, honestly admit an area of your own life where you struggle with rebellion. Your superior at work? Your mate or parents at home? The policeman in the squad car? Some "authority figure" who represents a source of irritation? Pray for one another, asking the Lord to assist your friend in that dilemma.

Strengthening Your Grip on the Family

In 1975 EDITH SCHAEFFER, wife of Dr. Francis Schaeffer, asked a question that deserves an answer every year. That question became the title of her book, *What Is a Family?*[1] It's a good question. Every twelve to fifteen months, each one of us would do well to analyze and evaluate our family, facing up to the truth of our answer. Certainly every generation would be wise to do so. It may surprise us.

Edith Schaeffer suggests several answers, each one forming a separate chapter in her book. For example:

A Changing Life Mobile
The Birthplace of Creativity
A Formation Center for Human Relationships
A Shelter in a Time of Storm
A Perpetual Relay of Truth
A Door That Has Hinges and a Lock
A Museum of Memories.

Good answers. Insightful answers. Beautiful . . . almost *too* beautiful. But we cannot deny that these are the ideal, the ones most of us would embrace. *But are they real?* To help us determine that answer, let's just change one word, "What is *your* family?" What terms would best describe the things that go on under the roof where *you* live, among the members of *your* family?

Today's Family: The Picture Is Grim

It comes as a surprise to nobody that the family is under fire these days. When one national periodical did a special report on the American domestic scene, the issue was not entitled "Strengthening the Family" or "Examining the Family" or "Depending on the Family." It was "*Saving* the Family."[2] Like the prairie bison and the sperm whale and the crane, the family is fast becoming an endangered species. For sure, it is a different scene from the quiet, heart-warming scenes of yesteryear when mom was always home, dad was the sole breadwinner, children lived predictable lives of ease and relaxation, and the lifestyle was laid back and simple.

From a combination of several television documentaries plus the popular program "60 Minutes," a couple of seminars I have attended in recent months, magazine and newspaper articles, conversations with authorities on the family, and a few books I have read on the subject, I have compiled the following list of facts. Without attempting to document each one, allow me a few moments to outline a general profile of today's family. I warn you, the picture is grim.

- 38 percent of all first marriages fail (conservative figure).
- 79 percent of those people will remarry and 44 percent of the *second* marriages will fail.
- During the 1970s, four out of ten babies born in that decade will spend part or all of their childhood in single-parent homes.
- 15 percent of all births today are illegitimate (also conservative) and 50 percent of the out-of-wedlock babies are born to teenagers.

- Approximately two million American children who do live with both parents are "latch key kids"... they come home from school to an empty house. Both parents work.

- Two hundred thousand American children are physically abused each year. Of those, between sixty and one hundred thousand are *sexually* abused.

- 15 percent to 20 percent of American families abuse their children.

- The No. 1 killer of children under five years of age is child abuse.

- Child abusers are in every category of our society. No social, racial, economic, or religious group is excluded.

- Only 10 percent of reported child abusers are classified "mentally disturbed." The rest are people who appear to be very normal but "cannot cope."

- 30 percent of all American couples experience some form of domestic violence during their lifetime. Two million (again a conservative estimate) have used a lethal weapon on each other during their marriage.

- 20 percent of all police officers who die in the line of duty are killed while answering calls involving family conflicts.

- An average of thirteen teenagers kill themselves each day in the United States—an out-of-date statistic... much higher now. Suicide is now the No. 2 killer among Americans aged fifteen to twenty-four.

- Wife battering is now reaching an epidemic level in our nation. In the opinion of one Los Angeles police official, "This is probably the highest unreported crime in the country. Approximately twelve to fifteen million women are battered each year."

A study completed at the University of Rhode Island described the American home as the most dangerous place to be outside of riots and a war. The scene is desperate. And I haven't even mentioned the impact of alcoholism, drug abuse, mental and emotional breakdowns, and the ever-present tension caused by runaway teens, runaway wives, walk-out husbands, and gross neglect of the aged by their family members. If ever there is a need for a nation to strengthen her grip on any one area of need, it is obviously *the family.*

HOPE FOR THE FAMILY UNDER FIRE

Enough of statistics and doomsday predictions! Let's spend the balance of our time thinking through some answers, getting help from the ancient, time-tested wisdom of the Scriptures. Here (and *only* here) will we find counsel that is inspired of God, workable, realistic, and full of promise. And best of all, the Bible is constantly relevant, never anchored to the lifestyle of a particular era. The things we are about to discover are for us today just as much as they were for the people to whom they were originally written.

To help us come back to some basics about the family and strengthen our grip on this vital area of life, we'll dig into a couple of the ancient psalms that appear back-to-back in the Bible, Psalm 127 and Psalm 128.

The Family in Four Stages

When we read through the eleven verses that comprise these two psalms, we have little difficulty seeing how they flow together. Actually, they cover four major stages through which a family passes... sort of a panoramic, time-sequence scenario of the family as it progresses from one stage to the next. We could call these psalms a domestic mural.

Stage 1: The family in its early years, from marriage to the birth of the first child (Ps. 127:1–2).

Stage 2: The family expands to include the birth of children (Ps. 127:3–5).

Stage 3: The family goes through the years of training, loving, discipling, and ultimately releasing the children (Ps. 128:1–3).

Stage 4: The family is reduced to its original condition—a husband and wife in their twilight years together (Ps. 128:4–6).

The Family from God's Perspective

Before going into each stage and drawing insight from God's Word for today's family, let's understand that we are interested in God's perspective, not man's. Bookshelves in stores are running over with volumes on every conceivable subject about family living. In a local bookstore I counted twenty-three titles on books for helping parents with their babies—just for parents with babies. I found another seventeen books promising help in raising teenagers. And, by the way, several of them suggest methods that contradict the counsel of other authors, so whom do we believe? Which philosophy should I adopt? And if I adopt *this* one, how do I ignore *that* one (since it is written by an authority of equal significance)? The scene gets increasingly more complicated the more we seek divided human opinions as opposed to divine counsel from God's Book.

In my more exasperated moments as a parent, I'm tempted to believe that Mark Twain's philosophy is the one to follow: When a kid turns thirteen, stick him in a barrel, nail the lid on top, and feed him through the knot hole. When he turns sixteen . . . *plug up the knot hole.* But not even that plan will work. Neither you nor I have ever seen a teenager who could get enough food to survive through the knot hole of a barrel!

No, what we need most is God's perspective on family life.

STAGE 1: THE INCEPTION OF THE FAMILY

These are the foundational years, the time when a man and woman join their lives together in marriage and learn to adjust to the new experience of living intimately with another

person. God says this about that important and often difficult
period of time.

> Unless the Lord builds the house,
> They labor in vain who build it;
> Unless the Lord guards the city,
> The watchman keeps awake in vain.
>
> It is vain for you to rise up early,
> To retire late,
> To eat the bread of painful labors;
> For He gives to His beloved even in his sleep.
>
> (Ps. 127:1–2)

Using word pictures from a Jewish mentality, Solomon, himself a Jew, compares the home to a city. In those days
it was not uncommon for an ancient city to be built by having its
walls finished first to keep out the enemy. After its completion
and dedication to Jehovah, the wall would be walked upon by
guards continually on the lookout for attack.

What is Solomon saying in this analogy? "Unless
the city officials and the military guards depend completely on
Jehovah, and not just the city wall, no enemy will be kept out."

Twice the writer uses the same words, "Unless the
Lord... in vain... unless the Lord... it is vain...." Here's
the idea. During those all-important early months and years of
marriage, make sure that the Lord your God is the heart and
center of your family! If He is not, the whole experience is a
study in futility—a wasted, empty, counterproductive effort. It
will all be in vain. He doesn't have in mind a home that hangs a
lot of religious mottos on the walls or a couple that simply goes to
church regularly or offers up a quick prayer before meals or places
a big Bible on the living room coffee table. No, the essential
ingredient is "the Lord." A family gets started on the right foot
when Jesus Christ is in each life (husband and wife are both born
again), and when the lengthening shadow of His Lordship pervades that relationship. When a couple makes Christ a vital part

of their life, in the terms of the psalm, that's when "the Lord builds the house," that's when He "guards the city."

But you know how we are, especially those caught in the grip and grind of materialism. We are so busy—anxious to get ahead, pushing and pulling for more, always more—that we begin to tell ourselves lies. Like, "What we need is more things, a nicer car, bigger-and-better stuff." The psalmist warns us that rising up early and dropping in bed late (hoping to find satisfaction in things) is vain. We "eat the bread of painful labors" when we worship the god of materialism. Interestingly, if that philosophy is adopted by a couple, it is often during their first few years together.

If you want a family that is different, distinctly set apart for God's glory—a family that enjoys life and reaps the rewards of His best gifts, then *start right*. And if you failed to start right back then, *start today*. As I mentioned earlier in this book, it is never too late to start doing what is right. Put your Lord back in top priority. As a husband-wife team, acknowledge the fact that you have sowed the wind and reaped the whirlwind. It will be a slow and tedious process putting first things first, but you can do it! And don't forget the closing statement of verse 2: "He gives to His beloved even in his sleep." God will work overtime helping you and giving to you the things that will make your renewed commitment stick.

STAGE 2: THE EXPANSION OF THE FAMILY

> Behold, children are a gift of the Lord;
> The fruit of the womb is a reward.
> Like arrows in the hand of a warrior,
> So are the children of one's youth.
> How blessed is the man whose quiver is full of them;
> They shall not be ashamed,
> When they speak with their enemies in the gate.
> (Ps. 127:3–5)

By now, the child-bearing years have come. Good years, but physically and financially exhausting. And I might add *surprising.* God often enlarges our quiver beyond what we expected (or planned!) and yet He calls each one of our offspring "a gift," "fruit," a "reward." Since I have already analyzed each of these terms in my book, *You and Your Child,*[3] I'll not repeat myself here. But it is worth noting that the birth of a child is not taken lightly by the Lord. Each one is significant. Each one is viewed by God as a transfer of love from His heart to the couple receiving the gift.

God never wastes parents. He doesn't inadvertently "dump" kids haphazardly into homes. Nor does He deliver "accidents" into our lives. It is exceedingly important that families place the same significance on children that God does. Again, this is contrary to the mentality of many people in our society today. We are considered as somewhere between weird and ignorant if we have this kind of attitude toward children, especially if we have a large number of them.

But the psalm says we are "blessed" if our "quiver is full of them." We'll also be busy and tired! And a minister's home is no different than yours, pal. It's amazing to me how many people have the idea that a divine aura hovers over the pastor's home, making it unlike the "average dwelling." Now *that's* weird and ignorant! Our home is no different from any other busy neighborhood dwelling. The scene is just like yours. Mounds of laundry—and a dryer that eats two to three socks per load. Dog messes on the carpet. Kids that sleep with their clothes on—shoes too. A garbage disposal that gets clogged on rubber bands and paper clips. Stopped-up toilets. Expensive orthodontist's headgears forgotten and left at restaurants sixty miles back while on vacation. I have kissed hamsters goodnight, rocked sick rabbits to sleep, helped raise new puppies, delivered newspapers in the rain, mopped up vomit, and often wondered, "Will we ever make it?" You see, just like you.

But in the meantime, my wife and I have a treasure of memories that will keep us warm through many years in the future, exactly as God promised. What a difference when the attitude is right. I love the story Gordon MacDonald tells.

> Among the legends is the tale of a medieval sidewalk superintendent who asked three stone masons on a construction project what they were doing. The first replied that he was *laying bricks.* The second described his work as that of *building a wall.* But it was the third laborer who demonstrated genuine esteem for his work when he said, "I am *raising a great cathedral.*"
>
> Pose that same question to any two fathers concerning their role in the family, and you are liable to get the same kind of contrast. The first may say, "I am *supporting a family.*" But the second may see things differently and say, "I am *raising children.*" The former looks at his job as *putting bread on the table.* But the latter sees things in God's perspective: he is *participating in the shaping of lives.* [4]

The "arrows" God delivers into our quiver come ready-made, needing to be shaped and pointed toward the right target, which brings us to the next three verses in our scriptural mural.

STAGE 3: CHILD-REARING YEARS

Perhaps the most taxing of all, are the years a family finds itself in and out of crisis situations. Little babies that cooed and gurgled grow up into challenging, independent-thinking adolescents. The protective, sheltered environment of the home is broken into by the school, new friends, alien philosophies, financial strain, illness, accidents, hard questions, constant decisions, and busy schedules. Throw in a husband's mid-life crisis (I've earned one, but I haven't had time to enjoy it) and a wife's awareness that there's a bigger world than carpooling and making lunches . . . and it isn't difficult to feel the pressure mounting—especially when you add dating, new drivers in the family, leaving for college, talk of marriage, and moving out. Whew! And what does God say about these years?

> How blessed is everyone who fears the Lord,
> Who walks in His ways.
> When you shall eat of the fruit of your hands,
> You will be happy and it will be well with you.
> Your wife shall be like a fruitful vine,
> Within your house,
> Your children like olive plants
> Around your table.
>
> (Ps. 128:1–3)

He says we'll be "blessed." We'll be "happy." It will "be well" with us during these years. A dream? No. Remember this is a domestic mural, one scene growing out of the former and leading into the next. In the family portrayed on this scriptural canvas, "the Lord" is still central. When children come, they are viewed as "a gift of the Lord," a reward, "fruit" provided by Him.

As they are reared, the process is carried out God's way.* Which means that even in the teen years, it can be fun and enjoyable. Believe me, it can be.

I don't know how many people, some years ago, told Cynthia and me, "Enjoy your children when they're small. When they grow up and become teenagers with a mind of their own—you're gonna hate it. It's dreadful!" I've got news for all those prophets of doom. We don't "hate it," and it has *never* been "dreadful." Challenging, yes. Stretching, always. Humbling, occasionally. Rewarding, often.

---

*In my book, *You and Your Child*, I explain in detail a philosophy of rearing children God's way, according to scriptural guidelines. If you are struggling with this process and want to read some child-rearing insights based on the Bible, I suggest you read this book.

Our quiver first began to expand twenty years ago. Now, as the Psalm states it, we have begun to "eat of the fruit of our hands." And our family grows closer together with each passing year. This does not mean it has been easy. Or simple. Raising "olive plants" and providing the necessary stability and wisdom so that each of our four could grow and become the people God would have them be has been no pushover. The father and mother in this family have had to flex and change. We have also had to stand firm on occasion and uphold the standard we established as a Christian couple. But we have had to be honest—painfully honest—with our children, admitting when we were wrong and apologizing for it; declaring how we felt, yet leaving room for each child to discover on his or her own; being vulnerable and open regarding our fears, our uncertainties, our disagreements, our weaknesses; loving and supporting one another through failure, mistakes, and sinful behavior.

The real bills come due at home, don't they? It is here that life ultimately makes up its mind. And it is during the child-rearing/adolescent years that a parent is called by God to carry out one major mission: the mission *to model authenticity*—authentic Christianity, authentic humanity, authentic vulnerability and approachability. Teens can handle almost anything except hypocrisy. Cynthia and I determined years ago that we would do everything in our power to resist hypocrisy. Although this meant our children would see and hear painful things, at times harsh reality, we determined they would not have to struggle through double messages and phony-baloney junk as they grew up. Above all, we would be real people... touchable, available, and approachable.

I was encouraged recently to read of an experiment with monkeys that seemed to affirm our philosophy of rearing children.

Dr. Harry F. Harlow loved to stand by the animal cages in his University of Wisconsin laboratory and watch the baby monkeys. Intrigued, he noticed that the monkeys seemed emotionally attached to cloth pads lying in their cages.

They caressed the cloths, cuddled next to them, and treated them much as children treat a teddy bear. In fact, monkeys raised in cages with cloths on the floors grew huskier and healthier than monkeys in cages with wire-mesh floors. Was the softness and touchability of the cloth an important factor?

Harlow constructed an ingenious surrogate mother out of terry cloth, with a light bulb behind her to radiate heat. The cloth mother featured a rubber nipple attached to a milk supply from which the babies could feed. They adopted her with great enthusiasm. Why not? She was always comfortingly available, and, unlike real mothers, never roughed them up or bit them or pushed them aside.

After proving that babies could be "raised" by inanimate, surrogate mothers, Harlow next sought to measure the importance of the mother's touchable, tactile characteristics. He put eight baby monkeys in a large cage that contained the terry cloth mother plus a new mother, this one made entirely out of wire mesh. Harlow's assistants, controlling the milk flow to each mother, taught four of the babies to nurse from the terry cloth mother and four from the wire mesh mother. Each baby could get milk only from the mother assigned to it.

A startling trend developed almost immediately. All eight babies spent almost all their waking time (sixteen to eighteen hours per day) huddled next to the terry cloth mother. They hugged her, patted her, and perched on her. Monkeys assigned to the wire mesh mother went to her only for feeding, then scooted back to the comfort and protection of the terry cloth mother. When frightened, all eight would seek solace by climbing onto the terry cloth mother.

Harlow concluded, "We were not surprised to discover that contact comfort was an important basic affectional or love variable, but we did not expect it to overshadow so completely the variable of nursing; indeed the disparity is so great as to suggest that the primary function of nursing is that of insuring frequent and intimate body contact of the infant with the mother. Certainly, man cannot live by milk alone."[5]

It might be good for you, my friend, to stop right now and think about the difference between being a "terry cloth" parent and a "wire mesh" parent. Even before you finish the chapter, it may be the right time for you to come to terms with the truth regarding your family. I must be honest with you, in most of the family conflicts I have dealt with involving trouble with teenagers, the problem has been more with parents who were either too liberal and permissive or too inflexible, distant, rigid (and sometimes hypocritical) than with teenagers who were unwilling to cooperate. When the modeling is as it should be, there is seldom much trouble from those who fall under the shadow of the leader. Strengthening your grip on the family may start with an unguarded appraisal of the leadership your family is expected to follow.

STAGE 4: THE TWILIGHT YEARS

Behold, for thus shall the man be blessed
Who fears the Lord.
The Lord bless you from Zion,
And may you see the prosperity of Jerusalem all the days of
    your life.
Indeed, may you see your children's children.
Peace be upon Israel!

(Ps. 128:4–6)

What will life be like when the dust settles and quietness returns? What will be the rewards for beginning and cultivating a family according to God's direction? How will it be in the empty nest?

To begin with, we will be "blessed" (v. 4). I take this to mean that we, personally, will be happy. There will be happy memories. There will also be the happiness sustained through good relationships with our adult offspring.

Furthermore, the psalmist states that "Jerusalem" will be a better place. That was the city where he lived. There will be civil blessings that come as a result of releasing into society a happy, healthy, young adult. The cities where our offspring choose to live will be better places if they emerge from a family that has prepared them for life.

Finally, "Peace be upon Israel!"—SHALOM IS-RAEL! Ultimately, the nation will be blessed of God. It is axiomatic. Healthy, well-disciplined, loving homes produce people who make a nation peaceful and strong. As the family goes, so goes the nation. When you boil it down to the basics, the pulse of an entire civilization is determined by the heartbeat of its homes.

When it comes to rearing children, every society is only 20 years away from barbarism. Twenty years is all we have to accomplish the task of civilizing the infants who are born into our midst each year. These savages know nothing of our language, our culture, our religion, our values, our customs of interpersonal relations. The infant is totally ignorant about communism, fascism, democracy, civil liberties, the rights of the minority as contrasted with the prerogatives of the majority, respect, decency, honesty, customs, conventions, and manners. *The barbarian must be tamed if civilization is to survive.*[6]

DISCUSSION QUESTIONS AND SUGGESTIONS TO HELP YOU STRENGTHEN YOUR GRIP ON THE FAMILY

• The family. Can there be anything more essential, more basic to healthy human existence than the family? See if you can name six or eight impressions of life we learn first in the family. Next, talk about how an unhappy, broken family relationship can affect initial impressions of life.

• Discuss some of the major problems families struggle with in this generation. How are they different from ten or fifteen years ago? Is there any scriptural support for the home suffering more as we move closer to the end times?

• Now let's get more specific. Let's talk about *your* home. Use several adjectives to describe family life within the walls where you live—like, "busy" or "peaceful" or "strained" or "accepting." Try to be completely honest as you answer this one: What influence do *you* bring into your family relationships?

• How has this chapter helped you with your particular relationship to others in your family? Which passage or verse of Scripture seemed especially relevant to your situation? Give an example of what you mean.

• If you could reach inside your own life and change one thing that would help with relationships at home, which one would it be? Talk about what it would take to start moving in that direction.

• As you have analyzed what has happened to hurt family relationships, maybe you've begun to wonder if there's anything good at home. Of course, there is! Be just as honest to name the *good* things as you were to admit the weaknesses.

• Finally, turn to the two psalms we examined in this chapter and share an application that encourages you and gives you hope. Thank God for that. Call on Him for assistance in the one major area you need help. Pray for one another.

Conclusion

A FUNNY THING HAPPENED after my book, *Improving Your Serve*, was released. A friend of mine up in the Northwest went into a secular bookstore in hopes of finding a copy. She patiently combed through the religious section, but it was not there. She was surprised because a friend of hers had picked up a copy the day before and had mentioned it to her. Puzzled, the lady asked the clerk if they had sold out. "Oh, no," she said quickly, "we just got in a new shipment of *Improving Your Serve* this week." As they walked back together, the clerk turned right as my friend turned left... just about the time the clerk was saying, "It's right over here in the sports section, among Connors, McEnroe, and Borg."

Smiling, my friend informed the lady that the book actually had nothing to do with tennis. To which the clerk replied, "Well, they're selling so well in this section, I think we'll just leave 'em here!"

As *Strengthening Your Grip* arrives at bookstores, it may appear on the shelf near Palmer, Nicklaus, and Hogan... but as you know by now, it actually has nothing to do with golf. And although the name seems to suggest a sequence volume to *Improving Your Serve*, it is not that either. This book was not intended to be another series of chapters encouraging the reader to serve better, but rather to think deeper. To think about what and how and why in a day when "who really cares" is fast becoming our world's favorite phrase. Hopefully, you have found *Strengthening Your Grip* provocative. But my main concern is that you found it relevant, not just another pile of words wrapped in dated religious garb. I *loathe* that thought!

The penetrating words of the German Reformer Martin Luther frequently flash through my mind:

> If you preach the Gospel in all aspects with the ex-
> ception of the issues which deal specifically with your time—you are
> not preaching all the Gospel.

Although he was a sixteenth-century monk, his cry was a plea for relevance. With boldness he addressed the things that mattered. He saw his church diseased and paralyzed by tradition, corruption, and apathy. He brushed aside the dry debris of meaningless formalities, he challenged inaccurate interpretations, he declared the truth at the risk of being branded a heretic. As the Spirit of God gave him refreshing insight and strength to continue unintimidated, he strengthened the grip of a new brand of Christians—"Protestants"—as he led them into a reformation, a movement that was destined to acquaint the world with the essentials of the faith. We admire his efforts to this day.

A "new" Reformation is in order, in my opinion. Christians in the last two decades of the twentieth century need a fresh, vital word for our times. Not further revelation. Not more doctrines. Not even a new system of theology, necessarily. What we need is a message, securely riveted to scriptural foundations, that has a ring of relevance to it—an authentic reality about it. Ancient truth in today's talk. In Luther's day that meant one thing—the need for clarification to dispel ignorance. *Today* it means another—a new style of communication to dispel indifference. *Strengthening Your Grip* has been an effort in that direction.

As I drive home on Sunday evenings after a full day of preaching and involvement with our flock here in Fullerton, I am usually exhausted. I drive slowly, thinking back over those hours I have invested. I ask myself many questions. Invariably, those questions include, "Was I connecting?" and "Did that make sense?" and "Is my communication relevant?" You see, I have this burning passion never to be out of touch with my times. God did not call me to be a prophet out of the time tunnel—one who looks and sounds like he was born two or three millenniums late. But I *would* like to have the commitment of the prophets, though not their style . . . because I need to connect with my day, not theirs. It is my wish that more and more of God's people would become a part of this "new" Reformation—committed to communicating divine revelation so clearly that the public is stunned to realize how eternally relevant God and His Word really are.

As I complete this book, I find myself, again, exhausted. Still asking those haunting questions: "Do these chapters make sense?" and "Can anybody understand them . . . even the uninitiated?" and mainly, "Will it make any difference?" You cannot imagine how much I care about these things.

Was the book worth the effort? If your grip is now stronger in an area of your life that once was weak . . . if Jesus Christ is more real to you than when you started . . . if you are more convinced than before that God's Word "connects" with wisdom and authority, then the answer is "Yes" . . . even for those of you who thought you were buying a book about golf, but discovered that you came home with a book about God.

Notes

Chapter One

1. Charles E. Hummel, *Tyranny of the Urgent* (Downers Grove, IL: InterVarsity Press, 1967), p. 4.
2. John R. W. Stott, *The Preacher's Portrait* (Grand Rapids, MI: Wm. B. Eerdmans Publishing Company, 1961), p. 31.
3. Ronald M. Enroth, "The Power Abusers," *Eternity*, October 1979, pp. 25–26.
4. *Your Churning Place* by Robert L. Wise. © copyright 1977, Regal Books, Ventura, CA 93006. Used by permission.
5. Charlie W. Shedd, *Promises to Peter*, copyright © 1970 by Charlie W. Shedd, pp. 12–13; used by permission of Word Books, Publisher, Waco, TX, 76796.
6. A poem by George MacLeod, taken from *Focal Point*, the Conservative Baptist Theological Seminary Bulletin, Denver, CO, Spring, 1981.

Chapter Two

1. Philip G. Zimbardo, "The Age of Indifference," *Psychology Today*, August 1980, p. 72.
2. From John Donne, *Devotions*, XVII, as quoted in *Familiar Quotations*, ed. John Bartlett (Boston: Little, Brown and Company, 1955), p. 218.
3. Philip G. Zimbardo, p. 76.
4. Leslie B. Flynn, *Great Church Fights* (Wheaton, IL: Victor Books, a division of SP Publications, 1976), p. 14.

5. *Up With Worship* by Anne Ortlund. © copyright 1975, Regal Books, Ventura, CA 93006. Used by permission.
6. James C. Dobson, *Hide or Seek* (Old Tappan, NJ: Fleming H. Revell Company, 1974), p. 134.

Chapter Three

1. Charles R. Swindoll, *Improving Your Serve* (Waco, TX: Word Books, 1981).
2. William Barclay, *The Letter to the Hebrews*, The Daily Study Bible (Edinburgh: The Saint Andrews Press, 1955), pp. 137–38.
3. Donald Bubna with Sue Multanen, "The Encouragement Card," *Leadership* 1, no. 4 (Fall, 1980): 52–53.
4. Lee Stanley, producer, *Mountain Top*, (Agoura, CA: Morning Star Film, Inc., distributed by Pyramid Film & Video Santa Monica, CA).

Chapter Four

1. William Barclay, *The Letters to Philippians, Colossians, Thessalonians*, The Daily Study Bible (Edinburgh: The Saint Andrews Press, 1959), p. 232.
2. Pitirim Sorokin, *The American Sex Revolution* (Boston: Porter Sargent Publisher, 1956), p. 19.
3. Ibid., pp. 21–22.
4. Frank E. Gaebelein, ed., *The Expositor's Bible Commentary*, vol. 11 (Grand Rapids: Zondervan Publishing House, 1978), p. 271.

Chapter Five

1. *The Third Part of King Henry the Sixth*, act 3, sc. 1, lines 62–65.
2. Taken from *Rich Christians in an Age of Hunger* by Ronald J. Sider. © 1977 by Inter-Varsity Christian Fellowship of the USA and used by permission of InterVarsity Press, Downers Grove, IL 60515, USA.
3. William Barclay, *The Letters to Timothy*, The Daily Study Bible (Edinburgh: The Saint Andrews Press, 1955), p. 152.
4. Alan Loy McGinnis, *The Friendship Factor* (Minneapolis: Augsburg Publishing House, 1979), p. 30.
5. Stanley N. Wilburn, "What the Next 20 Years Hold for You," *U.S. News & World Report* 89, no. 22 (December 1, 1980): 51, 54.

Chapter Six

1. "Voices: U.S.A. '80," *Life* 4, no. 1 (January 1981): 21.
2. Charles R. Swindoll, *Integrity: The Mark of Godliness* (Portland, OR: Multnomah Press, 1981), pp. 6–21, 23.

3. *Born Again:* Copyright © 1976 by Charles W. Colson. Published by Chosen Books Lincoln, VA 22078. Used by permission.

Chapter Seven

1. From *The Master Plan of Evangelism* by Robert E. Coleman copyright © 1972 by Fleming H. Revell Company. Used by permission.
2. From *The Pursuit of God* by A. W. Tozer. Copyright Christian Publications, Inc., Harrisburg, PA 17105. Used by permission.
3. *The Master Plan of Evangelism* pp. 59–60.
4. "I Met My Master," taken from *Poems That Preach*, ed. John R. Rice, (Wheaton, IL: Sword of the Lord Publishers, 1952), p. 18. Used by permission of the publisher.

Chapter Eight

1. Larry Dean Olsen, *Outdoor Survival Skills* (Provo, UT: Brigham, 1976), p. 4.
2. Lloyd Cory, ed., *Quote Unquote* (Wheaton, IL: Victor Books, a division of SP Publications, 1977), p. 15.
3. Reprinted with permission. *When I Relax I Feel Guilty* by Tim Hansel. © 1979 David C. Cook Publishing Co. Elgin, IL 60120.
4. Thomas Ken, "Praise God from Whom All Blessings Flow."

Chapter Nine

1. William Barclay, *Gospel of Matthew,* 2 vols., The Daily Study Bible (Edinburgh: The Saint Andrews Press, 1956), 1:191, 193.

Chapter Ten

1. Charles R. Swindoll, *Leisure* (Portland, OR: Multnomah Press, 1981).
2. W. E. Vine, *An Expository Dictionary of New Testament Words,* vol. 2 (Westwood, NJ: Fleming H. Revell Company, 1940), p. 248.
3. Alan Loy McGinnis, *The Friendship Factor* (Minneapolis: Augsburg Publishing House, 1979), pp. 93–102.
4. Charles R. Swindoll, *Stress* (Portland, OR: Multnomah Press, 1981).
5. Samuel Taylor Coleridge, "Youth and Age," stanza 2, *Familiar Quotations* (Boston, MA: Little, Brown and Company, 1955), p. 425a.

Chapter Eleven

1. Elisabeth Elliot, *Through Gates of Splendor* (New York: Harper & Brothers, 1957).
2. Merrill F. Unger, *Unger's Bible Dictionary* (Chicago: Moody Press, 1957), p. 997.
3. "Surely the Presence of the Lord Is in This Place" by Lanny Wolfe © (Nashville: The Benson Company, copyright 1977 by Lanny Wolfe Music Co. International copyright secured. All rights reserved. Used by permission of The Benson Company, Inc., Nashville.
4. F. B. Meyer, *David, Shepherd Psalmist—King* (Grand Rapids: Zondervan Publishing House, 1953), p. 11.

Chapter Twelve

1. William D. Longstaff, "Take Time to Be Holy," 1882.
2. Letter from an anonymous person to Dr. Charles R. Swindoll, April 21, 1981.

Chapter Thirteen

1. Dale E. Galloway, *Dream a New Dream* (Wheaton, IL: Tyndale House Publishers, 1975), p. 59.
2. Mark Kram, "The Face of Pain," *Sports Illustrated*, 44, no. 10 (March 8, 1976): 60.
3. Philip Yancey, *Where Is God When It Hurts* (Grand Rapids: Zondervan Publishing House, 1978), p. 142.
4. Douglas Colligan, "That Helpless Feeling: The Dangers of Stress," *New York*, July 14, 1975, p. 28.
5. Charles R. Swindoll, *Improving Your Serve* (Waco, TX: Word Books Publisher, 1981).
6. "Murphy's Law," (231 Adrian Road, Millbrae, CA: Celestial Arts, 1979).
7. Bruce Larson, *There's a Lot More to Health Than Not Being Sick* (Waco, TX: Word Books Publisher, 1981), p. 46.
8. Horatio G. Spafford, "It Is Well with My Soul," copyright 1918 The John Church Co. Used by permission of the publisher.

Chapter Fourteen

1. Billy Graham, *Quote Unquote*, ed. Lloyd Cory (Wheaton, IL: Victor Books, a division of SP Publications, 1977), p. 102.
2. Jeffrey L. Cotter, "Witness Upmanship," *Eternity* March 1981, pp. 22–23.

3. Jim Petersen, *Evangelism as a Lifestyle* (Colorado Springs, CO: NavPress, 1980), pp. 24–25.
4. Taken from *How to Give Away Your Faith*, by Paul Little. © 1966 by Inter-Varsity Christian Fellowship of the USA and used by permission of Inter-Varsity Press, Downers Grove, IL 60515, USA.
5. Taken from *Out of the Salt-Shaker and Into the World* by Rebecca Manley Pippert. © 1979 by Inter-Varsity Christian Fellowship of the USA and used by permission of InterVarsity Press, Downers Grove, IL 60515, USA.
6. Billy Graham, *Quote Unquote*, p. 102.

Chapter Fifteen

1. Richard Farson, *Birthrights: A Child's Bill of Rights* (New York: Macmillan, 1974).
2. James C. Dobson, *Straight Talk to Men and Their Wives* (Waco, TX: Word Books Publisher, 1980), p. 63.
3. Aric Press with Jeff B. Copeland, et al., "The Plague of Violent Crime," *Newsweek*, March 23, 1981, pp. 46–50, 52–54.

Chapter Sixteen

1. Edith Schaeffer, *What Is a Family?* (Old Tappan, NJ: Fleming H. Revell Company, 1975), p. 7.
2. David Gelman et al., "Saving the Family," *Newsweek* 91, no. 20 (May 15, 1978).
3. Charles R. Swindoll, *You and Your Child* (Nashville, TN: Thomas Nelson Publishers, 1977), pp. 52–54.
4. Gordon MacDonald, *The Effective Father* (Wheaton, IL: Tyndale House Publishers, 1977), pp. 183–84.
5. Taken from *Fearfully and Wonderfully Made* by Paul Brand, M.D. with Philip Yancey. Copyright © 1980 by Dr. Paul Brand and Philip Yancey. Used by permission of Zondervan Publishing House.
6. Albert Siegel, *Stanford Observer*, as quoted in *The Wittenburg Door* (San Diego: Youth Specialities).